KINDS OF WINTER

The Four Journeys 2002–2005

KINDS OF WINTER

*Four Solo Journeys by
Dogteam in Canada's
Northwest Territories*

DAVE OLESEN

WILFRID LAURIER
UNIVERSITY PRESS

Wilfrid Laurier University Press acknowledges the support of the Canada Council for the Arts for our publishing program. We acknowledge the financial support of the Government of Canada through the Canada Book Fund for our publishing activities.

Library and Archives Canada Cataloguing in Publication

Olesen, Dave, 1957–, author
    Kinds of winter : four solo journeys by dogteam in Canada's Northwest Territories / Dave Olesen.

(Life writing series)
Issued in print and electronic formats.
ISBN 978-1-77112-118-7 (bound).—ISBN 978-1-77112-131-6 (pbk.)
ISBN 978-1-77112-069-2 (pdf).—ISBN 978-1-77112-070-8 (epub)

    1. Olesen, Dave, 1957– —Travel—Northwest Territories. 2. Dogsledding—Northwest Territories. 3. Snow camping—Northwest Territories. 4. Winter—Northwest Territories. 5. Northwest Territories—Description and travel. I. Title. II. Series: Life writing series

FC4167.3.O44 2014   917.19'3044   C2014-904147-0
                                                    C2014-904148-9

Front-cover illustration by Graeme Shaw. Compass image © sergeiminsk, http://www.123rf.com/profile_sergeiminsk'. Cover design and text design by Daiva Villa, Chris Rowat Design.

This paperback edition 2016
© 2014 Wilfrid Laurier University Press
Waterloo, Ontario, Canada
www.wlupress.wlu.ca

"Kinds of Winter" and "So Long" and a line from "Our People," by William Stafford, from *The Way It Is: New and Selected Poems.* Copyright © 1959, 1970, 1998 by William Stafford and the Estate of William Stafford. Reprinted with the permission of The Permissions Company, Inc., on behalf of Graywolf Press, Minneapolis, Minnesota, www.graywolfpress.org. "Tasting the Snow" by Gary Snyder from *The Back Country* (1971). Reprinted with the permission of the poet.

This book is printed on FSC® recycled paper and is certified Ecologo. It is made from 100% post-consumer fibre, processed chlorine-free, and manufactured using biogas energy.

Printed in Canada

Every reasonable effort has been made to acquire permission for copyright material used in this text, and to acknowledge all such indebtedness accurately. Any errors and omissions called to the publisher's attention will be corrected in future printings.

RECYCLED
Paper made from
recycled material
FSC   FSC® C103567
www.fsc.org

For Kristen

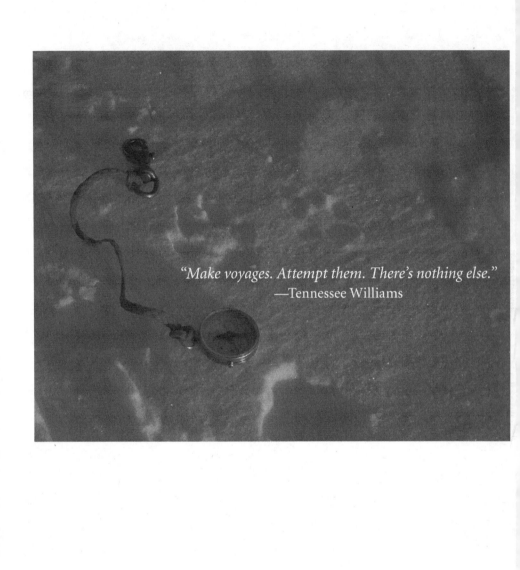

"Make voyages. Attempt them. There's nothing else."
—Tennessee Williams

Contents

List of Maps and Illustrations

Maps

Illustrations

Author's Note

Like many of my generation, I continue to be confounded by North America's split personality when it comes to everyday measurement of temperature, distance, volume, and weight. And this split does not split right at the Canada–U.S. border. As a pilot in Canada I still spend my working days conversing and calculating in miles and feet and pounds, for these are the worldwide industry standards. Meanwhile, as a Canadian citizen I am encouraged by Ottawa to think strictly in kilometres, litres, and grams. Alas, as an Illinois boy born in 1957, my mind will forever run in miles and inches and pounds.

In this book I have given temperatures and distances and other measurements in the way they now come naturally to me, and to many millions of others like me: Temperatures in degrees Celsius (for after twenty-seven years in Canada, I have at least mastered that changeover), distances in statute miles, smaller measurements in inches and feet, and weights in pounds. This is the way I think and the way everyone I work with, right across western Canada, still talks. Maybe in another generation or two we will all be converted and toeing the metric line.

As for the terms and slang of dog mushing and winter bush travel, a glossary is provided at the back of the book, along with several appendices, which might help the reader to understand some of the details of my travel and camping methods, food supplies, dog care, and navigation.

Compass Points,
Over the Boulders, Eager...

As the sun went down in late afternoon on the 28th of February 2003, I raised my voice above the roar of wind, calling out gently to the team of huskies stretched ahead of me: "Who-o-oa there now, who-o-oa." The low tone of my command was muffled by the ice-encrusted hood surrounding my face and it did not carry far. The dogs heard me but they hardly slowed at the sound. "What? Surely he's not thinking of making camp here?" I stood heavily on the sled's steel brake claws, forcing them deeper into the wind-packed snow. Our momentum fell off and ten frosty dog faces turned back, baffled, to see what I was going to do next. "Whoa," I said again, and dropped the snow hook. I kicked it down with my thick mukluk. "That'll do. Home sweet home."

It was time to camp, and the blank white sweep of tundra offered no shelter. The northwest gale had dominated our day, howling at us head-on, shifting slightly, probing for weakness like a tireless sparring partner, hour after hour. The rush of air had dropped perceptibly at day's end, but it still packed a wallop. With the temperature near 40 below zero, the wind was still eager to freeze any skin I might carelessly expose to it. I moved forward up the team and unhooked the toggle at the back of each dog's harness. Now my intentions were clear to them all and as they felt the toggles come free they each pissed, shook, circled, and curled up on the snow—tail over nose, furry shoulder turned toward the brunt of the wind. Work done, day over... call us when supper's ready, boss.

The dogs and I were about halfway between the upper Thelon River and the east end of Great Slave Lake. We were westbound for home, with about a hundred miles to go. It was time to stop the day's marching, dig in, pitch the tent, cook food for us all, and rest for the night. We would find no oasis of spruce trees, no cozy hut on these rolling plains. One barren hillside was as good as the next and darkness was coming on.

I started the chores. The dogs would sleep in harness that night, stretched out in pairs across a smooth blank slope, so I only had to secure the forward end of their gangline to one of the stout aluminum pickets I carried in the sled. I walked to the head of the team again, poked the 30-inch stake into the packed snow, and made the gangline off to it. That done, I set up and lit the two-burner camp stove, heaped big chunks of snow into a square cooker kettle, then sheltered the cooker and stove with a sheet-metal windscreen. Over the next half-hour or so that snow would grudgingly become hot water. With that hot water I could melt big blocks of frozen fat, then pour the water-fat soup over the dogs' dense kibble. I moved up and down the team, putting a bright blue windbreaker on each dog and taking off the cloth booties that they often wear on long runs in deep cold. Next I staked out and raised my red tent alongside the sled, only a few feet away from Jasmine and Schooner, the two wheel dogs at the very back of the team. Every time I set something down I secured it somehow or threw something heavy on top of it, and by doing so managed to make camp that night without losing any bits of my gear to the wind.

Through the two hours of dusk and deepening twilight I worked steadily. Finally, with everything done outside and the dogs all fed, I could retreat to the tent to cook and eat my own supper—a steaming kettle of caribou meat, rice, and butter, seasoned to simple perfection with salt and pepper. An hour later I could begin to get ready for sleep. This is a laughably laborious half-hour project when tent camping in winter: change clothes, arrange bedding, prepare the stove for quick lighting in the morning; wriggle into double mummy bags with their confounding tangle of drawstrings, cord locks, snaps, and zippers. At last I rolled sideways in my cocoon of goose down and synthetic fluff, and blew out the candle.

Pure blackness. The incessant wind still battered the fabric of the tent. Almost at my elbow Jasmine shifted in her snow bed, and sighed as she settled again. I marvelled, as I teetered on the brink of consciousness, at how utterly alone a man and ten dogs are in such a place on such a night. A warm glow of deep rest crept up and down my limbs, then deep, dreamless sleep.

And suddenly dawn—the first morning of March. Daylight tinged orange by the red-and-yellow fabric of my tent. And—could it be?—silence! For the first time in four days the wind had calmed.

Once I had the stove burning full bore I made a brief foray out from the warm tent. Tundra and sky all around, shaded pink to the east-southeast where the sun would soon rise. Forty-one below zero, according to the little thermometer slung from the handlebar of the sled. Dogs all drifted in, some completely invisible beneath the snow, and not one of them even stirring at the sound of my footsteps. After a couple of minutes outside in that ever-astonishing cold, I dove back into my little nylon haven and the comforting hiss of the camp stove. Just as I sat down and began to fuss with making coffee, one of the dogs barked, and another: short barks of alarm which told me something was amiss, something was moving or approaching our little camp. Reluctant to leave the warm tent again, I poked my head through the door flap.

Eighty yards or so beyond the lead dogs stood a truly enormous white wolf, thick with frost on his mane and pelt, staring at the camp and the dogs as if transfixed. A second wolf, tawny grey, stood just behind the white one. All the dogs were on their feet now, some with clumps of snow still clinging to the sides of their heads, shanks, and nylon jackets, giving them a dishevelled just-woke-up look. No one moved or made a sound. A third wolf, white and slightly smaller than the others, probably a female, trotted in from the northeast.

By then the tips of my frost-battered ears were going numb, and I pulled back into the tent to fetch my hat. When I stuck my head out again the two smaller wolves were ambling away, but the big white fellow still stood and stared. Finally he turned, stepped away, paused once more to study us, and slowly followed his comrades out of sight over the rise. I crawled back into the tent as the dogs settled into their beds again.

It seems necessary to begin every piece of writing about Canada's Northwest Territories with a refresher in North American geography—even for many Canadians. Because my family and I live in a little-known corner of these remote territories, we spend a lot of our conversations when we are "down south" in exchanges like this: "No, not the Yukon. No, not Nunavut. Not Alaska ..." Puzzled look, scratching of head. "What's next, going east ... Greenland? What the heck *is* straight north from Alberta and Saskatchewan, or straight north of Montana? Pass me that atlas, please."

That blank in popular geography is part of the wonder, and at times the frustration, of living in this place so far on the fringes of modern North America. It is an enormous stretch of land and waters over a thousand miles across, yet its entire human population could easily take seats to watch a ballgame in a metropolitan stadium. In 1999, when Canada officially established the territory of Nunavut to the north and east of us, the diminished yet still enormous Northwest Territories faded even further from the southern consciousness—perhaps not such a bad thing, considering the implications of the alternative.

The journeys I describe in this book took me out from and back to my home at Hoarfrost River, at the northeastern tip of McLeod Bay on Great Slave Lake. Once a year for four consecutive winters I hooked up a team of dogs and set out on long trips away from our homestead, travelling toward one of the cardinal points of the compass: south in 2002, east in 2003, north in 2004, and finally west in 2005. Having gone out, I turned home again. It was as simple as that. My narrative will make many digressions, but the days and nights and miles of those four trips are the main trail wending through the pages ahead.

As I look back on these journeys a steady stream of images comes to mind: that bare-bones camp on the tundra; the stunning cold morning after the wind died; those wolves. Other camps and fleeting moments are fixed permanently in my memory as all the little details begin to fall away: The headwaters of the Back River on a bright, amazingly mild day in late February 2004. I knelt to chip some ice with my knife, since I had boasted to my two little daughters that we would raise a toast to my return with lemonade poured over Back River ice chips. A moment on the first trip, south, on the divide between the Snowdrift and Taltson watersheds, standing alone on snowshoes miles from my camp and dogs, on a day so clear and frigid that the air was like some new solid, some surreal essence of cold. And a sunny pastel afternoon on the final trip, moving west across the enormous expanse of Great Slave Lake, mile after mile, slow hours passing, until the far western shore, a land of wood bison and sinkholes and poplar, rose into sight like a new continent in the distance.

———————

When a person lives in a place for many years, it becomes a *centre point*. Moving outward in any direction from that *physical* centre, the geographical place, one will eventually and certainly encounter change— or else all places would be the same. For my journeys and motives the four cardinal compass points provided suitable direct headings—I would hook up a team of dogs, and with them hold a heading *until something changed*. Vegetation, terrain, weather, animals, light, depth, distance— the specific parameters didn't matter. And then, having moved out to that perceptibly new place, the dogs and I would turn for home. Of course anyone, from anywhere, could undertake such a series of outings, and many people have probably taken such journeys in their minds. But it was important to me to actually set out and *do* it, to make it a part of my life—a life so firmly rooted to a place called Hoarfrost River.

The compass rose and its cardinal points provided a simple and appealing framework for my routes, year by year. Our little cluster of cabins and outbuildings, which we call our homestead for lack of a better word, sits just west of the mouth of the Hoarfrost, where that small river flows into the long arc of McLeod Bay. Here my wife Kristen and I have lived since 1987, raised our two children, and made a life and a living for ourselves. To journey out to each of the four directions, one winter after the next, rounding the compass and always returning to home, appealed to me. It was a simple plan, and that bare-bones simplicity was one of my goals. Over my years in the wilderness, I have often drawn wisdom from a snippet I first read in the mid-70s in *Mountain Gazette*, something like: "If you can't plan the thing on the back of an old envelope, it threatens to become an Expedition, and should be seriously reconsidered."[1] Of course my planning for these trips did entail more notes than I could fit on a scrap of paper, but that advice has always served me well, and over the years I have tried to remain true to it.

I was out for about sixteen days on each trip. Using my methods a lone musher with a sled and a team of dogs cannot travel more than about nine days (somewhere between 100 and 200 miles) without some resupply. Thus I needed to set out one or two resupply caches for myself prior to each journey. Being a bush pilot in my working life, I was able to set out these caches for myself, by ski plane, a week or two before each year's start.

I timed the first three journeys for the second half of February, and because of work pressures I made the final trip west in the middle of March. Given complete freedom to time the trips I might have taken them all in March, but that would have conflicted with my work as a pilot and guide. I intended these to be purely winter trips, not winter-edging-into-spring trips. The second half of February is the very heart of winter, analogous on the flip side of the calendar year to the second half of August. By February at 63° north the length of daylight does not impinge on a solid day of travel, and the equinoctial winds of March have not kicked in. So February it was, three times out of four.

Wild country rewards those who approach it without fanfare. I did not want corporate sponsors, online interactive education, or any of the other trappings of the modern Information Age expedition. And, to be honest, they didn't want me—the journeys I made were not intended to be dramatic or extreme. In Madison Avenue parlance, these trips just weren't very sexy. On the most prosaic level, I only wanted to take the time and make the effort to go out and immerse myself in some of the vastness that surrounds our home, and thus to fill in some of the blanks in my own mental geography. On another level, I sought a return to the original motivations of my long career as a dog musher. From 1985 to 2000, I had been intensely focused on long-distance sled-dog racing. Eight times I ran teams to Nome, Alaska, in the Iditarod, and I competed in many other races like it. Finally, coming home after the finish of the 2000 Yukon Quest, I sensed that I had scratched that itch, and I made the decision to turn away from competitive dog mushing. It was time to steer my dogteam and myself toward less tangible prizes, or risk finding that all of us—canine and human—had grown too old and soft to make the effort.

Early on in my ruminations about the four trips I decided to travel alone. Although the ideal companion would certainly have enriched these journeys in some ways, I never second-guessed my decision to go solo. For most of the sixty days and nights I spent on the trail I found that solitude could be, as Henry David Thoreau claimed, a pleasant and thought-provoking companion. It allowed me to sustain themes of thought over many hours without interruption, to linger over my journal writing on some mornings in the tent, and on other days to pack up and head out without any mandatory pause for introspection. I wanted time to think, to write, and to ask myself some questions; to mull things over all by my lonesome. Of course on a dogteam trip one is never completely alone. I could talk to my dogs, and with them I could savour—and at times simply endure—the ups and downs of our life on the trail.

Setting out in winter, I travelled by the only method that I, a veteran dog musher, could imagine setting out. Had I made these journeys without the dogs—travelling by ski and pulk, or snowshoe and toboggan—both the philosophy and the nuts and bolts of the trips would have been changed utterly. I would have sacrificed a huge amount of distance covered, and would have subtracted a measure of comfort from my already spartan camps.

And what if I had gone to the other end of the tundra-travel spectrum and set out by snowmobile—what then? I could have covered vastly more distance, hauled more gear along with me, and enjoyed the comforts of cozier camping night after night. And...at that vast distance, alone and unsupported, the machine might have broken down and demanded repair work far exceeding my paltry skills as a mechanic. What then? An ignominious rescue, a return home, a salvage, and a bill...failure and project over. The only thing I can say with certainty about the snowmobile option is that I never considered it even for a moment, because with every noisy, stinking mile I would have run that rubber track right over the essence of everything I treasure about winter and the wilderness. Harsh words, but true.

Sled dogs have been such a huge force in my life that I do sometimes take them for granted. I suspect that my time with huskies has shaped me more than I will ever know. I am a dog musher, and good mushers take pride in viewing dogs honestly, in trying to plumb the deep magic embedded in our unvarnished partnership with our dogs. "Critters are critters," as a friend of mine, a sort of horse whisperer in his own right, said one night as we sat and looked out at his pasture and herd. And in that simple statement lies a lifelong mystery.

Poet Augustus Merrill, once an English professor of mine, remarked after reading a draft of this book that he found himself interested not so much in *what* I did as in *why* I did it. Fair enough—setting out alone in mid-winter, for no apparent practical purpose, into some of the most desolate and unpopulated parts of the planet, is not, I admit, an entirely rational act. Yet to me and to my friends and family it never seemed completely *irrational* either, given my background and my lifelong fascination with the North. I tried to put it this way: for a man to make a home and live out his life at a place like Hoarfrost River, with a team of huskies and the savvy to drive them, and never to venture forth on such trips, would be like living on a sea-coast, with a capable boat moored in the harbour, and never to set sail.

Some people, told of my plans, simply nodded politely. Their bewilder-ment was obvious, though—it was as if I had announced "Over the next four winters I'm going to take a series of long swims in ice-cold water, just to see how it feels." For these puzzled people I can trot out reasons like those I have listed: the desire to explore my home territory; the chance to run the dogs without the pressure of racing; the urge to ponder, question, and write. Stacked up against the brute reality of a 40-below night alone on the tundra, huddled next to a camp stove in a flimsy nylon tent, words and reasons can all sound stilted and contrived.

It has taken years for me to complete this book, to work my scrawled-pencil notebooks into some coherent forms and chapters. As those years have passed my journeys have receded from the sharp clarity of recent memory into the slippery haze of the past. The essences of them, con-centrated or distilled like maple syrup or good whisky, have taken on a purity not apparent in the mundane details of days and nights, camps and weather and resupplies, routes and mileage. Those days and nights, that red tent on the tundra, those teams of dogs and miles of wind, have melded and become layers of my soul.

It is a primeval act, this setting out and leaving home—especially for a man alone, from such a remote home as ours, into the teeth of winter. Some lines from Gary Snyder's poem "Tasting the Snow" catch it perfectly:

Out the door:
Icy and clear in the dark.
    once I had thought,
    laughing and kissing,
      how cosy to be tuckt in bed —
let them sleep;
Now I can turn to the hunt.

Blade sharp and hair on end
    over the boulders
eager
    tasting the snow.

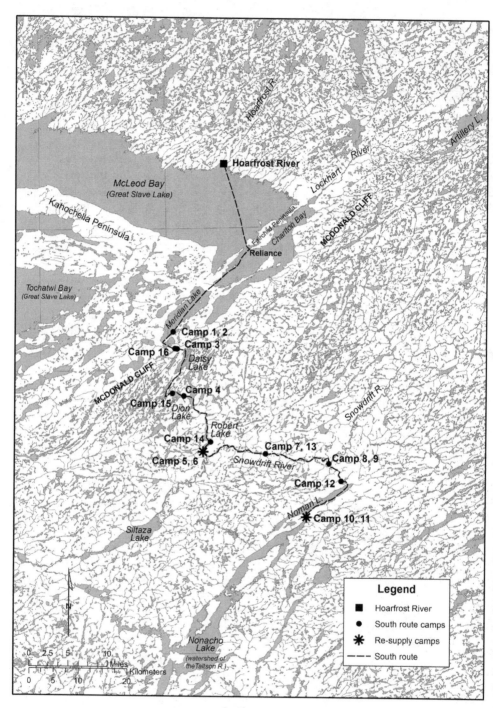

South 2002

South

Seventeen days, 20 February–8 March 2002
Hoarfrost River to Nonacho Lake (Taltson River watershed) and return:
 about 155 miles
Nine dogs, two resupply caches

I began by heading south.

My decision to go south that first year, 2002, was partly based in the need for a shakedown voyage, toward the compass point that I thought would be most forgiving in case of mistakes. Unlike the country waiting for me toward the three other cardinal directions, the route south lay entirely in timbered country, with its amenities of firewood and wind protection. Also, in apparent contradiction to that notion, I went south because I wanted to knock off the toughest physical effort first. I expected the southern leg of my four-year project to be gruelling, because of snow depth and unfamiliar terrain. Looking back with the unerring clarity of hindsight, both expectations turned out to be correct—especially the gruelling part. In fact my trip south in 2002 ranks among the most difficult dogteam treks I have ever made.

On 15 February, Kristen and our two young daughters, Annika and Liv, left our home at Hoarfrost River and flew in a small ski plane to Yellowknife, 165 miles away. There in the boomtown Arctic capital (population eighteen thousand) they settled in to our little houseboat cabin on the ice of Yellowknife Bay, to take up with four weeks of city life: public school for the girls, days filled with errands and appointments, visiting with friends—a welcome mid-winter change of routine.

As their plane departed my solo began. Although I would not leave home for days, and had no idea that first year how ridiculously long it would take me to get out on the trail, I was alone. I was free to focus entirely on the journey ahead of me.

———

Solitude stretches time. After months of keeping steady company with Kristen and our girls, the sudden silence of our homestead seemed to come barrelling in at me from every side. It brought with it a strange sense of slow-motion, freeze-frame movement along with a vague and unsettling emptiness. My first hours alone were spent in this oddly disoriented frame of mind. Suddenly there were no distractions. One task could lead logically to the next, without a plaintive little "tie my bootlace" or "I need a snack" to be heard. *Could* lead logically, that is, if I could just settle into a methodical and productive rhythm.

Afternoon, day one: time to set up the new tent I had purchased for these trips—a "three-man" (just right for one) Swedish arctic type that was beautifully strong, lightweight, and boasted a good pedigree of arctic and mountain expeditions. Over the next four winters I would come to deeply appreciate this tent, but on that first afternoon, on the hardpacked snow alongside the dog yard at minus 30 degrees, I struggled to politely make its acquaintance. Threading thin metal poles through narrow fabric sleeves, poking aluminum stakes into the snow, I clumsily rehearsed the process that would become so familiar over the coming weeks and years.

There is pleasure in using a piece of gear that has been well thought out, well designed, and well made. I can put up with all the intrinsic frustrations of winter camping—the dark, the cold, the tired impatience at day's end—if I am working with equipment I trust. That Hilleberg tent has become one of those pieces of gear, as familiar and comfortable to me now as an old parka, as trustworthy as a sharp axe. I *like* it, oddly, almost as if it were animate—even its red and yellow flamboyance is a source of real pleasure to me, a welcome contrast to the stark monotones of winter.

Tent up, and taken down again, I wrapped it tightly in its groundsheet, making a long slender bundle that would allow me to set it up again without re-threading poles through skinny fabric sleeves. I moved on down the long list. Stove fuel poured into jugs and bottles; lard and canola oil melted and spread out in flat boxes to freeze for the dogs' rations; a look at my homemade ski bindings...Soon it was dusk, and time to feed the dogs.

A month earlier I had made a seven-day, three-hundred-mile trip down the lake and back, to deliver fifteen of our twenty-four huskies to a tourist lodge near Yellowknife, returning with only the nine dogs who would be my team on the trip south. The others would be earning their keep for a few months in the care of the lodge's musher, giving short rides to guests. In that first twilight alone, my human solitude deepened my appreciation for my nine canine companions: littermates Ernie, Foxtail, Flynn, and Schooner; my main leader Steve; Murphy; Tugboat; Dandy; and old reliable Riley. They shattered the silence with their eager dinnertime barks. They were a strong crew, and they were tough as nails after our January trip to the lodge and back, when temperatures had dropped to minus 47 degrees on the way home.

The next two days passed in a seemingly endless checklist of preparations, from maps to meals to fuel to dog food. Each evening I worked on my sled in the old log shack that had been our first cabin at the homestead, and that had over the years become my workshop. As I tackled each detail of my preparation, waves of frustration came and went. I checked dozens of pieces of equipment, and made some important discoveries: the Coleman stove leaked fuel at the tank outlet, the ten-gallon kegs for my food caches needed new sheet-metal covers, the high-frequency (HF) radio needed its battery terminals scraped and cleaned. Every piece of gear, right down the list, seemed to need some sewing or fixing or troubleshooting.

Finally on a sunny cold morning, February 18th, I went through the winter ritual of heating up the airplane, using a portable generator and three small electric heaters. Once the engine was warm enough to start I crammed all my resupply provisions into the plane's tiny cabin: metal kegs of dog food and my own food; plastic pails of dry goods like crackers and cereal; an old canvas wall tent and a small wood stove for use at my far cache site; jugs and bottles of white gas for the Coleman stove; spare dog booties; extra socks, books, and gloves; batteries for the HF radio and for my headlamp. Still saddled with the habits of my fifteen years on the race trails, where checkpoint bags bulge with items to meet every imaginable competitive contingency, I really loaded up that first year's resupply caches. If I had seen need for a kitchen sink, there would have been a big one *and* a spare in that cache bundle.

Somehow, just barely, it all fit into the little two-seat plane with its backseat removed. I squirmed into the pilot's seat wearing my bulky winter flying suit, taxied out, and took off. I felt tense, lonely, and—truth be told—a little uncertain. Why, I asked myself, had I decided to do *this*?

It was a perfect day for winter flying—clear and not bitterly cold. The airplane was another of those trusted old inanimate friends, its control stick as familiar to my hand as the stanchion of a sled or the shaft of a paddle. So why that enervating tension? I have no good answer to that, but every year prior to setting out it was there, like a weight around my neck as I made my preparations.

Once airborne and southbound I faced a choice with enormous influence on the days ahead: where to put the caches? If I put the resupplies too far out, I would not be able to reach them at all, or the effort of doing so would turn the trip into a grinding struggle dominated by time and mileage. Put the caches too close to home and the trip would be cut short and robbed of some of its potential. I would reach the caches before I really needed them, and the first of my four expeditions would become a mere outing. The choice was all mine—nobody else would care what I decided. I was both the drop-off pilot and the recipient of this airdrop, and on a day in February I could land the little ski plane on almost any small patch of snow and ice.

I flew very low and tried to glean all possible hints as to travelling conditions on the land and lakes below me. My gut feeling was that the route south was going to be slow and difficult, the snow deep and soft, the terrain rugged and utterly trackless. Mile by mile as I flew along I took small clues from the look of the landscape and the texture of the sunlit snow on the lakes. I could tell there had been a few caribou drifting around, but only a few, and I saw none that day. There were no signs of human travel—that is, no snowmobile tracks, which nowadays are the only signs of local winter travel other than my own.

I settled on two cache sites. The first, an intermediate stopover with about five days' supplies, I decided to place on Robert Lake just north of the Snowdrift River. The second, my major resupply, with the wall tent and about ten days' supplies, I placed at Noman Lake. Noman lies just across a short portage from the north arm of Nonacho Lake, in the Taltson River watershed. As I circled over a little rock island on Noman, I spotted an old cabin on the Nonacho side of the portage. This brought a sudden flash of hope: maybe someone, from somewhere, had an active presence in the area and there would be some trails broken through that deep soft snow. (As it turned out, the cabin was a wreck and the country untouched, but I would not know that for another twelve days.)

I landed only briefly at each of the two cache sites that afternoon. I am never completely at ease when I shut down an airplane motor on a cold day far from home. I am always eager to hear it roar to life again, always happy to climb back up into the sky. On the island in Noman I clustered the kegs and pails along with the bundled canvas tent. At Robert Lake I took time to dig a pit in the deep snow along shore. There I buried my wooden crate of supplies and marked the spot with a red jug of stove fuel. I lifted off from Robert Lake in a prop-wash blizzard of powdery snow, feeling much more at ease and confident than I had that morning. I made the short flight home, still studying the route that would pose such a challenge in the coming days, and landed at Hoarfrost. As the sun set I put the wing and tail covers on the plane. Securely tethered to logs frozen beneath the lake ice, it would be safe while I was away.

That night the trip began to feel more real to me. There *was* an end to all this "getting ready," and I chuckled at a remark often quoted on preparation days around our place. It came from a Wyoming dog musher named Ray Gordon, who had lost parts of his throat to cancer by the time

The Husky ski plane and the cache supplies on Noman Lake.

I knew him. "Haarrumph," he had croaked to me one night before a race in Montana, "Homehtimes hyou hujus' hagotto ghuit ghettin' haready anh' hujus' hafukkin'haGo!"

Before I could "hajus' haGo," though, I spent yet another full day immersed in details of preparation, and another long night in the workshop, struggling to get my old warhorse of a sled up to some minimal acceptable standard—patches over patches, splines under lashings. At last the items on my lists were all crossed off. I could start closing up the homestead: a few token padlocks, some boards nailed over shed doors. It had been five days since Kristen and the girls had left, the longest it would take me to get on the trail over the series of four journeys. Finally I could harness up the team and start south.

February 20th dawned overcast and mild. I woke early, feeling rested and calm. I savoured the little luxuries of cabin life as I sat and read for the first time an obscure essay by Thoreau, "A Winter Walk."[1] "We sleep," he begins, "and at length awake to the still reality of a winter morning." Bare feet, porcelain coffee mug, the pulsating glow and soft hiss of gas lights. It would be several weeks, I knew, before life would again be so physically luxurious. I was finished getting ready, and I had made my peace with the long delay of the preparation days just past. A person can only do so much in a day, in a year, in a life. In middle age I desperately needed to accept that, or I would wind up rushing forever, in a foul and frustrated mood, with lacklustre results.

I was still nagged with worry about my sled, though. I had finally pushed it out the door of the cluttered workshop the night before. It was a long narrow sled I had built twelve years earlier. Its unorthodox slenderness (16 inches instead of the usual 20), along with its yellow nylon cargo bag, had quickly earned it the nickname "The Banana." Kristen, who has always disliked driving it, has other names for it, by far the most polite of which is "that horrible yellow thing." Its long ash runners are cracked and splinted. In a desperate last-ditch fix, I had bolted on a pair of three-inch-wide, half-inch-thick runner shoes of high-density polyethylene. When I finally launched it out the workshop door that night, it did not slither gracefully across the snow. It landed with a thud and stuck there like something inert until I put a shoulder to it and heaved it toward the dog yard. New cold snow, fine-grained and windblown, is more like dry sand than frozen water. I could only hope that milder weather would ease the laws of physics for the first few days, while we climbed heavily laden out of the basin of Great Slave Lake. The main thing, I had to remind myself, was that I was going. If a man always postponed departure until every last thing was perfect, he would never leave home.

Over the morning my innards gradually tightened, and the peace of that Thoreauvian dawn was replaced by tension. I had set out on enough big trips and long races to know that the easing of that tension would only come a few days down the trail—if I could find the trail. "Well, if we can't find a trail," I said out loud to the puzzled dogs, "We'll just have to make one." At a few minutes past noon I stepped onto the runners and yanked the snub line free of the hitching post. The yelping dogs fell silent as they instantly shifted their efforts from insane barking to a smooth slow lope. We crossed the ten-mile breadth of McLeod Bay in just over an hour. It was the fastest, easiest ten miles we would make on the entire trip.

At Reliance, the home of our nearest neighbours sits on the prominent point across from the abandoned weather station. Beside the weather station is a cluster of buildings where the Royal Canadian Mounted Police (mounted on dogsleds instead of horses at this location) maintained a detachment for nearly forty years. Those buildings are now a sport fishing lodge and retreat, but the lodge is open and occupied only in summer. The manned weather station closed in the early 1990s, replaced by an automated weather device that transmits its data via satellite. There is also an old trading post at Reliance, now occupied by mice and voles, and a cache of aviation fuel in drums that are delivered by barge. Little by little, year by year, the entire outback of the North is losing its year-round human presence, and on no route of mine would this be more apparent than on the trip south.

I tied off the team and walked up the steep rock point for a coffee break with our neighbours Roger Catling, Miranda Casaway, and their two young children. All of us who live in remote places take a vicarious pleasure from almost any passing traveller. It is always a breath of fresh air to see a new face at the kitchen table and to hear of someone's adventures, whether in the past or future tense. Like neighbours everywhere, our two households perched on either corner of McLeod Bay's east end are aware of our differences, but we are strongly bound together by our isolation and our common interests—the weather, hunting and fishing, the ebb and flow of water levels and caribou herds. We share an appreciation for the seldom-seen aspects of this landscape—beautiful glimpses to be had only by those who are fully immersed in a place, and not available to the passing tourists. There is solidarity in that, ample enough to ground an ongoing friendship.

After goodbye and good luck, I was away again. As the dogs and I started south from the first portage out of Charlton Bay, Roger suddenly zoomed up behind us astride his enormous snowmobile and passed with a friendly wave. I waved back happily for I knew he was doing me a big favour. He would drive south about ten miles to the tip of Meridian Lake and set a spruce-tree marker out on the ice of a smaller pond. There, "as near as I can remember," he had said over coffee, an old route started up for Daisy Lake. It had been used "years ago."

"How many?" I asked.

"Oh, maybe twenty? Nobody has gone up that way in a *long* time."

I camped at dusk, a mile or two short of the south end of Meridian Lake. There was open water close to the tip of a wooded point, and ice that was much thinner than I suspected. This caught me by surprise since the point was only a peninsula jutting out from the shoreline, with no obvious flowage. Studying the map later that night I could see that in fact there is a flowage there, into the lake from the east, which explained the thin ice. Ice, like bears and many other facets of wild nature, is steadily finding ways to surprise and mystify me as the years pass. As the saying goes, "When is the ice *completely* safe? Never."

Safely accessible open water, or ice thin enough to break with a few strokes of an axe, is a welcome attribute for any winter campsite, especially when travelling with a team of dogs. As amazingly efficient as sled dogs are, a working husky requires at least a litre of water every twenty-four hours—and much more than that in deep cold or on long endurance races. This is in addition to the "metabolic water" which they (and we) generate in the digestion of fat-rich trail food. In the old days all of this water came, in winter, by way of the dogs' fish-and-meat diet. Also the dogs ate snow as needed (and of course they still do), but eating cold snow is a metabolically costly way to get water in the Arctic. Today, with dried kibble as the dogs' main ration, providing liquid water along with their food is essential to the team's well-being, and I concur with that practice.

Melting enough snow to produce several gallons of hot water is a long process that consumes precious fuel or hard-won firewood. Thus over the course of my four journeys, the desire to *find* open water or thin ice, and to camp near it, was a theme of my days. Alongside that, always, was the desire to *detect* open water and thin ice, and to keep myself, my sled, and my dogs safely clear of it. The Arctic in winter is a desert. Although dry snow replaces the sand, and deep cold replaces the intense heat, the pressing concern with water—whether discovered as liquid or melted from snow and ice—is always looming. Water must be found, or manufactured with copious amounts of heat, at every campsite—and avoided like the plague all day.

The night was mild, and humid in a way that often surprises me after a long stretch of deep dry cold. The dogs were happy and energetic as I fumbled in the half-darkness to get them fed and to finish all the camp chores. Only with time would my new tent, and the routines of my camping methods with it, become second nature. I had travelled too late to finish setting up my camp in daylight. The night was cloudy and there was no moon. At last the tent was up, the team was fed, and the sled load was lashed down for the night.

———————

Day two, 21 February. Up and out of the tent for what the Saskatchewan farmers call "a coyote's breakfast: a piss and a good look around." *A month until the equinox*, I thought, as I stood outdoors in the first dim light of dawn. The date struck me as being the mirror image of 21 August, with the equinox a month away and the full richness of the season still at hand. In late August, with summer easing toward autumn, it could still be hot, but night brought full darkness after the twenty-four-hour daylight of June and July. Now, in late February, winter was past its deepest and darkest. The nights could still get bitterly cold, but day by day the sun gained strength.

A light snow was falling; the air was calm and mild. I could have packed up and moved south that morning, but the first priority was to locate and break open the route up to Daisy Lake. I decided to go by dog-team as far as Roger's tracks led, stake out the team there, and scout ahead on snowshoes. A short run brought us to the end of the snow-machine tracks. I paused on the little lake just off Meridian Lake to photograph the sled and team with the imposing rise of elevation looming in the background. "McDonald Cliff," noted the topographic map, along a distinct band of tightly spaced contour lines running northeast-southwest. The geologists call it the McDonald Fault, leading to jokes about everything that goes awry in that area being McDonald's fault. It is the single most distinctive feature of the landscape just east of McLeod and Christie Bays. The terrain rises sharply from the 500-foot (above sea level) elevation of Great Slave Lake to the 1,200 to 1,600 feet of the surrounding terrain. There are no mountains in this part of Canada, but the land is fractured, steep, and much more rugged than most people imagine.

All that first day was spent struggling about a mile, up the steep rise into a small unnamed lake. I was grateful that Roger had put me onto the foot of what was plainly an old route up the hill, but a hundred yards or so into the dense bush I had reached an impasse. The barely discernible swath of the old trail had petered out to nothing. I made my best guess, but it was wrong; a crucial 50 yards divergent from what, two weeks later, I would discover to be the remnant old trail. Through late morning and into early afternoon I floundered methodically back and forth on snowshoes, in the deep powder and thick deadfall that covered the steep hillside. Two hours of effort left me frustrated and sweat-soaked. I returned to the sled and the dogs. I ate some lunch, drank some warm orange Tang, and started off again up the hill. I could find nothing resembling an old axe-cut, a blaze, or a trail. It was time to abandon the effort of searching for the old trail and turn the rest of the afternoon toward creating a new one.

At last, late in the day, tired and exasperated and much wetter than I should have allowed myself to get, I dropped over the brow of a steep rock onto the snow-covered ice of the little lake. The route was in. There was no time that day to go any farther, up toward Daisy. Had I done so, I might have seen—over my shoulder about 600 yards west of my crude steep trail—a weathered old axe-cut marking the upper end of the old trail.

I returned to the dogs, who had enjoyed their day of ease in the mild weather. At a full gallop they whisked me back up Meridian Lake to our campsite. In the twilight a cold north wind was driving some snow ahead of it. As I finished my chores in the fading light and fed the dogs, an otter poked its head from the pool of black water alongside the tent and snuffed a short bark at us all.

That night, fed and warm and feeling metaphorical, I jotted in my journal the day's "Lessons for Finding Old Trails":

1. The easiest place to pick up a trail is at either the beginning or the end. In the middle, deep in the thickets, everything—and at the same time nothing—looks like a route.

2. One must avoid the pitfall of having a constantly revised "theory" as to the trail's route. One must simply move around on various headings, and scrupulously avoid jumping to conclusions, while examining every possible detail for some sign of man-made passage: an old blaze, an axe-cut stump, or a tree with branches trimmed on only one side.

3. Finally, at some point you just have to get on with it and say, "Well, I'm sure they had a way through here, but what *I* need right now is just to get *through* here!"

The night was windy with snow falling steadily, and still mild, certainly above minus 20 degrees. It was a pleasure next morning to break that camp and move south. The sky cleared quickly as the sun rose. The dogs had enjoyed an easy couple of days, and they pulled me at breakneck speed down the short stretch of trail to the south end of Meridian.

At the southeast tip of Meridian stands a cabin belonging to Lawrence Catholique, a Chipewyan man from Lutsel K'e whom I knew for many years. That day his little log cabin was cold and empty, surrounded by red fuel drums, shreds of blue tarp, a log sawhorse, and some spruce-pole tripods. The frosted window panes sparkled in the sunlight like trays of jewels, as did the surface of the fresh snow all around, and as I flew past on the sled runners it struck me that the most stunning diamonds the Arctic holds will never be mined. "Thank goodness for that," I said aloud to no one. The dogs, long accustomed to my mutterings, paid no attention. I imagined Lawrence off at a distant, boring meeting that morning—land claims, caribou management, a diamond-mine proposal—while his little cabin, a symbol of his other life and his heritage, sat forlorn and abandoned. Sombre thoughts. The passage of a man's years.[2]

In a flash we had rounded the turn beyond the cabin. I was glad to put it out of sight. I sometimes fear for the future of this land now that people like Lawrence, who know it best, have deserted their day-to-day lives within it. Others, in brightly lit offices hundreds and thousands of miles distant, knowing little but firmly convinced that they know nearly everything, lay siege to it on all sides.

Alaskan poet and essayist John Haines wrote: "The land lives in its people."[3] I have thought long and hard about this profound sentence. Yes, the land lives in its people, but only in those people who live *on* and *in* that land, day by day, sunrise to sunset, equinox to solstice: gathering wood and water, fish and berries and meat; celebrating births and childhoods and comings of age; enduring illnesses and hardships; living to old age; marking graves on hilltops. The land does not "live," in this profound sense that I think Haines intends, in those people who launch off and arrive in it like platoons of astronauts, set up their base stations replete with lobster and green-pepper stir-fry. Nor does the land endlessly "live"—and here is the rub for a non-Native inhabitant like me in northern Canada these days—in those people who once lived there, no matter for how long. The land resonates with echoes of its past inhabitants, no matter their colour or creed, but these *echoes* of lives are not life. Echoes reverberate, but they eventually fade to silence.

––––––––

Our effortless morning sprint ended abruptly. We had reached the start of the day's work. "The Banana scales the Matterhorn," I quipped to myself, as we hit the first steep pitch of the snowshoe track I had made the day before. Up and up we went through the morning—grunting, sweating, heaving, and cursing.

I took my inspiration that day almost entirely from old Tugboat, one of my wheel dogs. The *wheel dogs*, a term borrowed from mule and horse drivers, are the dogs at the rear of the team, closest to the sled. (I suppose they should be called the "runner dogs" since there is not a wheel in sight.) The wheelers often bear the brunt of heavy work in tight quarters, because the weight of the sled is forever jerking them from behind while the momentum of the team pulls forward. Tugboat was an exemplary wheel dog, brutish and strong. A thoroughly unlikable fellow, ever first to steal another dog's supper or to instigate an utterly pointless brawl, all but blank in his relations with the human race, he was in his glory on that climb that day. Doing what he did best, inch by inch, hammering away at his tugline like a creature possessed, he made short work of every tough pitch. For a few fleeting moments I caught myself thinking I actually *liked* the old devil. Perhaps his work that day was my reward for all the Amoxicillin tablets I had dispensed to Tugboat and his hapless victims over years of scrapping, as I nursed them back after treating their

Tugboat and Dandy cast a doleful eye back at the load, partway up the climb to Daisy Lake.

wounds and suturing their gashes. For much of his bellicose dog-yard life, Tugboat must have thought antibiotic pills were some sort of bland after-dinner mint.

By mid-afternoon the dogs were parked and resting again, on the little lake above the climb. From the west end of the lake I floundered ahead on snowshoes and found a usable route up the next leg. I came back to the team. It was late in the day by then, so we turned east a short distance and found a spot where I could get water from the small creek. It was 25 below zero, breezy and snowing lightly as I stamped out a tent site in the dusk. We could reach Daisy early the next day, and I looked forward to that. Four caribou had been standing on the ice of the little bay when I reached Daisy on my scouting of the next stretch of trail. From the high ridge I had savoured a stunning view northward, across the sweep of McLeod Bay, past home and beyond to a horizon at least 50 miles away.

Tent up, dogs fed, supper done, I settled in for the night. My leg muscles kept cramping up badly, and I must have downed two quarts of water that evening. Journal notes: "I am impressed with the dogs…they are very strong. Wildlife so far: one otter, some crossbills, a whisky jack, a squirrel, a raven, and four caribou…This in three full days, lest anyone think it's a petting zoo out here."

My evening journal entries make an interesting contrast with the morning writings. At night my words are terse, blunt, and on some nights they simply fall off the page in illegible scrawls. Fatigue, a full belly, and a warm tent often brought sleep right in mid-sentence. In the morning, rested and relaxed with the new day ahead, my journal wanders off on frequent side trips, tries to wax poetic, and fills page after page.

It was now night three. I was already south of all territory familiar to me. With the day's trail barely wide enough in places for the sixteen-inch Banana to pass between tree trunks, we had essentially slammed the door behind us. No one would be driving a snowmobile up a trail that narrow, and no one would see any reason to follow us on foot. We were on our own.

I had been alone for just over a week, but I realized that I was still travelling with a host of mental companions and one foot in each of two worlds. I was nowhere near any state of meditative solitude, caught up as I was with leg cramps, the challenge of each day's trail-breaking, and my nagging awareness of days passing without significant mileage made toward the first resupply cache. I kept thinking of Kristen and the girls and their time in town. I looked forward to "radio night" on day six, when I would try to contact them. Strangely, I was troubled by a vague concern over events half a world away. "Open talk of war," the voice on CBC radio had solemnly intoned on the morning I left home, beginning a report from Palestine. Odd as it may seem, this forecast of an escalation in bloodshed troubled me deeply way out there, alone in my creek camp below Daisy Lake.

Perhaps because I was alone, this vague foreboding was always there, even after days back of beyond. We are all conditioned, I think, to carry with us that notion of a "real world," or "the big picture" that *really matters* and forms a grandiose backdrop to our puny daily lives. Out there, churning away on CBC and CNN and Google News, across the pages of the *Times* or the *Globe and Mail*: bloodshed, threats, diplomacy; crises, elections, floods, famines, and bombings...day and night the *news* pours in. It is a genie's curse, this ability to know about and to be instantly, incessantly "updated" on events which have no *immediate* significance in our daily lives. At the start of my wilderness journeys, and off and on throughout the trips, the "news" festered in one corner of my mind. A man sits alone in a little red tent in the snows of the subarctic forest, sewing up a rip in his parka, and finds himself wondering about Gaza— where he has never been, will likely never go, and where he knows not a soul. How strange. How absurd.

Day four came up grey and windy after a light dusting of overnight snow. I had long dreams of friends in the hours before waking, but like most of my dreams they seemed to be only silly scenes tossed up by a mind at restful play, rather than dramas weighted with deep significance. A long-time friend, hearing of my solo journeys, had admonished me to pay close attention to the portent of my dreams as I travelled, and I was trying to do so. So far I was not finding much insight there.

The miles ahead were the persistent theme of my waking thoughts. I could still not gauge the pace of our progress accurately, since so much time had been spent on the climb between Meridian and Daisy Lakes. I was accepting one cold hard fact of these wanderings, a fact that at first I tried to resist: time and distance were of enormous significance. It is all well and good, from the comfort of the cabin or the city apartment, to imagine an idyllic state of mind oblivious to mileage, time, and their correlation, speed. In the bright glare of sub-zero reality, though, once the resupply caches are placed, they become very insistent and concrete goals. Steady progress toward one's next food cache is a necessity, not a distraction.

The day's miles led the dogs and I steadily and pleasantly south, across Daisy and onto a lake called Dion. Caribou surrounded us on Daisy Lake, leaving fresh trails carved into the deep snow, from which I could choose the ones most in line with our heading. There were hours of intense pleasure that day, the first of the trip and—although I didn't know it—the last I would have for many days. Nine strong dogs pulling powerfully, the sun bright before us and the north wind strong at my back, a tow rope in hand, my wide wooden skis strapped to my mukluks, the narrow old Banana snaking almost gracefully along, little bands of caribou trotting ahead of us down the lake.

It had been years since I had travelled with that technique, wearing skis to take my own weight from the sled runners, shuffling along to help the dogs, letting them tow me when they could. No sign of a snowmobile track anywhere, and wild country all around. "What freedom!" I exclaimed to my journal that night.

The air was gradually cooling as the sky cleared from the north. My fourth camp was at the second narrows on Dion Lake. There I had hoped to find thin ice and easy access to water, but instead found—and finally chopped through—thirty inches of clear blue ice.

Morning brought minus 30 degrees, and I woke to the solo recital of a raven somewhere close to camp: a croak, a caw, a gulp, or ga-loop, then a ga-loop with a fancy flourishing trill, and a couple more work-a-day caws for punctuation. Maybe there is language there; there is surely playfulness and imagination.

I sat a while with the stove purring, hot instant "coffee" in my mug, thinking about how similar dog mushing is to sailing. I had spent the previous winter enrolled at a school of wooden boat building, and my thoughts were never very far from boats in the aftermath of that. I was utterly infatuated with sailing, as decades ago I had been infatuated with dog mushing, and my daydreams were filled with nautical images of gaff cutters, scow sloops, cockpit coamings, and birdsmouth spars. Parallels seemed plain enough—the graceful curve of wooden hull and sled runner, the magic of being drawn along by a quiet force other than your own muscles. "So silent when it labored hardest, so noisy and impatient when least effective," wrote Thoreau about his mainsail, on his short voyage down the Concord River.[4] How perfectly true of a dogteam.

And water, in all its forms, dominated my days. At times the management and interaction with it seemed to *be* my entire day. I was forever hauling, melting, and heating water for the dogs and myself, trying to drive moisture out of my clothing, piling snow around the tent walls for extra insulation, fighting condensation as my dinner pot boiled in the tent's outer vestibule. All day, every day, we plowed our way through the cold fluff that covered the land and lakes to a depth of two feet or more, and carefully skirted those treacherous places where all three forms of water lay together in ambush: a wisp of steam, a pool of black liquid, and a bordering shelf of fragile, treacherous ice. Even in camp I sometimes felt as though I was aboard a small vessel—the same notion of a safe harbour at nightfall, the same snug but cramped life demanding careful attention to detail. No surprise that so many mushers become sailors when winter ends, or when they finally tire of seven-month arctic winters. There is a deep connection between the two pursuits.

I was about ten miles from my Robert Lake cache. By mid-morning we were under way again, and the day held a few surprises. The portage out of Dion into some smaller lakes to the south brought us to the edge of a huge stretch of country that had recently burned. Every summer, in the area we were traversing, dozens of wildfires are started by the lightning bolts of brief thunderstorms. Once ignited the fires burn unfettered, changing their size and direction with each shift of the breeze. No attempt is made to put them out, for the country is far beyond any of the marked "values at risk" (cabins, fuel caches, fishing lodges, known grave sites) on the maps at the Forest Fire headquarters. In the country south of Great Slave Lake's eastern tip, the fires of many summers overlap, forming a quilted patchwork of new growth and charred snags for hundreds of miles down toward the Saskatchewan border.[5]

I left the team on Dion Lake and snowshoed ahead to find a route through the jumble of blackened spruce trunks and deadfall. The dogs waited patiently—they were getting used to this pattern of stop-and-go progress. When again we were mushing south together, a small drainage of ponds, thin ice, and flowing water demanded careful attention. I made it through with one foot slightly wet, and came to another bushwhack portage through charred snags, into the north end of Robert Lake. Again I left the team and went ahead to make a trail.

The crossing was short. I walked forward to test the snow conditions on this last lake of the day. Without warning one snowshoe suddenly sank into a slushy layer of water lying beneath the snow and atop the ice. *A soaker this time*, I thought, and cursed out loud. I would have to bring the sled and team forward, and once we were through the slush I would have to unlash the load and find some dry socks and woollen boot liners.

These hidden layers of slush, called "overflow" in the north, are an insidious hazard. Water rises from beneath the ice, usually from a narrow crack or small open hole, and then spreads out. Over a winter each new snowfall pushes the ice surface downward. The ice sags under the weight of the snow, and if given an opening the water beneath flows up to balance the equation. If exposed to the air in cold weather, this overflow water quickly freezes to a milky white, and poses no threat. Often though, it lies well insulated and unfrozen, hidden beneath a deceptive layer of fluffy snow. With the first unexpected step into overflow my nerves are always on edge, since I instinctively feel as though the ice beneath my feet might fail completely. Once it is obvious that it is only a patch of overflow slush, the surge of panic gives way to exasperation.

That day I was lucky. Sometimes even a short stretch of overflow can translate into hours of misery. (For sheer delight try getting a 500-pound snowmobile mired in a foot of slush at 40 below zero.) After pushing the sled and cajoling the reluctant dogs through the slop, I sat down atop the load and got my footgear back in working order. We set off down Robert Lake with daylight rapidly running out. I put on skis again and alternately led and followed the dogs. It was an ordeal for us all. The dogs were confused about the persistent lack of a decent trail and they were tired of my petulant whining. I was desperate to reach the cache site before we camped for the night. There was no help from the lake that evening—not a trace of an old caribou track or a helpful patch of wind-packed snow to be found. Late, cold, tired, and hungry, we reached the cache in the very last vestige of twilight. I was relieved to find my big wooden box of supplies still untouched in its snow hole, with the bright red fuel jug alongside it. There was relief too in the thought of taking the next day off, to repack and repair and rest.

That night I tried to call Kristen on the two-way radio. It was the first of our scheduled calls. While calling home sounds simple, and in this era of pocket-sized satellite telephones it can be simple (though expensive), I was still using a type of high-frequency radio that for decades was the communication standard in the northern bush. Thus every six nights on the trail my radio check-in calls involved stringing a long-wire antenna, running the wire into my tent, warming the radio transceiver and its batteries, and finally, at the pre-arranged time, transmitting my attempt. Kristen, about 180 miles away in Yellowknife, had a similar radio and antenna already set up.

That night on Robert Lake I had the times confused and tried my call at 9 p.m., when Kristen had been listening for me an hour earlier. I knew I could try again in the morning, having everything all set up, if I kept the radio warm. So that night, the two warm water bottles and my camera were joined in the depths of my crowded sleeping bag by the radio and its eleven C batteries. After a day of hard travelling, though, I could have slept comfortably with an anvil and a roll of barbed wire tucked in beside me.

The temperature dropped to the trip's new low that night, and I slept until past seven in the morning. I was gradually refining my technique in the tent, with my two-burner Coleman camp stove, and that morning I got the heat started without even getting out of my sleeping bag. "Luxury, pure luxury!" I remarked in my journal. I was happy to have a layover day ahead. As I stepped out of the tent to hang my sleeping bag from the tip of an upright ski, six caribou trotted up the trail we had plowed in the deep snow the night before. Those were the first caribou I had seen since Daisy Lake, and a welcome sight. I thought briefly of shooting one to bolster our food supply, but while I mulled over that opportunity they paused, caught wind of the camp and the dogs, and swiftly disappeared. They were the last mammals I would see for ten days.

Got through to Kristen on the radio and passed along my location. We exchanged some small talk about my progress and her time in town, and I had a chance to talk with Annika and Liv. They pressed me for complete details about their favourite dogs, most notably my young leader Foxtail, who was Annika's favourite. Kristen did not report any enormous new wars in the Middle East or elsewhere, so I could only surmise that there had been no momentous change for the worse in that realm. We signed off, with a plan to talk again in six days.

The layover day was busy. This was no surprise—the first layover after days of steady travel is always full of chores. I got a big campfire going alongside the dogs' picket line, there being an unlimited supply of burned

Wet gear hung to dry at the layover campfire, Robert Lake.

standing trees for fuel. "Firewood with prior job experience," I chuckled to my only audience. I dried all my gear and melted huge chunks of overflow ice from the Banana's runners, my snowshoes, and the sled bag. I warmed some Furacin salve and slathered all the dogs' footpads with it, finding only three dogs with tender paws: Foxtail had one, her brother Ernie had several, and irascible old Tugboat either had four sore feet or simply disliked my fussing with him—perhaps both.

At the height of the day's warmth and sunlight, about 2:30 p.m., I set off on snowshoes to break a trail south to the Snowdrift River. As I descended a long slope through burned snags and deep powdery snow, my mind's eye flashed up memories of other dramatic northern rivers: the Thelon, the Yukon, the Liard and the Coppermine. The Snowdrift is unique among the rivers flowing into the east end of Great Slave, in that it has a classic riparian character. Most small rivers on and through the Canadian Shield run through such shattered rocky country that they have no lazy S-curves, sloughs, cutbanks, or sandbars. Although it is a small river by any standard, the middle stretch of the Snowdrift, from Wolf Creek down to Siltaza Lake, has all of these, like a miniature Mississippi or Mackenzie. I was full of energy that afternoon, strolling downhill into the valley of the Snowdrift. There is an inherent rightness in the running of a dogteam up a winding frozen river, for a river makes one of nature's most obvious trails. Such a river can be, on good days, a wide avenue of snow and ice, connecting all of the landscape with an elegant, Taoist grace.

That evening I noted to my journal, with what turned out to be accurate premonition, that "perhaps by tomorrow night I won't be so nostalgic about river travel. I've had many miserable miles of river mushing over the years, with headwinds and punchy trail, in darkness and bitter cold—for the cold air always sinks to the lowest places on the landscape. Eight times on the Iditarod I have climbed off the Yukon at the village of Kaltag, and twice on the Yukon Quest at Circle and Dawson City, and every one of those times I have headed up the bank thinking, 'Am I ever glad to be off the goddamned Yukon River!'"

Still, I was touring, not racing, there was a river ahead to follow upstream into new country, and that all felt good as the day ended. I cooked my supper outdoors at the open fire, but darkness, deep cold, and fickle smoke took some of the pleasure out of that. Once finished with the fuss of cooking I stoked the fire high. Radiant heat soaked luxuriously through my heavy clothing, deep into flesh and bone. Out beyond the ring of firelight the sky was speckled with a million stars. A gibbous moon cast its glow over the lake and the snowy fire-scarred hills. Before heading into the tent, I put nylon jackets on all the dogs. On this second night in the same campsite their circular lying places had frozen hard and crusty, and the cold was feeling deeper by the minute. They seemed happy to have me bring them their jackets. Even Tugboat let me wrap him up and tuck him in.

To my surprise a mass of slightly warmer, moister air must have moved through overnight. It was only minus 26 degrees the next morning, and the visibility was reduced in an icy haze. "8 miles vis.," I noted in my journal, as if such precision mattered to anyone. I did not write for long in the tent that morning. It was day seven. It was 35 or 40 miles to the next cache, the big one I had left at the outflow of Noman Lake. I was glad it was not any farther, and I thanked myself for the choice I had made in the airplane, not to set the cache on Hjalmar Lake, 100 miles farther south. Had I done so, the prospect of reaching it would surely have looked impossible. I would probably have been forced to return home.

I broke camp quickly, with a short stretch of broken trail ahead as incentive. Meanwhile the northeast wind built to a gale. Just out of camp the dogs and I came quickly into the shelter of the burned-over slope with its thick swath of charred tree trunks. We crossed Robert Lake's outflow creek and paralleled its north bank down toward the Snowdrift. On my snowshoe hike down that slope the previous day, I had seen an amazing juxtaposition—amazing to me at least. Jack pine seedlings were sprouting in the burn. As is taught in every grade-school ecology class in northern North America, jack pines are perfectly adapted to reforesting an area following a fire. The dense waxy cones are opened by the heat of a wildfire, releasing the seeds. Nothing too remarkable then, in the sight of those seedlings, except the welcome sight of a tree which does not grow at all on the north shore of McLeod Bay, and which for me always carries memories of my years in Minnesota. Here and there among the little jack pines was something I found truly odd: big clumps of muskox wool hung from the bright green needles of the seedlings. I knew that there were muskox down in the Snowdrift valley, but the sight of that wool festooning the pines was striking. Like most people I always think of the muskox as a creature of the high north, the tundra, and the Arctic archipelagos. In the years since that journey, though, my flying work has brought me to those Snowdrift valley burns for many days in summer and early autumn. There are large herds of muskox throughout that area, right in with the moose and the beaver, and those herds seem to be growing. Those muskox show no inclination ever to wander north and east, out past the treeline. If anything they seem to be migrating south. In fact, at this writing, muskox have surpassed every other large mammal as our most common sighting around the Hoarfrost River, and muskox roasts now grace our table more often than caribou.

I stuffed some of the muskox qiviut into my pocket along with a jack pine cone, to show Annika and Liv back at home, and enjoyed the final few minutes of downhill travel on a broken trail to the bank of the river. The fun was about to begin.

———————

The Snowdrift valley, the same valley I had so happily admired twenty-four hours earlier, had become a wind tunnel of frigid, fast-moving air, flowing downriver out of the northeast, directly against us. Through the morning the sky had cleared and the temperature was steadily falling. We reached the river just past noon. For the next five hours the dogs and I alternated in the lead, heads down, churning upriver into the wind through deep and drifted snow. Total gain for those five hours: about nine miles.

We were immersed, the ten of us, in a familiar struggle. All my naive visions of a pleasant sojourn up the winding river valley seemed pretty laughable by the time I set up camp. The cold was still deepening. I made a spruce bough bed for each dog, as a full moon came up in the north-east.[6] My notes that night end simply, "I am very tired. Dogs too."

The deep-freeze had begun. I knew another thing from my past travels farther upstream on the Snowdrift River: this valley could get much colder than the surrounding uplands on any winter day. A few years back, I had flown a couple of mineral-claim stakers, a tough spry Newfoundlander and an equally tough Dene man from Fort Liard, out and back from our homestead to the upper Snowdrift. The weather at dawn on December 30th, at our place, was clear and minus 36 degrees: cold but not desperately so. When I landed eighteen minutes later, about 23 miles to the east, the thermometer showed a bracing minus 44 degrees—about 50 below Fahrenheit for those who prefer that scale when the cold really sets in. This pattern prevailed day after day for the duration of that job. The stakers finished their work, and I made a mental note that the valley of the Snowdrift River might well be the coldest place in this part of the territories.

––––––––––

The days were changing, and changing me. I had been out a week, and I knew that in another week I would still be out. My solitude felt comfortable, and the dogs had so far proven themselves equal to everything the country had thrown at us. As mushers often do I took my inspiration from them, and envied at times the apparent simplicity of their lives. We were making progress together, even if slow and gruelling. It was good to be immersed in that unfamiliar landscape, uncertain from hour to hour what lay beyond each fresh bend in the river.

That was the up side.

A lesson regarding the solitary life, which I was relearning daily, is that it has a definite down side. When travelling with others in a tight-knit group a person does not have the perverse luxury to truly plumb the depths of a foul mood. But alone—even if in the company of nine eager dogs—there are no social niceties barring your descent into the doldrums. I am not by nature a moody man. I am generally optimistic—some might even say irrationally so. I have a good sense of humour, tending toward the ribald and sardonic. Alone in the wind and cold and grunting effort of those days between Robert Lake and my far cache, my optimism and humour were hard-pressed to match wave after wave of frustration and fatigue. I was getting cranky.

Truly cold weather is not conducive to knee-slapping hilarity, no matter the circumstances. As I write this, years later and back home at Hoarfrost River, it has turned Cold. *Cold*, with a capital *C*, is not a term used flippantly around here. It starts, generally, when the temperature hits 40 below zero.[7] Such temperatures, especially when they come during the darkest winter period around the solstice, sap strength and resolve. Outdoor chores and travel take on an air of desperation; indoors, one feels besieged by the frigid air beyond the windowpanes. As the mercury sinks, a primal instinct rises in every creature's brain: hunker down, stay put, wait it out.

You can, for a time, flip this instinct on its head and draw strength and power from the cold and darkness. A good dose of gallows humour and a few like-minded companions can make the cold, like a mountain wall or a storm at sea, an inspiring adversary. Racing to Nome, or running for home, you can just grind it out. Heading away from home, though, alone on a self-inspired "adventure"...well, that's another kettle of frozen fish.

Those miles up the Snowdrift River and south to Noman Lake demanded that adversarial, black-humour survival strategy, so I dug it out, dusted it off, and carried on, cursing like a Jack tar and throwing myself almost violently at each new challenge. I chuckled aloud at night, trying to read a long-winded New Age commentary on a Mayan parable, something a friend had sent me for inspiration on my trip. "What the hell?" I muttered, "Tropical wisdom at 42 below zero? Gimme a break, man. Bring on Thor and Odin, ice and snow, Väinämöinen and Valhalla, but spare me the flippin' jungles and palm trees!"

Thoreau expressed a similar frustration, more politely, toward the end of his "Winter Walk" essay: "Is there no religion for the temperate and frigid zones?...Let a brave, devout man spend the year in the woods of Maine or Labrador, and see if the Hebrew Scriptures speak adequately to his condition and experience, from the setting in of winter to the breaking up of the ice."[8]

We worked our way up the Snowdrift for two full days—long slogs in the steadily deepening cold—upwind and upstream. Hour by hour I traded off trail-breaking with my stalwart lead dog Steve and several of his younger proteges. I shuffled ahead of the team on my wide wooden skis. (I hesitate to say "I skied" because it was not really skiing— "Norwegian snowshoeing" is more apt.) The dogs became good at following along just behind me. Whenever a patch of wind-packed snow gave them slightly better footing, I dropped back to a tow line behind or alongside the sled.

Early in the evening of 27 February, day eight of the trip, we reached a big horseshoe bend in the river and climbed a steep bank. My map showed this as the spot where the Snowdrift curved closest to the watershed of Noman Lake and the Taltson River. I planned to strike south

overland from there. I made camp on a level bench of widely spaced jack
pine, almost a city-park setting, which must be stunningly beautiful in
the warm days of late summer. I did the chores, jacketed all the dogs, and
dove headfirst into the tent. "The Snowdrift is aptly named," I scrawled in
my journal.

At dawn on 28 February my little thermometer read minus 44 degrees.
That was four degrees lower than the lower limit of the tiny numbered
markings on its scale, so I was just guessing. By the behaviour of my camp
stove and the nylon fabric of the tent, I could tell it was all of 44 below,
and then some. At such temperatures there is no volatility left in gasoline,
and a big puddle of it can be set alight with impunity when priming a
stove. Nylon tent fabric crackles like heavy aluminum foil.

Grasping the metal fuel bottle with gloved hands, my lower body still
encased in my sleeping bag, I doused the stove top with fuel and put a
match to it. I watched as the raw gasoline slowly caught and flared in the
vestibule of the tent. As I slowly opened the control knob, burner number
one sounded off with a comforting roar. The auxiliary burner soon followed. Ah, blessed heat! Mr. Coleman of Wichita, Kansas, purveyor of the
time-honoured two-burner stove, should have long ago received a Nobel
Prize in Applied Thermodynamics.

Outside, the dogs were curled up, their jackets frosted over, nine perfect circles in the snow. They would have the day off while I broke trail
south over the divide. In such deep cold it would be good for them to
spend the day resting quietly, conserving energy. Several of them were
afflicted with an odd malady that I had seen only a few times before. The
fur on the backsides of their shanks, just above the paw for six inches
or more, was being stripped away by the combination of deep snow and
extreme cold. Iditarod slang for this is "chicken legs." The condition
baffles me, being so obviously detrimental to creatures otherwise so
perfectly adapted to the North. It is an inherited tendency, seen only in
certain bloodlines of sled dogs. Perhaps it is a genetic tag-along, linked to
one of the non-northern breeds that have added diversity to the Alaskan
husky stock over the years: hound or retriever or pointer. Conditions such
as we had—the deep cold with many miles of breaking trail through deep
snow—are so rare nowadays even for teams working in the Far North,
that I suppose the trait has never been purposely bred out of the more
recent husky strains.

Ernie, a two-year-old then, along with his brother Flynn and their
sire Riley, were hardest hit by "chicken legs" on that trip. By the time we
left the Snowdrift valley southbound, the back surfaces of Ernie's hind
legs were bald and red. I had used up my entire supply of stretchy gauze

The team in deep soft snow, breaking out the trail along my snowshoe tracks.

on him the previous day, and I knew I would have to try something else. Ernie, for his part, was bouncing and barking with eagerness at every pause in our progress, and he was eating like a creature possessed. Appetite is always a good barometer of a dog's well-being. As I tried to bandage his shanks on the river the day before, he was wagging his bushy tail so hard that I had to force it off to one side with my leg in order to work. He was making his point plainly enough: ugly and painful as his shanks might look to me, he did not intend to quit any time soon.

An ominous foreboding crept over me in camp that morning. I tried to discern its origins and came up with only the bare facts: I was completely alone, it was very cold, and the success of the coming day was entirely uncertain. Somewhere down the river the tips of my ears had been frostbitten, along with the tips of two toes, and I could feel the morning's deep chill stinging those places. I felt as if the cold had become a predator, waiting and watching, probing my defences, poking and prodding as I secured the tent and packed a light backpack for the day's hike.

Muttering "See you later, guys," to the dogs, I stepped off into the woods, axe in hand, a compass on a lanyard around my neck, and a folded one-to-a-quarter-million topographic map in my anorak pocket. As always, there was comfort in action. My foreboding and tension faded into the effort of movement, and the constant mental monologue of trail-breaking: "Left or right around this pile of windfall? Up the slope here, or farther down the shore of the pond? How are the dogs going to pull that damned Banana sled through this minefield of boulders? Here's a nice stretch, must be a sand flat in summer. Wait a minute, what the hell? This must be the big hill on the map, the one I thought I had already passed…and if it is, then where does that put me?"

The sun shone and the day was calm. I was constantly adjusting my clothing, stuck in the paradox of hard exertion in bitter cold. Sweat dripped from my brow while inches away my ears stung with frost. For most of the day I wore an odd-looking hat made from my neck warmer. The tall polyester-fleece fez rose high above my head, giving me the look of a subarctic Shriner on parade. All I needed was a miniature car. Step by step I climbed the hills south from the river and the hours passed. The muffled swish and thump of snowshoes in deep powder, my hard breathing and mumblings were the only sounds. A world frozen, silent, brightly lit and abandoned, untouched by man since the start of time…that is how those four miles felt to me.

I had looked at the map with my neighbour Roger back in Reliance. He had been to Noman Lake decades ago, and he told me that the old route he recalled was reached from farther up the Snowdrift, making a longer traverse southwest along a creek. I had considered this, and had decided to punch straight south, partly to avoid more miles of hard slogging on the river. A phrase from our conversation rang over and over in my ears that day: "They [the Natives and old-timers] always took the easiest way." He had not said it in a disparaging tone, but in simple recognition of a fact. Over the years an unspoken consensus had been informally reached about every such route. I was flying in the face of all that wisdom, cutting across the grain of the country by forcing a more direct passage, and I was paying for my stubbornness.[9]

A lovely steep-walled lake and a climb through some thick timber brought me over the crest of the watershed divide. I could not see Noman Lake, but I could tell in which fold of the horizon it lay. By just after 2 p.m. I was standing on its ice. Six miles or so to the southwest was my big cache—wall tent, wood stove, frozen doughnuts and all. The next day, with luck, we could get there. Happier than I had been for three days, I turned and started back up into the hills toward the camp and the dogs. My energy was waning. I was glad for the broken trail to follow and for the sun's barely perceptible mid-afternoon warmth. I made only a few minor efforts to fine-tune the route of the trail as I backtracked, despite some major revelations that showed the route I *should* have taken. I was too worn out to break open new chunks of the route. We would have to make do.

That day and that stretch of country still strike me as a crux. Every journey, like every climb, has a crux—sometimes obvious, sometimes subtle. I knew we would have a hard time, the dogs and I, getting over to Noman on the rough trail I had made. But the battle—for that is what, like it or not, the trip had felt like for most of the past week—was won. Now there was a trail to the lake, a lake to the cache, a trail back to the river, and so on, all the way to home. I could relax. I hoped I could remember how.

I was back in camp in two hours, hardly stopping on the way. I was teetering on the edge of exhaustion then, and I felt the lightheaded swooning that comes when the bottom of one's reserve is reached. Momentum carried me over the final mile. The dogs all stood up and barked, happy to see me emerge from the forest.

I built a campfire, in order to save some stove fuel for heating the tent, boiled a big pot of instant soup, downed it, melted snow and soaked the dog food, fed the team, and crept into my hidey-hole. I did not re-emerge for over thirteen hours—rudimentary indoor plumbing being one of the perks of solo winter travel.

The weather stayed clear and the cold eased a little. It was minus 38 degrees the next morning, the first of March. It was check-in day, and I learned from my brief morning radio conversation with Kristen that it was warming up in Yellowknife, and forecast to continue doing so. Yellowknife was 180 miles west of my Snowdrift campsite, lying in a different climate area, so I knew it might not warm up where I was. Often, though, the weather that comes to Yellowknife does eventually move east and southeast.

After the radio call my thoughts turned to times past. The trail-breaking through new terrain had once again left me with a profound respect for the old-timers and their journeys. Whether Native or newcomer, a hundred or a thousand years ago, theirs was a different North; an utterly different world, in fact. It is easy for us to forget this fact, and it is thought-provoking to try and remember—or at least imagine—their world. Without aircraft, without radios, long before satellite telephones and accurate topo maps and GPS, human life in the Far North hung from a completely different set of balances. Survival could hinge on the existence or obliteration of one thin ribbon of packed trail, one chance sighting and skillful stalking of an animal, one shivering attempt to strike a spark and make a fire. Viewed in this way no modern journey in wilderness is ever *for real*, so to speak, because even if one eschews various levels and layers of technology, one does so in the knowledge that they do exist. Whenever we venture out nowadays we pick and choose our own level of playing the modern version of wilderness travel. We take this but leave that; we use one layer of technology (an aircraft for resupply) and spurn another (a satellite telephone). I was doing this myself—setting rules for my own approach to the game. In the North a few hundred years ago wilderness travel was not a game. It was life and death—plain and simple.

On my trip south I had with me several forms of modern technology as hedges against the direst scenarios. A friend from the government wildlife department had loaned me a little VHF tracking collar, of the size put on wolverines, which I had bolted onto the handlebar of my sled. It just hung there, emitting a weak radio signal of a specific frequency, day and night. Were I to suddenly keel over dead in the snow or disappear through a hole in the ice, a search plane could tune a set of telemetry equipment to that frequency and home in on that signal, just as wildlife researchers would home in on a collared wolverine. At least they would be able to find the sled, and thus perhaps my frozen carcass. The country being so vast and empty, it seemed like the least I could do to help my loved ones solve the mystery of my disappearance. None of this was pleasant to contemplate, but I was happy that the little radio collar was there, and I would bring it with me again on my journeys to the other compass points.

I did not carry a GPS unit on that journey south, and I was content to be without that. In the relatively small scale of that south journey, my trail tromped out step by step through thickly wooded country, with obvious lakes and drainages as markers, I did not once miss the nuisance of computerized navigation. In the coming years' solos, with greater speed of travel and much greater distances over open country, I did use the GPS to check my progress, and I made an uneasy peace with it as a part of my gear.

I discovered on that morning that I had left my extra rolls of film at home. I had by then shot up the first roll of thirty-six exposures (with what turned out to be lacklustre results), and had tried to record a few memorable scenes along the way. Having no more film, I would just ditch the camera at the cache site for retrieval later. I did not consider this to be much of a loss and in looking back I still hold to that view. Photography, like GPS navigation and two-way radios and satellite telephones, can all too easily become a distraction for me. (Now a voice pipes up in the back of my mind and says, "And what about all of your scribbling in the journal—isn't that a distraction, too?" Not in the same way, is my answer.)

At mid-morning we set out for Noman Lake and the cache, following the twisting snowshoe trail up toward the watershed divide. As we left camp Ernie was decked out with a goofy apparatus that I had designed to protect his horrible-looking shanks. I had cut the bottoms out of a pair of my wool socks, put one of his hind legs into each sock, and strung the top ends up over his hips through the rear webs of his harness. It worked poorly and looked ridiculous. For his part, Ernie seemed downright embarrassed. After a half-hour I put the entire rig away. I knew there was some soothing salve in the cache supplies, and I hoped a few applications of that would help him.

Noman Lake lies southwest-northeast in a rugged defile, the forest along its north shore burned by a recent fire. It is about eight miles long and a half-mile across. It was the biggest expanse of open ice we had reached since leaving Great Slave and Meridian. I arrived on it hoping to find it firm and wind-packed enough for some fast sledding. It was just barely firm enough to allow the dogs to go forward without a broken trail, but we still moved slowly down it as evening came on. Beyond Noman, over a short portage trail, was Nonacho, a truly enormous lake by most standards, at least 40 miles from end to end, with arms and inlets spreading in every direction. From our home up on McLeod Bay, just the name "Nonacho" has always epitomized the country lying to the south. I had flown over Nonacho many times, but I had never been on the ground there long enough to truly see it.

At twilight, about half past six, we arrived at the big cache. I dumped the contents of my sled in a clearing on the Nonacho side of the short portage, and returned to Noman to ferry the drums and bundles that made up our resupply. The dogs were confused by this, and they balked at first, then tore off through the woods at breakneck speed when they realized that the sled was virtually weightless. Much vehemence.

Finally we got ourselves settled. Camp making progressed haltingly in the blackness of a cloudy moonless night. A tree branch had given me a bad poke in the eye sometime earlier in the day, so the darkness brought with it even more fumbling than usual. It was midnight before the big canvas wall tent was up, with a fire crackling in its sheet-metal stove. I laid back on the boughs I had cut for the tent floor and watched the steam pour out of my clothing and the outer shell of my sleeping bag. My weary brain worked in short bursts: Nonacho. South. Cache. Get in the sleeping bag. Blow out the candle.

Nonacho Lake epitomizes south for me in several ways. Come morning I watched the sun light up the austere ranks of dead trees that form its shoreline; trees not killed by wildfires but by the rising water of the lake as it became a reservoir behind the dams of the Taltson River hydroelectric project. Built to generate electricity for a lead-zinc mine on the south shore of Great Slave Lake at Pine Point, the dams still exist although the mine shut down years ago. In recent years there has been talk—and even some sporadic action—to do with revamping the generating stations and sending electricity north to the diamond mines, or south to the tar-sands developments in Alberta, or across Great Slave to Yellowknife.

Noman Lake, just to the north, does not have the bathtub ring of dead timber, so the portage where I was camped marked the upper limit of the reservoir effect. The ghostly dead trees, along with a dismal-looking plywood shack perched on the knoll across from my camp, the huge expanse of fire-killed forest rising from the north shore of Noman, my jumble of metal cache barrels and gear all in disarray, lent that camp—viewed out of my one good eye in the cold light of dawn—a dismal ambience it took me most of the day to shake. My long-awaited day of rest was off to a bleak start.

A woodpecker began to tap on a tree near camp. That sound brightened my mood a little. On the journey thus far I had seen very few birds, very little life of any sort. Not surprising at that season in that region, but a fact that made every sign of life all the more welcome.

I loafed and puttered. Supply caches reached in the midst of a journey always entail hours of mundane chores: opening and emptying, refilling and repacking. At that camp I was glad to make some choices on items I could trim from my load. The pile of discarded gear grew steadily larger and heavier. With my mind's eye set on the steep climb north out of Noman, I culled ruthlessly. By early afternoon I was in the tent, baking a skillet of bannock, when I suddenly realized the place was stifling. I stepped outside. A southwest wind was up, the sky had turned cloudy, and the temperature was rising rapidly. *Ah*, I thought, *a change!* After lunch I went for a short walk on snowshoes and took a look at the shack across the cove. It must have been built as an overnight stop for summertime fishermen. There is a fly-in fishing lodge down on the central peninsula of Nonacho, so this had likely been an outpost camp. Nowadays it is just a hideous, useless eyesore, wrecked—mostly in winter, it seemed—by passing hunters and trappers. What a penchant for mindless destruction these places so often showcase! What could have been a haven for a passing traveller, whatever the agenda, was just a squalid heap of old snow-machine parts, torn-up foam mattresses, ransacked kitchen utensils, mildewed magazines, and on and on. It reminded me of my arrival at the old cabin at Hoarfrost, many years earlier, when I came ashore on a summer night to take up residence and start my new life there. Even the heaps of old garbage bags and broken glass looked familiar.

The mess dragged my lifting mood downward again, and I fled from the shack. On the way out I pilfered six pans and bowls usable as dog dishes, and once back to my camp I heated up a rich soup for the team. They slurped it down eagerly. I thought about carrying the bowls with me on the trip home, but decided to stick with the method I had used so far on the trip. (See Appendix B for notes on the feeding and watering methods I used.) Deep cold brings more danger of dehydration for both people and dogs, and the dogs were feeling its effects—I could see this plainly by the deep yellow of their urine in the snow. I decided I would continue soaking their kibble–fat mix with copious amounts of water, and attempt to stay ahead of the problem that way. I did not want to resort to packing and carrying a clumsy pile of mismatched pans and bowls.

As I crossed between my camp and the shack I noticed lynx tracks out on the narrow arm of Nonacho. Lynx are rare up around the Hoarfrost River and McLeod Bay. They become steadily more commonplace— along with beaver lodges, jack pine, and poplar—as one travels south away from the taiga and treeline, into true boreal forest.

My injured eye was improving and by late afternoon I could see clearly again. Back at camp I laid out a spruce bough bed for each dog. They were enjoying this rare luxury and I was finding it pleasant to take the time for their extra comfort. In the alders across the creek mouth a trio of ptarmigan clucked, feeding and roosting. Their meat is as tasty as partridge. I considered shooting one, but I had ample food and so did the dogs. I decided to let them be.

At last, imbued with the relaxation of the rest day, I wrote that evening: "I walk at dusk. The silence and solitude more intense now that the goal is reached. A woodpecker tap-taps on a flood-killed spruce trunk, soughing of wind in spruce tops, burble of creek. Firewood cut for night and morning. Supper to cook, reading, tugline repair, sleep. Tonight the journey deepens."

Morning, 3 March brought calm overcast with light snow and a tropical minus 15 degrees. A good sleep had worked wonders on my mood. Even the shoreline's dead bathtub ring of old snags could not dampen my optimism. I spent the morning in a final effort to pare down my load. I hooked up three dogs and shuttled the discarded gear and the remains of the cache back over the portage to Noman, where I could pick it up by plane sometime in coming weeks.

North toward home: I would now be heading away from the sun, yes, but also away from the first visible vestige of that sprawling industrial civilization that dominates the southern two-thirds of the continent. And which, given ample incentive (translation: money) will surely come north to take a shot at dominating what remains. I could have wandered south on Nonacho for a day or so, but such an effort held no interest for me. I had accepted by then that there would be no good fast sledding conditions for us on that trip. No trapper's trail was going to suddenly appear, and even the big lakes were not packed hard by the wind. The snow was just too deep and soft and no one else was afield in that part of the world. We would have to break every foot of the trail, and if wind and snow had filled in our back trail we would be obliged to break it all a second time.

Here was a situation where travelling alone was clearly a disadvantage. With a string of several good dogteams, with one member of the party on snowshoes or skis out front breaking trail (that person could set off each morning while camp was being struck), and a frequent rotation of everyone's position as the day went on, a steady 15 or 20 miles would be possible. So ran my thoughts... would, could, should, might. I was just theorizing, and still stuck in the trap of trying to justify to my ego the paltry map mileage covered on the trip thus far.

Gradually the final pieces fell into place. Everything to be left behind was cached for pickup and my sled load was lashed down. The Banana looked even trimmer than I had dared hope—hell, it looked almost racy. It carried a full seven days of rations for us all, fuel for the stove, and a pared-down complement of camp gear and spare clothing, bedding, tent, and tools. I had jettisoned a good amount of weight and bulk, with eight days left to travel and a clearer notion of my daily routine. There were still some supplies up on Robert Lake, so we were in good shape. Ounces pared from a load always add up to pounds. Kristen gets a laugh out of watching me cull even the papers in my briefcase before setting off in the plane for town, and the same mindset is helpful for all travelling, whether by boat, backpack, aircraft, or dogsled. Backup gear and "spares" so easily become impedimenta. One thing I do know is that any non-essential item left behind is rarely missed. Ingenuity and substitution can carry the day nine times out of ten, and there is time and energy saved for every piece of extraneous gear left behind.

After a two-night layover camp and all the sorting and repacking of my supply cache, I looked at the campsite with a wry smile. Green spruce boughs lay in heaps at the tent site and the dog beds, stripped saplings were scattered about, dog shit in big frozen clumps marked the perimeter of the piss-stained picket line, stumps of deadwood marked the ends of a spider web of snowshoe paths out into the surrounding forest. *No "minimum impact" camping here,* I thought—it was more like "dig in and rest and regroup, and no one is going to camp in this spot again for a hundred years," which in this particular part of the world may well be true. A fresh snowfall, a spring thaw, a summer's growth, and this little patch of swampy shoreline would be ready for another weary winter traveller. We had not done any lasting damage, but the place sure looked trampled as we left it that day.

My final quick entry in the journal record of those rest days, written just before I took down the big canvas tent, was: "More than anything, I just want the country to crack a little smile!" As if on cue, the land and sky did flash us a fleeting grin that afternoon. As we mushed up Noman Lake the clouds broke open into bright blue, and despite a rowdy north wind it was a pleasant afternoon.

Leaving the cache site on the island in Noman, the dogs balked briefly at the prospect of heading out onto the punchy, windswept expanse of the lake. I marched forward and "discussed" our options with Steve and his partner Foxtail, my leaders that day. The discussion took the form of mitten waving, stern exhortations delivered in a gruff tone, and a firm swat to each of their hind ends. Following this presentation they *understood* our situation and our objectives more clearly. Up the lake we went, into the wind. For the first time since day one of the trip, I rode on the sled runners. We were moving at a glacial four miles an hour or so, but we were moving more easily than we had in days. Climbing off Noman we took a short break on a sunlit slope of white birch, then grunted and heaved our way up the first quarter of the crossing to the Snowdrift. The dogs—rested, rehydrated, and trail-hardened—put on an amazing performance out in front of that heavy sled. My worries faded a little, but I knew I was teetering on the ragged edge of prudence as we moved across those hills that day. With so much power and momentum, on such a crude trail, the risk of breaking the sled, smashing a hand, or putting out an eye was right there minute by minute. I could not let my guard down.

That night the red-and-yellow tent felt like home again. Everything was back in its familiar place and all within arm's reach. It was a welcome change from the clutter and confusion of the big wall tent at the layover camp. Tugboat Lake, in honour of the old grouch himself, was my name for that camp on night thirteen, partway over the divide between Noman Lake and the Snowdrift River. Tugboat had been in his glory all afternoon, hammering away at his tug line like a furry piston, preserving and amplifying every shred of the Banana's momentum.

It came to me, finally, late that day—the sense of rhythm I had been craving. The journey was my entire world, and it was good, and I was grateful. That state of mind is so elusive, and consciously *striving* for it only pushes it farther away. It comes on its own when and if it will. As I did my chores that evening and the sun slid below the high ridge to the west-southwest, an unusual colour tinged the pink-and-orange sky. It was—and I had to look for a long time to confirm this—a delicate green, like the green of a new birch leaf, just edging the plumes of cirrus cloud. It was the same ethereal green as the aurora borealis, but it appeared to be a part of the sunset's spectrum, not a twilight showing of the aurora. I smiled about it later, thinking "red sky at night, sailor's delight" and imagining what a *green* sky might portend for a sailor on a stormy passage.

The sunset, the day's progress, and that beautiful campsite had put me in a reflective, appreciative frame of mind, but my dreams that night were the usual mix of silliness and banality. In my journal I wrote, "No spirit world messengers, animal totems, or dog-driving shamans come to me at night. I am firmly bound to this straightforward world of snow, tent, trail, dogs, friends, airplanes, boats, books, wife and children and—*out there*—all the sundry nuts and bolts of my life. What does this mean? I guess maybe that I am just happy, and damned lucky, and not *seeking* or *searching*."

Yet immediately I knew that could not be true. Alone, at 30 below zero, in the midst of one of the most remote tracts of land on the planet, with no respectably *practical* agenda like trapping, prospecting, or even race-training, I had obviously come in search of *something*. So next was this: "Yes I am. I seek a sense of place, tired as that cliché is—a gut feeling, when next I stand on our beach at the Hoarfrost on a warm evening late in summer, my bare skin drying in the last puff of breeze after a dip in the lake, and gaze *south* to the ridges on the horizon. Then my mind's eye will conjure up the country here with a well-won familiarity: the burns, the river, the forlorn flooded shoreline of Nonacho, the boulder fields of this divide I camp on tonight."

Filling pages in my mental atlas, mile by mile. I had, as of that year, lived longer—sixteen years then, now twenty-seven, and on from here—

at Hoarfrost River than at any other place in my life, including my boyhood home in Illinois. The place had become my life, and my life was immersed in it whether or not I tried to make it so. It seemed fitting, that evening, to be having that coyote's breakfast at last: the "good look around" part. The *waking* dream, the journey itself, was sufficient, and I could not muster much concern over the ridiculous themes of my *sleeping* dreams.

———————

Two weeks on the trail, and my thoughts were easing toward cabin life. In this way cold-weather camping contrasts sharply with outings in summer. I was not craving pizza or beer, but instead the small niceties of life in buildings: windows, thawed food, bare feet, chairs, and—most of all—the chance to sleep with my head uncovered, not shrouded in layers of nylon, fur, wool, and an irksome patina of breath-frost.

Dog morale was decidedly upbeat. The dogs had obviously surmised that we were homeward bound. They could sense, too, that I was happy about that, and that I had finally relaxed. Their pesky chicken-leg troubles had been eased by the rest days, some salve, and the firmer broken trail. Foxtail had come into estrus on the day we hit the cache, but so far it appeared that the boys were oblivious to her condition. A good thing, too, since such situations always hold potential for a complete breakdown of a dogteam's work ethic. (I will float no sweeping anthropomorphic generalizations.)

Twilight, 4 March, found us back at camp seven on the north bank of the Snowdrift. The wind had strengthened yet again, and the temperature had dropped to 34 below. On the first leg of the day we had finished off the crossing from Noman, and the dogs had been amazing. On the very steepest slope I had resorted to a technique used often by mushers cresting Eagle Summit on the Yukon Quest trail. I had used it myself on that climb during the 1998 race, but had not needed to resort to it since then. It had come in handy on one short pitch just out of camp that morning. At each slight pause in the team's upward progress, I grabbed the snow hook and leaped forward to plant it, essentially *backwards*, alongside the wheel dogs. Anchored by the hook, the sled could not slide back, and the dogs did not have to fight gravity as they took a short rest. With each such kedging of the anchor hook a few more feet of the climb were gained, and everyone, four-legged and two, could catch their breath. Tugboat was working alone in wheel, in order to give him a little more side-to-side freedom than he would have with a partner, and he continued to do a huge proportion of the grunt labour. A strange critter, that one, and at this point in his checkered career a tremendous dog whenever the going turned slow and steep. That day he had again forced me to recant some of the nasty things I had said about him over the years.

About 2 p.m. we had reached the river. Oh, the river. Our upstream trail was still discernible, just barely, but it was now only a narrow trough packed full of cold windblown snow—snow which, as mentioned already, is more like dry sand. The sled's runners rasped and squealed on it, while the wind—which had swung 180 degrees around to the west—came straight at us again. It was a wearisome three-hour trudge to our old campsite. I was cursing foully at one moment, when suddenly I stopped and said aloud, "Oh fer Chrissakes, Olesen, snap out of it—it's not as if anybody *told* you to come out here."

Yep.

My patience, like my reserves of body fat, was wearing thin. Every passage had held some element of down-and-dirty struggle. My mood was swinging wildly and for hours of each day I was not getting so much as a flicker on the needle of the fun-o-meter. That night, warm and tucked into my sleeping bag at last, I wrote:

What life we must have passed today, all of it unseen except for three ptarmigan peering down at us from the steep sand-and-clay riverbank. Lynx tracks joined our trail on the small pond just before we reached the river—big paired prints bounding out from the forest and turning down our trail. There is animal life around, but it is sparse and invisible. Surely somewhere we have passed a few caribou, a moose or two, some muskox, wolves, and wolverines, perhaps a bear asleep in its den (as any creature with an ounce of sense would be!). Surely there are fish beneath the ice, drifting along like the bears in some semi-aware state, just biding their time, waiting for spring.

It is difficult to convey, or to recount honestly, the essence of such days as those on the Snowdrift. The theme of those slogging, half-numb river days does not jive with those romantic (and often citified) legions steeped in the outlook of Nature as Benevolent Mother. The journey had been, for the most part, Nature as Merciless Adversary, and I was on the home stretch. It was getting a little late for there to be any substantial shift in theme. I felt as though I had once again been offered a glimpse of an older, truer vision, and shown a facet of wilderness that is not often championed or celebrated. I kept thinking of a line from William Stafford's poem "Our People": "and the north wind felt like the truth." Indeed it did.

———————

"Day Fourteen—calm, clear, –35°, a light skiff of snow overnight, some haze in the sky to the east." I began my journal entry, and as I typed it months later I saw that I had written "Snowshoe River" instead of Snowdrift River. I was restless that morning in the pre-dawn darkness, my mind running in bizarre loops and twists. I was relieved that the day's travel would, with luck, see us off the river. I was struck by how *days* of such travel often boiled down to just a few fleeting *moments* of satisfaction, the essence of which was their brevity. Ahh, *right now* everything is working—trail firm, dogs pulling, ears and nose and body warm, and the entire caravan is "firing on every cylinder," as my fellow Iditaroder Dewey Halvorson once put it. And then it passes, everything changes, some unforeseen obstacle looms, something to be untangled or broken out or chopped down or set up or lit or thawed...the *moment* is over.

Two brief interludes of luxury and peace came at the beginning and end of every day, though: in the tent, stove hissing, vents adjusted for fresh air, piss can nearby, warm puffy booties on my feet, hat and mittens and outer layers shed at last, legs stretched out and tucked under billowy folds of parka. Considering my days objectively, I wondered if I spent more time looking at my surroundings—really *looking* at treetops and horizons and sky—in a day at the homestead than in a day on the trail. At home, though, it was always the familiar trees and the known vistas. Out on the trail, after all the effort of travel, all the details and chores of camp making, there came that one single reward: a glimpse of new country. Most days, that fleeting glimpse still seemed to be worth the effort.

Still musing about the three ptarmigan huddled on the riverbank the day before, I wrote, "There is a popular perception of the North as a steady parade of wildlife, a *National Geographic* or Discovery Channel montage, but it is simply not so. Yet on its own terms it is a land of wonder and beauty. Its terms are Vastness, Purity, and Silence." I am not the first northern traveller to rail against this false stereotype of the Far North as a vast Serengeti of wildlife. In his book *Sleeping Island*, canoeist P.G. Downes, writing in the 1940s and describing his journey north to the tundra, writes: "The popular notion that the North is teeming with wild life is completely erroneous. A region may in certain seasons, or for a very brief time seem to be overrun with game, then just as suddenly there is no trace of any, and often the farther one goes north the more inexplicably empty it becomes."[10]

I don't think it "inexplicable," considering the vicissitudes of climate with increasing latitude. These are, of course, similar to the changes that occur with increasing altitude, and obviously people don't climb high peaks expecting to find more wildlife up on the summits. But I agree with Downes, and when I came across that passage I was happy to see such honesty shine through the prevalent clichés. My outlook on wild nature was shifting day by day on that trip, just as I had felt it evolve year by year at Hoarfrost River. As I hacked down spruce boughs for the dogs' beds, and for laying beneath my tent—since the site was hard and icy after our recent camp there—I joked to the dogs, "Down where I grew up they throw people in jail for this kind of thing nowadays!"

And that was almost literally true, but I did not feel even slightly criminal as I made camp that night. It all boils down to scale, and to density and use and justifiable need. Our modern urbane culture despises the thoughtless transgressions of the litterbug and the spruce-bough chopper, while at a mighty arm's length we pollute entire watersheds, seed the upper atmosphere with the contrails of our beloved jetliners, mow down entire forests for toilet paper and cardboard and plywood (and books!), and to some as-yet-unmeasured extent, poison the entire planet. The older I get, the less black and white it all looks. And while we're standing here, pass me that axe so I can chop some spruce limbs—it's gonna get bloody cold again tonight and the dogs deserve a good sleep after everything they did today.

———————

Soon the windless morning of lofty soul searching and journal writing degenerated into—surprise!—another gruelling march into a blasting headwind.

I clearly recall a moment of that day: I was shuffling along on skis beside the sled. It was excruciating to watch the sheer step-by-step exertion of the dogs. Slowly but steadily they dragged the load over that dry, fine-grained snow. They slogged along like a troop of battle-hardened soldiers and I could almost hear them belting out some foul-mouthed call-and-response marching song as they forced their way downriver, heads low, muscles bulging through thick fur, their muzzles and eyelashes rimed with frost from the rhythmic huff-huff-huff of their breath.

Once we were off the river and onto the climb to Robert Lake (feeling, in double helpings, the relief I had forecast a week earlier), the day's travel turned pleasant for a while. We paused at the old Robert Lake cache just long enough to pry open the lid of the wooden crate, shove in some empty food sacks, and retrieve my Thoreau anthology. For the pared-down load on the stretch since leaving Nonacho, my only reading material had been Peter Steele's *Backcountry Medical Guide*.[11] It is a good text on wilderness first aid, but now that my sled load had lightened I was eager to add some fresh, if familiar, reading to it.

A storm was brewing as we left the cache in late afternoon. Wind from the northwest brought low cloud and some granular pellets of snow. Dusk came early. I tried to break trail on skis ahead of the dogs, but they had just enough good footing to move faster than I could, and they were constantly running up on me. I dropped back to my position beside and behind the sled, and we slowly covered the final mile. A narrow peninsula juts out from the west shore of Robert Lake and it offered a little shelter. The timber there was nothing but scrawny burned black-spruce stems, but it deflected the wind. I made camp, did my chores, then set to work on the extra half-hour task of setting up the HF radio's long antenna.[12] I got it strung in the final dusky light and hoped that after a night with eleven C batteries and the loaf-sized radio transceiver as my lumpy bed partners, I could check in with Kristen on schedule come morning.

To a stubborn Luddite, there is satisfaction in establishing such an unpredictable link to a distant familiar voice, entirely free of per-minute charges, passwords, digital text, and profit for some corporation. By way of contrast, and to shed more light on modern communication from the trail, let me digress briefly to describe the events of an evening six weeks or so after my final camp on Robert Lake.

I was guiding a father–daughter pair on a dogteam trek northeast of our homestead. Annika, who was seven years old, was with us. We were camped on a broad rock slope overlooking a small snow-covered lake about 16 miles from home. It was a fine evening in subarctic springtime, mild and calm, and the dogs were sprawled along their picket lines in postures of blissful lounging. The four of us humans were circled around the camp kitchen on the bare granite: camp stove, pots and pans, and a small campfire.

I don't remember what sparked the notion, but suddenly the father, Larry, asked his daughter, Adriana, "Hey, would you like to try to call Mom?" Mom being, presumably, somewhere back home in California, and I being unaware that Larry had actually brought along a satellite telephone, I grinned at the humour of his question.

"Oh, yeah, that would be fun," came the reply.

Out came a little orange case, and from it the six-inch telephone, up went the little side-mounted antenna, and after a short pause and a few beep-beeps, Larry was pressing numbers on the keypad. We could hear the ring tone. He handed the phone to Adriana. A voice answered and a short conversation ensued. Mom, it turned out, was away on a business trip somewhere in the Midwest. Yes, she had her cellphone. Bye-bye. Another round of number-punching, more ring tones.

"Hello, Mom?...Oh yeah, we're having fun...No, we're out at a campsite...Where are you? Chicago?" And so on.

And I still can't put my finger on it precisely, but for me that campsite and the ambience of that evening were, and have remained, irreversibly changed by that brief connection to a cellphone in Chicago. Changed ineffably, in a way that my morning at the campsite on the west shore of Robert Lake—where I worked in the dusk and the wind to set up the HF-radio antenna, and slept all night with the radio to warm it up, all to pass a brief "all's well" to Kristen over the crackle of static—was not. Talking to Chicago that night was perhaps just too easy and nonchalant for my taste. It stole some of the magic from that remote campsite. It's all one connected world now and there's no "away" left. Perhaps I had better get used to it.

———————

My journal notes that night were predictably terse, but the tone of them is conveyed by two paragraphs. This: "Wildlife sum total, entire day—1 whisky jack, 1 unidentified sparrow-sized bird, 1 raven, circling and leading and following us down the river." And this: "I cannot *love* this landscape of spindly burned trees swept in the dark by this bitter wind. I can only be glad it's still out here, untrammeled and 'un-developed,' and I can try to know and respect it."

Dawn broke calm, minus 32 degrees, and after a dusting of snow overnight only a thin high overcast remained. I could feel the trip winding down. The mixture of sounds in the little tent carried some tentative hints of reconnection to the wider world: hiss of the Coleman stove, so constant that it had become a given; the rumble-roar of an airliner passing overhead; the familiar crackle of static from the HF radio. For ten years at our home that faint crackle had been our only long-distance connection to the land of phones and distant callers. The sound, for Kristen and me, is still loaded with nostalgia for those early Hoarfrost years.

At 8:30 a.m. I picked up the little microphone and keyed it: "Houseboat Bay Yellowknife, Houseboat Bay Yellowknife, copy Robert Lake?"

"Robert Lake, this is Yellowknife, you're loud and clear, go ahead."

I told her that since last we talked I had made the far cache, resupplied, and was now turned north for home. I expected to be home in another three or four days, five at the most. She told me everything was fine in town, and then signed off in order to get the girls on their way to a dentist appointment. I left the radio on for a few more minutes, hopeful that she might come back on to tell me something else, but she was gone. I finished my familiar trail breakfast ration: a quarter-pound of bacon fried crisp and a cup of toasted oats with raisins and warm instant milk. I began melting snow for the day's Thermos bottle of cocoa and my two litres of hot Tang, and started on the daily ritual of breaking camp.

My solitude had become a habit and mostly a pleasure. I had been more beset by pangs of loneliness in the days at home before my departure than at any time out on the trail. At a few moments during the crux passages of the journey I had been struck, and frightened, by the daunting magnitude of my isolation. "What if I have a stroke out here? What if a sharp spruce branch pokes into my eye and continues right on into my brain?" But the next thought after these was always, "Yeah, what if? And what if that happened and somebody was out here with you? Would such dire catastrophes turn out any different with a companion or two along to watch you gasp and shudder and slip off into a coma?" Maybe. Maybe not. Probably not. The gifts of solitude had far outstripped the burdens it brought.

It was especially nice to be out with those nine hand-picked dogs. It was fun to be running the "A Team" for a change. When I am guiding I often need to give the best dogs to the rookie mushers in the caravan, and assemble a team of high-maintenance troublemakers for myself. Driving "F Troop" all the time gets tiresome. This selfish facet of solitude cannot be discounted: no one else to look out for can sometimes be as big a plus as its flip side—no one to look out for you—can be a minus. I was free to think, free to muse, free to follow trains of thought however convoluted or banal, without the jabber that inevitably creeps into camp conversation: "Have you seen the movie where…?" Not that my solitude kept me constantly up on some lofty philosophical high ground, but at least I could follow the ups and downs of my thoughts as I chose.

Day fifteen of the trip was bright and cold, but the breeze was light from the north and the miles fell away more quickly than I had expected. Up Robert Lake, through a winding chain of small lakes and flowages, onto Dion Lake, and north through the narrows to a sheltered cove I had noted on the southbound trip. The pulling remained slow and difficult and I stayed off the sled. I followed behind it on my skis, steering it only on the portages. The team was so strong and so accustomed to our modus

operandi that they seemed to have accepted three and half or four miles
per hour as a normal speed. I wondered how it would be for them when
they finally regained the hardpacked fast trails around home. On a short
half-mile of frozen overflow between Robert and Dion, I laughed out loud
because it looked to me as though they were all trying to recall just *how* a
loping gait was performed. Huskies, like all dogs, instinctively shift from
one gait to the next as speed increases. The gaits and the speeds for "shifting gears" vary from dog to dog and breed to breed, but in a nutshell they
are, from slow to fast: walk, trot, lope, and gallop.

I stopped early and enjoyed a leisurely pace of camp making in the
sunshine of late afternoon. I made another bough bed for each dog and
laid a thick mattress of boughs beneath my tent. I wanted a warm night of
sleep. My sleeping bag had built up another heavy load of condensation,
and the tiny red line in the thermometer looked like it was in free-fall
again. Having finished my chores, I puttered around and opened a little
water hole at the creek. The days were lengthening. The spring equinox
was only two weeks away. Eight weeks from that and it would be light
twenty-four hours a day. I stayed outside the tent that night until the stars
came out. On snowshoes, I strolled the portage trail and back in camp I
sauntered along the line of dogs dispensing pats and shoulder rubs.

I was struggling to shift mental gears; to force myself out of the
Nature-as-Merciless-Adversary outlook and into some more generous
frame of mind. The transition was not easy on a moonless night at 35
below, miles from home, but it felt as if that day the country had shown
us a hint of a smile. I did not want to emerge from the trip with my mind
calcified into battle mode. Deep down, I knew that Ma Nature didn't
give a hoot whether I lived or died or froze in the dark. The trip had
underscored that view of things, and it is a stance that serves a traveller
well in the Arctic, out at sea, or high in the mountains—anywhere that
the north wind feels like the truth. Still waffling between world views, I
went into the tent, lit up Mr. Coleman, and pulled the flap-zipper down
on the black sky full of stars. After dinner I read by flashlight. "In winter,
warmth equates all virtue," Thoreau reminded me.[13] Bang on, Henry.

The night stayed clear and calm and the temperature surprised me by
creeping upward a few degrees. This, along with my extra preparations
with spruce boughs and spare clothing, resulted in the best night of sleep in
nearly a week. My dreams, as trivial as ever, were entirely pleasant. As I lay
in my warm sleeping bag before dawn my thoughts drifted north to home.
I wondered how the house had fared after three weeks standing empty in
such deep cold. I was glad once again that our water and plumbing systems

were Stone Age simple. Not much can go wrong with an empty pail, an outhouse, or a cold wood stove in a cold cabin, even at 45 below zero.

———————

That morning as I sipped coffee in the warm tent, I thought and wrote at length about the dogs. They slept out on the picket line curled into nine frost-covered mounds, each nose tucked under each bushy tail plume. We had come through a lot together in the past two weeks and our working relationship was solid. It was not warm and cuddly, though, that relationship, and it confounded my attempts to define it.

From my journal: "No one leaps up to lick my face when I come down the line. In this weather, no one leaps up at all. In their minds I am the Alpha animal, if I can make a stab at popularized science. I am also Provider: of food, of a trail to follow in deep soft snow, of decisions and direction, of spruce boughs for bedding and salve for sore feet."

The team had been remarkably quiet throughout the trip. Even at feeding time (the decibel level of which, at home, seriously requires hearing protection) there had been hardly a sound—just a bark and the obligatory selfish growl from Tugboat. At departure time each morning they all wagged their tails and lunged into their harnesses, and at stops along the trail Murphy sometimes barked with impatience. Mostly though they had been silent and watchful, carefully studying my every move around camp and on the trail: Is he getting out his snowshoes or his Thermos? Is this a brief stop or are we taking a real break?

I tried to take an objective view and I concluded that I was a leader trusted, followed, and passably well liked by my troops. My main lead dog on the trip, Steve, stood out from the rest. He was the kind of dog best suited to my own mushing personality. He could take some reprimands for bad behaviour, yet still greet me at the next pause in the proceedings with a happy grin and no trace of lingering distrust.

I will venture this: the world of dogs is a physical world, and the milieu of the working husky is the paragon of that physical essence. Huskies are strong aggressive animals. Like all working dogs, they thrive on work. They want a job to do and they want to get on with it right away, thank you. The team is a domesticated wolf pack of semi-socialized hunters, a loose alliance driven by instinct to co-operate and compete, all at the same time. (This loose alliance reminds me of the hard-core cadre of mushers who run the Iditarod or the Yukon Quest year after year—allies when necessary, competitors to the bone.)

To watch huskies scrap with each other, or to watch dogs go after a teammate who has for some reason become a scapegoat, is sobering to anyone who tries to mould dogs to a human model, or to elevate them to a preconceived notion of furry nobility. They are physical, and we must relate to them on that level.

I often remember a moment during the 1991 Iditarod. Dave Allen, Mark Nordman, and I were heading for the Inuit village of Shaktoolik in a storm, following a low spit of beach which juts into the Bering Sea. Arctic blizzard conditions prevailed: visibility near zero, temperature well into the danger zone, wind howling. We three were travelling together, taking turns in lead. Dave's team was out front and he was trying to command his leader to move up from the ice edge and run along the crest of the spit. From just behind him I watched him suddenly stop, throw down his snow hook, sprint to the front of his team, pick the little lead dog up and half-carry, half-toss her up onto the trail. Even without his giant suit of arctic clothing Dave is tall and imposing—he was once an Olympic-calibre wrestler. To the little dog, the lift-and-toss must have felt like a visitation from Thor himself.

On we went. It was a pithy little "teachable moment" for the dog, and she kept to the trail flawlessly from there on. Dave turned back to me and shouted above the roar of the wind, "I'm still training that young leader!" I smiled. To those unfamiliar with the intensely physical world of dogs and mushers, it would have looked like "dog abuse." It was not. The leader was not harmed or hurt; it was only surprised and it was that sudden, very physical surprise that drove home Dave's message: let's run up on top of the spit, not down here on the beach. Dog and musher. Just another day on the trail.

There is a steady conversation always under way between a musher and the main lead dog. It is spoken, and sometimes physical, and with the really good leaders it can become telepathic. A few days earlier, Steve had balked at the prospect of leaving the cache site and retracing our way down Noman Lake. I sprinted forward just as Dave Allen had done years ago, pounced on Steve, bit him once, very hard, on the tip of his left ear, shouted "Straight ahead!" into his face like a drill sergeant, and ran back to the sled. He carried on, straight ahead. I could have said, "Now Steve, you see, if we don't go down this lake into this wind, we won't get home before we run short of food," but that would have been like the *Far Side* cartoon by Gary Larson, where the dog Ginger hears the man saying only "Blah blah blah Ginger blah blah blah Ginger..."

Mushers learn to take up with dogs as dogs, and then try to be perceived as the big, respected two-legged member of the team. In a culture that is becoming almost completely unfamiliar with animals as working partners, many people take up with their dogs as furry little surrogate children—children who somehow just happened to come into the world with fangs and four legs, and who, left to their own instincts, will raise one leg to piss in their dinner bowl after they have finished eating.

———————

That night we camped below Daisy Lake, on the little lake I had earlier named for Riley, the oldest dog of the team. As darkness fell a lone wolf with a quavering voice howled from nearby. It was minus thirty-something, and a light northwest wind was rising and falling in the darkness. The wolf howled again and again, as if intent on getting a response from the dogs. I fully expected the entire team to howl back in unison at any moment. For reasons known only to them, not one of them replied.

I knew it was likely our last night on the trail. By the next night I would almost certainly be either at home, or ten miles short of home, parked on a couch at Roger and Miranda's house watching television. I hoped to be home. The thought of television was more than I could bear.

It had been a good day, the sixteenth of the trip, and it ended on a high note, for I had found the portage trail down to Meridian Lake. This was the trail I had searched so hard for on the second day of the trip. From the upper end, approached from the east along the shore of Riley Lake, the trailhead was fairly obvious. It was even marked by a monstrous old axe blaze, but the blaze was on a big tree that had toppled over years before and was half-buried in snow. After I found that first clue in late afternoon, I tied off the team and walked ahead on snowshoes, down the slope north and west, blaze by blaze, clearing after clearing, enjoying the unravelling mystery and the detective work it entailed. Once I had a firm idea of the trend of the trail I returned to the dogs and set up camp. The final connection to my already-broken lower end of the trail would be made in the morning.

There were caribou by the hundreds on Daisy Lake that day, and their trampled tracks had given us some fast, easy sledding. As I had thought they might be, the dogs seemed entirely surprised by the opportunity to trot and lope along at a good clip. The hardpacked caribou trail did not last for long, and we finished the day in another powder-and-crust march.

With the trip nearly done, I realized I was feeling some sheepishness over its limited mileage. It would only be 150 trail miles all told, in seventeen or eighteen days of hard travel. As the raven or the airplane flew, it was a mere 45 miles from home to the far cache, our turnaround camp at Nonacho. That was a big slice of humble pie for someone who had openly mentioned Lake Athabasca to friends, back when these compass-point journeys had been conceived. Yet only the dogs and I would ever know those miles and what they had meant and held. There was a solipsistic satisfaction in that. I was glad we had "locked the door" behind us weeks earlier on that first narrow climb out of Daisy Lake, when I had failed to locate the wider, more gently sloping trail we had just discovered. Had I found the proper trail on that second day, Roger and possibly others might have zoomed south to say hello or to hunt. With a broken trail to follow, it was only three or four hours by snowmobile from Reliance all the way to the Snowdrift valley.

Snowshoes, ample time, and the combination of mushing and skiing— along with a very solid team of dogs—had allowed us to go the way we had. We *had* been to the South—into country of pines, lynx, and beaver, none of which were found around home. Just by setting out and slogging, and sticking with it, we had started the round of four trips to the compass points. We had made a start, and for every project that is always one of the hardest steps.

In a lighthearted mood that night I chuckled about my beat-up old snowshoes, and all the verbal abuse I had heaped on them over the course of the trip. There is nothing worse than snowshoes, I had decided— except, of course, *no* snowshoes. The fur-trading voyageurs knew this, and they coined the phrase *mal de raquette* for the painful inflammation of the Achilles tendon that often afflicted them after many miles on their *racquettes*. I could see a tie-breaking question on the boreal-forest version of *Who Wants to Be a Millionaire*: "What does *mal de raquette* mean? (a) I am sick of snowshoeing; (b) I got sick on my snowshoes; (c) my snow- shoes are evil; or (d) that is Mal's tennis racket.

Snowshoes can seem to be instruments of torture at times, but would I venture out without them, in winter, in this part of the world, as I have so often watched the modern "locals" do? No thanks. I can only surmise that their motto must be "In Bombardier, Polaris, or Pratt & Whitney We Trust," but it is a motto to which I cannot subscribe. Snowshoes, please.

I thought of the days just past, and of the trip's lessons, and wrote: "The emptiness of the country is deep and profound. It is a hostile, silent, enigmatic landscape dominated by ice, snow, rock, and scrawny, stunted trees. It can seem lifeless for days at a time. There is nothing welcoming or warm or inviting about it, but there is this—it is a reservoir of silence and darkness, in a world intent on obliterating both."

Time for bed, one last time. The wolf finally gave up its efforts to engage the dogs in a singalong. Perhaps it trotted off. I started the famil- iar ritual of contortions and squirming involved with going to bed, and soon I was bundled in my layers and ready for sleep. Out with the light and done for the day. *McLeod Bay tomorrow*, I thought as I drifted off.

––––––––––

Twenty-four hours later I was home, upstairs in the chilly cabin, sitting in my favourite chair.

The final day held a little of everything. It began with a wonderful descent on the "found" trail, piecing together the final few hundred yards to join my old trail on the lower end. Vistas of the broad basin of McLeod Bay rolled away to the far horizon, with the steep wall of McDonald's Fault rising to the south and southeast over my shoulder. Bright sun, cold snow, a lightly loaded sled, happy dogs…what a life.

Just over the portage from Meridian Lake to Charlton Bay of Great Slave, I met up with two snowmobilers. Roger, heading south, who greeted me with "I thought you might be near here by now"; and Alfred Lockhart from Lutsel K'e, out on a long day trip, hunting caribou or muskox—whatever meat might show itself first. We traded snippets of news. Alfred's eyes lit up when I mentioned the scores of caribou I had seen up on Daisy Lake, and—of course—my hardpacked trail that led right to them.[14]

Our packed trail, the result of so much effort, was there, but a winter trail is a fleeting thing. It would not be there for long. Come spring, it would show up plainly for a day or two, as a line through the woods and across the surface of the melting lake ice, and then it would vanish into rivulets of cold water, like a Tibetan monk's mandala of coloured sand, days and weeks of work swept to oblivion.

After a stop for tea at Roger and Miranda's, the dogs and I set off across McLeod Bay for home. It seemed fitting that those final ten miles became a long grind, steadily more difficult toward the last. Deep snow blanketed the north side of the bay, and there was no trail to be seen. In the very last light of day we pulled into the yard and began the long process of settling in to a frozen homestead. With no water hole open, I set up the Coleman stove one more time and melted snow for water. Then I went up to the house, unlocked the door, and started a fire in the wood stove. The indoor temperature had at some time in my absence hit a low of minus 44 degrees, according to the recording thermometer on the second floor, but everything in the house appeared to be unscathed. The massive log walls of the house would take several days to warm up. The satellite telephone seemed to be seriously frostbitten, so I was unable to tell Kristen of my arrival. No radio call had been pre-arranged, and

I was too worn out to set up the HF radio that night anyway. I did turn on the AM receiver in time to catch the 10 p.m. news. Intense fighting in Palestine, elections in Zimbabwe...

I sighed and switched off the radio. I poured a double shot of Jack Daniels into my favourite steel goblet. In a maudlin journey's-end gesture I raised a toast to the cold blackness out beyond the cabin's main window. Tactical error—my lips stung at the touch of the super-cooled whisky, and stuck firm to the metal rim of the cup. *Ouch, and cheers*, I thought, peeling free. Pain and pleasure. Perfect.

Next year, east onto the Barrens.

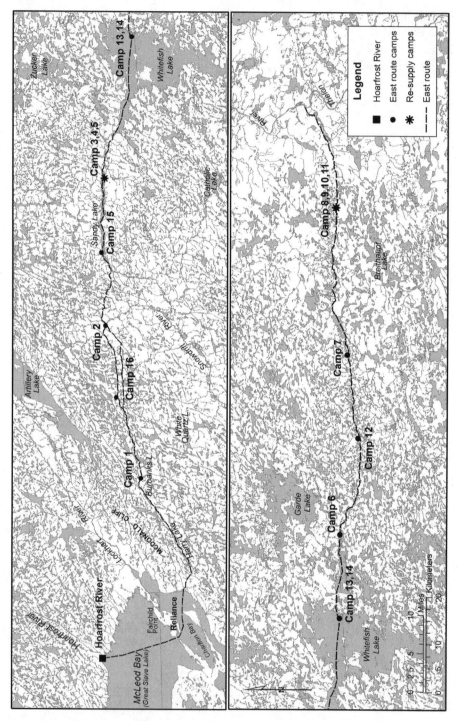

East 2003

East

Seventeen days, 17 February–5 March 2003
Hoarfrost River to upper Thelon River and return: about 380 miles
Ten dogs, two resupply caches

In the weeks leading up to my journey east I was haunted by a dream. As I have already mentioned, dream messages are not my usual cup of tea, so this one kept me wondering. In my dream I saw a parka-clad figure sprawled in the snow on a blank patch of winter tundra; only that and only a glimpse—no dogs, no sled, no tent in sight. I knew, though I never saw clearly, that there lay yours truly, frozen stiff. That was all, but it was enough to put me on edge. Perhaps it was prompted by a rereading of a poem by William Stafford, a poem I have always liked, called "Kinds of Winter":

> It was a big one. We followed it over
> the snow. Even if it made no mistakes, we
> would have it. That's what The World means—
> there are kinds of winter that you meet.
> And that big one had met us, its big winter.
>
> But there was a hill, and when we rounded
> it the tracks were gone. We had used up
> the daylight. The wind had come and
> emptied our trail, back of us, ahead of us.
> We looked at each other. Our winter had come.
>
> This message I write in the shelter of the overturned
> sled. Later someone may find us
> and mail this letter to you. Let me tell you something:
> it doesn't make any difference what anyone ever said,
> here at the last, under the snow.

I kept the dream to myself—it seemed like one of those intuitive four-o'clock-in-the-morning warnings that are best just filed away for reference.

If I took every scary dream as a portent of impending doom I would never leave home. As February days brightened and truly cold weather settled in, the ritual of packing and preparing went along in its mundane familiarity. Kristen and the girls left home again for a stay in Yellowknife; I prepared to shut down the homestead and head out.

My resupply loads prepared, I fired up the airplane one morning at daybreak and flew east to place the caches. The distance from the Hoarfrost to my planned location for the far cache near the Thelon River showed up as 113 nautical miles on the airplane's GPS: about 130 straight-line statute miles. Accounting for the meanders from an airborne straight line, which overland travel always dictates, I guessed it would be about 180 miles out to the far cache by trail. The intermediate cache I placed about 75 miles out, at the far end of Sandy Lake. My two flights out and back that day (I made a separate trip to place each cache) left me deeply thoughtful about what I would be attempting. My thoughts ran along two paths: one lofty, full of adventurous inspiration; one more basic, fraught with intimidation and coloured by that dismal dream image. Rattling along in the little cockpit at minus 32 degrees, with the plane stuffed full of supplies, the utter *emptiness* of the white tundra beneath me was most intimidating. No checkpoints, no cabins, no mining camps or trapping shacks, mile after mile after mile.

Yes, I knew there *were* a few camps and cabins out that way. To the south of my planned route was Lynx Lake, and on its northwestern arm stood the cabin of two long-established trappers and hunters, Richard Black and Lance Leubbert. But Lance and Rick had retired south in 1993 after twenty-some years in the country, leaving their cabin and much of their gear behind. Their old place was the most obvious bail-out for me, but it was 25 miles south of my planned route, long deserted, and stone cold. There were a few other places like it: a plywood shack up on the shore of Artillery Lake, belonging to my neighbour Roger, recently remodelled by a grizzly bear and now sporting a big hole in one wall; a summer tourist lodge on the north end of Whitefish Lake; an old drill camp at Boomerang Lake ... but all of these stood empty, drifted in, and about as cozy and comforting as a collection of walk-in freezers.

Having chosen the precise spot for my far cache I circled overhead and set up for a landing. My groundspeed dropped below twenty-five knots on final approach, so the wind had to be blowing at well over twenty knots. Suddenly four big muskox appeared out of the spindrift alongside the lakeshore and took a few hurried steps as the plane dropped toward them. Keeping an eye on them I touched down and taxied toward shore in a blizzard of prop wash. They stood still and watched. Sheer bafflement seemed plainly written on their prehistoric faces, or so I imagined. This was *their* country. I was the interloper here. They had been napping pleasantly in the sunny breeze, at a balmy 34 below, until I showed up overhead and disrupted their halcyon afternoon.

I unloaded my cache supplies at the base of a little clump of stunted white spruce. In just a few minutes I was airborne again and westbound for home. There was no sign of the muskox, or of any other living creature. Only the white plains, the drifting snow, and tiny dark threads of spruce along the eskers. These eskers, which are essentially upside-down riverbeds formed by glacial meltwater thousands of years ago, are the only reliable landmarks in the winter Barrens. They snake for miles across the tundra, even crossing lakes underwater where they are obvious when viewed from above on a summer day. Because in winter they form giant snow fences, they trap deep snow along their margins, and often this is just enough of a change in microclimate to let a few stunted trees take hold and grow. Wolves and foxes den on eskers, and all sorts of tundra creatures, including us two-footed types, use the eskers as walkways through the tundra.

I wanted to move capably and confidently into that vastness, and to arrive again at the cache without the speed and sputter of the plane. I wanted to travel adeptly, making miles behind a strong team of happy dogs. *If I could accomplish that*, I thought, *I might be able to look a muskox in the eye with some shred of credibility and understanding.* Could I? I did not know, and that *not knowing* was at once inspiring and frightening.

During the final days of preparation I was alone with the dogs, the ten who would go with me this year: Steve, Dandy, Foxtail, Gulo, Murphy, Jasmine, Schooner, Riley, Edelweiss, and Ernie. The rest of the kennel was again at the tourist lodge on Blachford Lake, a hundred miles to the west, working for wages. The dogs I had chosen for the trip were solid, and I knew we stood a good chance of some long steady miles of wonderful running, out beyond the deep soft snows of the forest, out on the hardpacked tundra where dog sledding truly thrives as a means of transportation.

There was one more dog at home: fourteen-year-old Bim, a stalwart veteran born and raised in our kennel. Two days before Kristen and the girls had left for town, he had suffered something resembling a stroke (though I am told by veterinarians that dogs do not often suffer strokes, per se). Old dogs can get something called idiopathic vestibular disease, which Bim seemed to be showing. He was lurching sideways, the left half

of his head and torso sagging, his appetite and liveliness gone. He was well
past ninety years old by "human" measure. Old Bim, clown of the team
for so many years. I led him off into the woods and said goodbye and did
what needed to be done. As Stafford wrote in his poem "Old Dog," "our
days together were the ones we had already had."[1] I had known this was
coming, but putting a dog down never gets any easier, only more difficult
year by year. The next day an honour guard of his teammates hauled his
carcass up the steep trail northeast of the homestead. There on a hilltop
I laid him out to become raven, wolverine, soil, and moss. I nailed Bim's
wooden name tag to a spruce trunk already festooned with the placards
of others long gone, yanked the hook, and turned that strong team back
toward home.

————————

Once again I found myself cobbling together a less-than-perfect sled for
this, the trip of the year. "How can this be?" I asked my journal. In the
back of my mind I could hear the legions of dilettantes cluck-clucking
over such flawed preparations. It reminded me of a baffled look at my sled
from a fellow musher somewhere along the trail of my rookie Iditarod in
1986: "You came all the way here to run the race with *that* sled?"

"Well, yes," I had answered him, and I recall thinking to myself,
"Because, you see, my sled may not be the latest or the greatest, but I'm
here and I'm going to Nome with these dogs, and that is the real bottom
line of what is going on...the sled is just a detail. The real wonder is that
we are here at all."

Over the course of these four journeys I learned to accept this
bottom-line approach: year by year I could only manage to pull the
hook and leave the homestead—north, south, east, west—by setting my
sights somewhere short of perfection. A bar set too high will only dis-
courage the jumper, sometimes forever. Good old Ray Gordon—sometimes you have to stop getting ready and just "hafuckin' haGo." Just
carving out the time and making the commitment to the journeys was
a bigger hurdle than fussing endlessly over the various parts and pieces
that needed to be assembled to pull them off. It has been a lesson of my
life that, if we let them, little everyday imperfections can easily become
an excuse for delay or even for retreat and surrender. On the flip side of
this, one neglected detail of sled preparation would come to bear heavily on my trip east. In those days before departure I did not spot it, but I
should have.

Deep cold hung steady through the days of preparation: minus 38,
minus 36, minus 41. I felt like I was plodding at times, although all the

preparations were going smoothly. With a jolt I realized that my foot-
dragging was just plain common sense at work. I began to think of it as
my Basic voice. It was the part of me—of anyone, for that matter—that
needed convincing, that held out as perfectly sensible the desire to stay
warm, comfortable, and well-fed...in short, to *just stay home.* To step
out into minus 40 degrees, lock the door, harness the dogs, and head
east onto the tundra, was to fly in the face of every "normal" human
instinct. It was like planning a spacewalk, and a part of me was shouting,
"What the fuck?" (for Basic voice always speaks in what my grandfather
called "Saturday-morning English"). "Aren't we close enough to the goddamned wilderness already? Why the hell are we doing *this*?!"

With Mr. Basic on similar rants every few hours, the days of final
preparation passed. Two became three, and—surprisingly, embarrass-
ingly—four. Little details filled the hours: finding all the maps, repairing
snowshoe bindings, transferring bottles of lemon juice and vinegar stored
in the pantry downstairs, lest they burst when the entire cabin froze solid
after my departure.

At last I was ready for blast-off, and the *other* part of me, which I began
to think of as my Lofty voice, was scoffing at the quivering worshiper
of heat and light, bare feet and warm wooden floors. Saying, along with
Gary Snyder from his poem

Now I can turn to the hunt.

Blade sharp and hair on end
   over the boulders
eager
     tasting the snow.

Morning, 17 February, minus 41 degrees. Thick frost fog down near
the river mouth, where the flowing water plunging over the falls lifts an
enormous billow of steam into the frigid air. This fog coats every tree and
bush with the thick hoarfrost that long ago gave the Hoarfrost River its
name. I was rested and well prepared—or at least I had convinced myself
I was, which is just as good sometimes. I was tense, though, and deeply
thoughtful as I paused to write a note to Kristen and the girls. Without
intending to be dire, I suppose that farewell paragraph was a nod to that
awful dream image, and to the real risk of the days ahead. I left it on the
table alongside a map and a more prosaic outline detailing my route,
resupplies, and planned itinerary.

The dogs were eager and watchful as I locked up the buildings and lashed the sled. They had been crowding into my thoughts in a new way over the previous several days, ever since I had said goodbye to old Bim. As I thought back over his years as a sled dog, I realized that I had been mushing dogs for no less than twenty-five years, and that through all those years I had been driven forward mostly by my own momentum. Never had I made a serious effort to step back and examine the running of dogteams from any detached perspective. I resolved to spend some time examining the ethics and the foibles of this human–husky partnership, honestly and objectively, during the days and miles ahead.

Just before noon on the 17th of February, I was finally ready to leave. The ten dogs shot out of the yard in a burst of trademark sled-dog insanity—ethical or not, the launch of an eager team of dogs has to be seen to be believed—and we flew south onto McLeod Bay. "Thirty-eight below?" they seemed to be shouting. "Eastbound a few hundred miles? Tundra? No trail? Sounds perfect, boss, and by the way, what the heck has been the delay around here these past few days?"

Another ritual stop at Roger and Miranda's house on the peninsula opposite Reliance, for a cup of coffee and a careful look at the map. This year I was headed right into the heart of a region that Roger had known intimately for many years. In the 1970s and '80s, Roger and his first wife Theresa trapped and hunted each winter from a cabin on the upper Thelon, just a few miles from my far cache. Theresa died of cancer in 1993. When Roger talks about those seasons on the Thelon it is clear that he treasures them. The route I would follow was familiar to him from those years, and I gleaned as much about it as I could. Then away, with a wave and "good luck."

It is five miles across Charlton Bay to the base of the first link of Pike's Portage. The route is named for Warburton Pike, an eccentric, wealthy, and very hardy Englishman, who in 1890 came down from the tundra using the stunning thoroughfare now named for him. He described it vividly in his 1892 book, *The Barren Ground of Northern Canada*, as "by far the prettiest part of the country that I saw in the North."[2] Pike's Portage is a natural progression of lakes and portages that join the northeast tip of Great Slave Lake to the Barren Lands beyond. It is safe to say that in the past two or three centuries, perhaps for a millennium or longer, not a single season has passed without at least some traffic on the route—by canoe, by dogteam, and nowadays most often by snowmobile. It is by far the best route eastward and upward from Great Slave Lake.

The climb from lake level begins immediately. Up a progression of short steep hills, 300 feet of elevation are gained right away. Pausing to look west from the crest of the first big hill, all the points and islands around Reliance and the broad sweep of McLeod Bay are laid out in raven's-eye view. After short drops into a couple of creek bottoms and some steadier climbing, the first link of Pike's chain ends at Harry Lake. The lake is named for a crew member on J.W. Tyrell's 1900 journey of map-making and exploration. Harry, French, Acres, Kipling, Burr, and Toura were all among Tyrrell's men, and their names live on as the main lakes on "Pike's."

I first passed this way in late March 1981, eastbound by dogsled. By August 1983 I was back again, sweating and giving blood to the local blackflies as I portaged an old wood-and-canvas canoe up to Artillery Lake and back. Those fly bites must have left a deep impression, because except for a few summer day hikes, I have been strictly a winter traveller on Pike's ever since. In winter, with a good string of dogs and a packed trail, the fearsome first climb to Harry Lake is not much to write home about. In just over a half-hour the dogs and I were on the ice of Harry Lake, and I planted the snow hook for a rest.

My load at departure was, in pilot's vernacular, "over gross." In mushing slang my sled had a classic affliction known as "rookie bulge." Not being a rookie, I was unhappy about this. The sled I had chosen to go east was shorter than the previous year's Banana, but it was four inches wider. Its load-carrying capacity was theoretically similar, but its sled bag was literally bursting at the seams. I spent the first few miles of every morning mentally reviewing and winnowing the various components of that load: bulky dog jackets, heavy spare headlamp batteries, and a full spare set of outer clothing that stayed in the sled every night in case of a tent fire. Solo travel is always bulky. Most of the basic items of winter gear are easily justified, but even in a group of three or four people only one of these essentials is needed—the bowsaw, for instance, or the rifle, the axe, the windscreen for the camp stove, and so on down the list. I needed them all and there were no partners to divvy them up with.

Overgross or not, the load did not faze the dogs. A broken trail lay ahead of us, packed down by some Native hunters on snowmobiles within the past few days. A mile down Harry Lake I passed close to a wood-framed wall tent belonging to Noel Drybones. Noel was a Chipewyan hunter, father of Roger's first wife Theresa, well into his seventies but still active in that winter of 2003. He died in 2005 and his grave now lies in a cluster of others at the mouth of the Lockhart River north of Pike's Portage. Truly the last of his kind in some ways, Noel stayed out at Reliance and Artillery Lake as long and as often as he could, even as health problems piled up on him in his final years. Considering his experience and his many decades of life on the land, Noel's camps and cabins were always remarkable to me for their threadbare, ramshackle ambience. He was a living example of a world view that cared little for what most people now consider basic amenities. The mainstays of Noel's store-bought supplies were bullets, gasoline, Redman chewing tobacco, snow-machine parts, and mantles for gas lamps. His final years were hard, with his eyesight and his heart both failing, and every season it became more difficult for him to move around in his vast domain.

Despite our fifteen years as distant neighbours, I didn't know Noel Drybones well. Every now and then our paths would cross and we would talk, have tea, and trade news. Sometimes I would fly him somewhere or pick something up for him in town. As the trail approached his tent on Harry Lake that day I wasn't sure what to expect. A dog began howling and barking excitedly as we drew near. By its desperate tone I surmised that it had been left alone. A few hundred yards out, abeam the camp, I paused and shouted. My dogs set up a loud ruckus. I could see a little smoke rising from the tent's stovepipe, but there was no sign of life apart from that one frantic tied-up dog. Fresh snowmobile tracks led into and out of the camp in several directions but I could not decipher all their passages. I watched the tent for a minute or two. When no one appeared we moved on.

From Harry Lake the good trail continued northeast up narrow French Lake, and over another short portage to the third lake, Acres. Here it forked, one fresher set of snow-machine tracks leading left—the main route to the narrow south fjord of Artillery Lake. The other trail, not as fresh but still perfect for sledding, turned east and crossed a short portage into a lake called Burbank Lake. This was our route.

Mile by mile we were leaving the forest. The treeline is rarely a sharp, definite boundary, but as one begins to cross it the signs are obvious: all the low-lying timber smaller and more stunted, the ridges and hillsides increasingly barren and windswept, the snow firmer and no longer fluffy. At the northeast tip of Great Slave Lake, this ecological gradient is very steep—from thick stands of jack pine at the start of Pike's Portage to wide-open tundra on the east shore of Artillery Lake—a dramatic change within 18 straight-line miles. From Burbank Lake the short climb east on a winding uphill trail removes any doubt that a change is imminent. As the dogs climbed and I kicked, still holding to a good firm trail left recently by someone on a very wide snow machine, the vistas opened out to north and south. A long grade up a boulder-studded hillside put the last real forest below and behind us. We had crossed over.

I was very happy that afternoon. It was a pleasure just to be out there, and to be headed east. Sunshine, cold air like shots of pure oxygen in the lungs, and a spirited team of dogs who were so obviously enjoying the day right along with me. As the trees fell away and the Barrens opened out ahead of us, my resolve strengthened and only a vestige of my earlier trepidation remained. Over a broad hilltop and down into the valley of a twin lake called M'clorree (partly swallow the *c*)—which, I am told, is the Chipewyan word for the plant non-Natives call "cloudberry" (*Rubus chamaemorus*). It grows around the world at northerly latitudes, but it is less common than the various strains of *Vaccinium* (blueberry and lingonberry.) It thrives on boggy, poorly drained patches of level tundra. The thumb-tipped-size berries are pinkish orange. They ripen in mid- to late summer and pass quickly through their voluptuous prime. The Scandinavians make a sweet liqueur from them.

No cloudberries for us on the Cloudberry Lakes that February night. I camped in a patch of spruce and tamarack at the foot of another long white slope. We had come 31 miles from home. The dogs, all but two of them veterans of the previous year's trip, seemed to sense immediately what we were up to. For me too there was a pleasant familiarity to the whole routine, even more than I had expected. My first journal entry from the trail began: "It is as if I have just finished last year's trip. Here I am again, in the tent, stove hissing, candles lit, all warm except for my toes. I'm working on them, with both feet stuffed under the folds of my huge blue parka and a hot bottle of water cradled between them. I don't think many people would believe just how comfortable it is out here, on these evenings and mornings in the tent..."

A dusting of fresh snow fell overnight, and in the morning the moon was dimly visible, one night past full, behind a thin overcast. It was minus 27 degrees. My thoughts ran to that comforting familiarity, and how a routine, *any* routine, can be a pitfall on the path to a broader awareness. Small details of tent life—where to place the stove box, when to fill the water bottles for the night—threaten to become somehow *too* important, especially when one is alone. Simple tidiness can morph into an obsessive, tyrannical fussiness. This leads to a new challenge; to look beyond the mundane details of tent life, and remember *why* one has ventured out in the first place.

Summer and winter camping differ dramatically at day's end. In summer, once supper is done and the campsite is set, a paddler or hiker is still outdoors. The outdoors is still relatively warm, and in summer the world is still awash in daylight or twilight. There is time for a stroll, a long sit on a hilltop, or a few casts with the fishing rod. On a winter journey the day's looking-outward ends abruptly with the decision to stop for the night and make camp. Night after night, from the moment I gave the word to the dogs and planted the snow hook, I was all narrow focus and mundane repetition. With the long cold night bearing down like an unlit freight train, there is snow and fat to melt and pour over the dogs' food, the tent to pitch and a dozen chores to finish. Finally, all done, supper eaten, and ensconced in the tiny haven of the tent, a bit of time to reflect on the day and make some notes, perhaps to mend something, and then to prepare for sleep.

In the morning it all gets repeated in reverse. A brief interlude of pleasant "indoor" reflection, followed by hustle, melt, feed, eat, roll up, dismantle, load, harness, and at last—hours later—*go*. So the days go, and so mine went. For long stretches I was completely wrapped up in the management of fuel, food, dog care, navigation, moisture in clothing, and on and on. Mulling this over, I noted in my journal that second morning: "You cannot expect to come out here and live for 18 days in a safe, predictable routine. No. The land will have its say, like it or not."

I had camped once before on the Cloudberry Lakes, on a canoe trip in August 1983. I was alone then too. My friend Mitch Gilbert and I had a base camp on McLeod Bay that summer. We had a boat to look after down there, along with supplies and ten huskies, so we had to take turns making solo forays out and back into the country beyond the lake. My journal from that night twenty years earlier gives some feel for the landscape in summer:

August 22, 1983, north end of 'M'cloree Lakes'

And what have you seen?
The tundra at evening
The way the long light carves the low hills
After the heat and flies of the day
The breeze now cool
Sky clearing…

It continues, trying to be poetic, for in those days I still fancied myself the next Snyder, but I will cut to this:

An odd day, the gung-ho ambition of yesterday slowly winding down. Wind and dark thunder clouds gave me an excuse to camp and rest early, in mid-afternoon. Pitched the tent and gathered

wood, slung the binoculars on and walked east along the ridge
top. Far views in all directions and—until the wind dropped—no
blackflies to annoy me. Glassed the long bare slopes slowly from
several high points. Nothing moving in all those miles. On toward
"Barrenland Lake," the next lake east, savouring the firm rock and
dry lichen underfoot, little blue lakes spread out in all directions,
all ruffled by the steady breeze. A mile out from camp the wind
dropped, and suddenly the walk changed. The flies now found me
at each brief pause, bouncing off my shirt and pants like tiny pellets of sleet, crowding into my eyes as I tried to glass the hillsides.
I was moving steadily faster, driven on by the miserable prospect
of stopping; even the late-afternoon sun began to feel oppressive. I
turned directly toward camp and came cruising in at a trot, across
tussocks of marsh grass, through thick swales of dwarf birch and
spruce, wild-eyed and harried. Here, to quickly light a fire and lean
close above it, letting the smoke flow over me. Gradually the flies
eased and I pulled back from the fire, barefoot and relaxed, to put
on a pot of water for tea and supper.

By 1988 I had been living at Hoarfrost for a little over a year, and I had
twice come this far east by dogteam. The first was an April outing with
my friend Sam Cook, during which we tried to follow the route I was on
now, but were stopped short by a four-day spring blizzard. Then in the
short cold days of December eight months later, with twenty-some dogs,
Mike Dietzman and I had made a training run out to Richard Black and
Lance Leubbert's winter outpost at Lynx Lake, and returned to Hoarfrost.
For both of those trips there had been the luxury of a snow-machine trail
leading all the way out to Whitefish and Lynx Lakes—our only real challenge had been to hang onto that trail across the tundra and lake ice. This
time around I knew there would be no trail after the first hour or so of the
second day. I thought I had learned quite a bit about winter navigation on
the Barrens over the past fifteen years, and I was eager for the test.

Before leaving camp that second morning I had to catch a couple
of loose dogs. Two females, Jasmine and her young sidekick Edelweiss,
had slipped free of the picket line at dawn and had been running loose
around camp all morning. I kept thinking I would get a chance to put
them back on the line, but as departure time neared they were still at
large, playing a combination of tag and hide-and-seek with me. Putting
on a cheery tone, I knelt and tried to call them to hand, but no—this was
just too much fun. The rest of the dogs were in an uproar, and there was
a firm open slope to scamper up and down, and for the time being they

were the absolute centres of attention. What dog would willingly put a stop to such sheer pleasures? Finally an old ruse worked. I started lavishing attention on the other dogs, the ones already in harness and strung out along the picket line. Jealous curiosity brought the two girls in close, and once I laid a hand on them they each seemed to say, "Okay, that was fun. Let's get started."

Another dog-catching episode came later that morning, this one brief but far more serious. We had made a few miles and we were well past the last vestiges of old snow-machine tracks. By the sun's position, and with map and compass, I was navigating as best I could. The day was perfect, with no wind, a bright blue cloudless sky, and the air cold and sharp. Partway up a long slope I stopped the team and kicked the snow hook in. I needed a moment to compare my *hypothesis* of where I was with the paltry clues offered by the map and the rolling white landscape. Head down, mukluk-shod foot resting lightly on the snow hook, I studied the map. Was this rise *this* hill on the map or could it be *that* hill? Meanwhile the dogs were going berserk. The day's perfection was not lost on them, and it had inspired them to new heights of enthusiasm. Suddenly they did it. The hook gave a quick jerk beneath my foot, I lost my balance, and they were away.

This was not good. A runaway team is never good. This time I was lucky and the odds were in my favour: we were not following a trail, there was no herd of caribou or flock of ptarmigan out ahead for the dogs to chase, and most importantly the heavy sled was heading directly up an even steeper portion of the steep hillside. I made a brief but very inspired sprint up that hill, caught up to the sled, kicked in the snow hook, and muttered something soothing and poetic like, "Whoa, you fucking goddamned crazy sons of bitches."

The dogs would settle down as the trip went on. I knew that and I looked forward to it. For a dog musher that settling-in process is one of the joys of a long trip or a long race—to be out long enough to let the dogs' bred-to-the-bone insanity mellow into a quiet, rock-solid but more *subdued* willingness. But this was only day two, and they were still in phase one: completely bonkers. A lost team, on such a nice day, would not likely lead to disaster. After all, where could they go? Just on and on and on, leaving a plain set of tracks as they went. Finally they would stop, or get tangled, or circle back, or a tine of the bouncing snow hook would catch by chance on snow or rock and bring them up short. Hours later, along would come the exasperated, overheated musher. It was no big deal, most days. But if things went wrong the outcome of a runaway team was not pleasant to consider. Some of them even led to that parka-clad figure sprawled in the snow... "there are kinds of winter that you meet." Thinking along those lines, I slipped a loop of nylon cord from the handlebar around my mittened wrist. Doing so, I chuckled—*that* was something I hadn't felt a need to do on the southern slog a year earlier. "You guys might be able to pull my arm out of the socket," I said out loud, "but I bet you can't tear it off!"

———————

Route-finding on the Barrens, in winter, is not a precise affair. At times it becomes almost surreal, because it is so hard to maintain an accurate sense of scale. A boulder that looks to be a mile away suddenly looms up alongside in mere seconds, or it takes a half-hour to reach a ridge that looks like it is a hundred yards ahead. On days when the sun is visible, even if only as a fleeting shape through overcast or blowing snow, it is my favourite point of reference. Knowing local noon, which is about 12:15 p.m. or so in the area of my home, and knowing that the sun arcs through the sky at about fifteen degrees every hour, a musher can hold to a fairly accurate heading. I have found it best to avoid too much concern with precision, and instead to keep revising my estimated position as new clues become apparent. (See Appendix C where I have included my formula for measuring speed by using a stopwatch and the passage of the dogs' long gangline over a fixed point—a sort of chip log on a frozen ocean. This is surprisingly accurate.)

What I did *not* want to do—on these or other trips—was to replace the subtle, intricate art of dead reckoning with a stupefied reliance on the global positioning system, and thus join the ranks of what a bush-pilot friend of mine calls "the GPS junkies." I could imagine that scenario: the little computer screen flashing its numbers, while I struggled with mitten-clad hands (or freezing fingers) to punch in new waypoints, scroll down endless "menus," and so on, trusting the satellites of the Pentagon to guide us over the tundra. So the little GPS unit—for this trip I had decided to carry one—was stowed away deep in the sled with my camp gear (until one day later in the trip when it disappeared forever). I carried on by sun and pocket watch, revelling in the day and the dogs and the absolute freedom of it all.

Early afternoon found us deep in a sunny bottom alongside a tall esker, flanked on every side by spindly white spruce. It was a refuge in the midst of the Barrens, perhaps the very same spot that Helge Ingstad discovered in his travels through this same small watershed—now named Ingstad Creek—in the early 1930s: "Then it was that I fell upon my oasis in this vast snowy desert—a hollow through which flowed a river and a lake…Driving in across the Barren Lands, I did not suspect the existence of this hollow until I was fairly upon it. Quite suddenly it smiled up at me like a veritable scene from a fairyland."[3]

In brilliant sunshine the little thermometer showed minus 18 degrees. The dogs had finally calmed down enough to curl up and take a nap. I poured myself a cup of cocoa from the Thermos and perched like a sultan atop the bulbous sled load. I knew I was somewhere south of the "exact" route, but simply knowing that was good enough. The day's work would see good progress east no matter what. A half-hour rest for the dogs, and onward. We were crossing the upper reaches of Ingstad Creek, seventy years after Helge. I was feeling my way toward what Richard and Lance used to call Bablet's Draw, after another 1930s-era trapper of that name.. I knew that somewhere in the area we were crossing there stood a tiny board-and-frame shack built in the 1950s by the RCMP for use on their winter patrols. The fallen-down shack is of no practical value to a traveller now (except perhaps as emergency fuel), but I remembered it as an important landmark from the 1988 trip and I wanted to find it. Just east of it, I recalled, on the shore of Police Shack Lake, stood a big lone tamarack tree, its broad limbs distinct from the conical spruces. I must have passed south of both landmarks that day—as I would again on my homeward trip two weeks later. It was not until I flew east in April to retrieve my leftover cache supplies that I succeeded in relocating the shack and the tree. They both looked obvious, viewed from above, but even with the aerial view from several thousand feet I was unable to spot the lovely little hollow where I had paused for lunch. It is a big country, devoid of prominent landmarks.

Gradually we were moving into more wildlife, after what had been a very desolate winter back home on McLeod Bay. I had not seen a caribou for over three months when suddenly the dogs topped a rise and scared up a dozen of them. There were tracks of larger groups by then, too, showing plain and fresh on the snow in all directions, and just before halting for the night I spotted a herd of ten muskox, like square black boulders spread across a distant slope. So there was life and food out here, just a couple of days' travel east of Reliance. It occurred to me again how utterly crucial *mobility* is in this part of the world. To become too firmly rooted in one place is no advantage for animals or hunters of the North, if we aspire to live on what the land provides. The country is too vast, and its resources too widely scattered, for a homebody to make a living from it.

That night I found myself wistful over the fact that Richard and Lance were no longer living out at Lynx Lake. I will never forget arriving there by dogteam in the dark of a December afternoon in '88, and glimpsing that yellow lamplight in their cabin window. The poet John Haines could have been writing of them in lines from his poem "On the Road":[4]

There is a light through the trees—
it is only a simple place,
with two souls strung together
by nerves and poverty.

I caught myself thinking, time and again as I made my easting into the empty Barrens, how wonderful it would be to run into someone else out there. Finally I had to force myself to think through this longing a little more thoroughly. I asked myself whether I would truly welcome, for instance, the contact with humanity I was most likely to make out there, *circa* 2003. There were two choices, really: one, a Native hunter roaring up on a purple or fuscia snowmobile with yellow tongues-of-flame decals on the plastic cowling, a cooler in his toboggan filled with thawed cans of soda pop; or two, the *whock-whock-whock* of a helicopter, hovering and then touching down in a cloud of snow and the scream of a turbine engine, half-crouched figures scurrying out of the spindrift with bundles of geophysical gear or claim-stake pickets in hand, running over to holler at me, "Are you all right? Where are you headed?"

Would I welcome these? No, I supposed not. The first meeting with either apparition would be a pleasant change of pace, but if repeated over the course of a trip both would quickly become a dreaded nuisance. I ached only for that remembered warm lamplight in the cabin window, on a night in early December fifteen years back, two modern old-timers happy to see us, bottles of home-brewed beer around the pallet-board table. Aloud to the dogs as I made camp that night, thinking about all of this, I grunted, "Well, Olesen, they're gone. There's nobody left out here. Now just get over it." And mostly, for the rest of that trip, and the next two as well, I did, and I have. This land lived in its people, but the people have all moved away.

Making camp, night two, at what I figured to be the east edge of Bablet's Draw, was a far cry from the pleasant ritual of the first night out. Tired, clumsy, cold, and losing the race against darkness, I struggled through it. After chopping down through two feet of ice I hit gravel instead of water with the ice chisel, dulled the blade badly and so ended up melting snow to soak the dogs' food. Next, I found that Foxtail had chewed her harness while waiting for me to put the team out on the picket line. The stretchy rubber inserts of the tent poles, and the rubber inner-tube loops of my snowshoe bindings, were stiff and troublesome in the deepening cold. My toes were numb and my feet ached. At last I was settled in my little hutch of warmth and light, with Mr. Coleman purring at my side.

A clear cold night and a wondrous warm deep sleep. This year I was using a new light overbag to encase my goose-down mummy bag, and it made a big difference. Minus 36 degrees at dawn, 19 February, with a north wind and clear sky. I remembered asking in Reliance whether my neighbours had seen a weather map on their television. Roger had replied, "Just one big high after another, stacked up all the way to Siberia."

Day three was short and sweet. I lazed and puttered through a slow morning in the tent, and did not pull out of camp until just before eleven. By noon we had dropped onto the narrow west end of Sandy Lake. In that first hour there were moments again of the intense beauty that, I claimed to my journal that night, "I will remember as long as I live. Dogs in February sun, climbing smooth white slopes into an azure sky, past a rock cairn placed by someone years ago to mark this route, then dropping swiftly downhill dodging and careening past boulders and outcrops, into the western outlet of Sandy—headwaters of our old nemesis, the Snowdrift. Dogs so fast and eager, a joy to drive."

East down the 16 miles of Sandy Lake, relishing the passage and our arrival at this first big landmark. A group of caribou along the south shore watched us pass. Three wolves appeared and scattered at a lope up the creek leading in from Marge Lake, Summit Lake, and the ominous-sounding Lake of Woe. By mid-afternoon that day we had come 25 miles and had reached the intermediate cache: metal drums of dog kibble and fat, along with my own resupply—bacon, butter, crackers, fuel, and all the rest. This was a two-way cache, partly for use eastbound, the remainder to be left in reserve for our passage home. I dug the drums out of the drifts on the lake, loaded them aboard the emptied sled, and ferried them up to the campsite.

I did not know it yet, but that first cache site was to be our home for the next three nights. By dusk a fierce wind was roaring in from the north. Beyond the shelter of the spruces the air was a blur of wind-whipped snow. It did not seem to be snowing—in fact a star or two winked down if I looked carefully. The snow was blowing off the hilltops around us. I was glad we were not pinned down somewhere out there on the treeless plains we had crossed for the past two days.

The storm droned in the spruce tops all night, and all the next day. It was 39 below zero in the morning. After a deep sleep I was ready to roll over and continue with another round of such pleasantness. Only one thing inspired my emergence from the warm tent: the soaked dog food I had stored overnight in a buried cooler (in this usage actually a warmer) would begin to freeze if I did not retrieve it. I dressed, crawled outside, dug up the cooler and ladled out breakfast to the troops. That done and the spare fuel tank for the stove refilled, I retreated happily to the tent again. The dogs were snug and sound, and they were all clearly as pleased as I was to be tucked down in this haven while the wind howled overhead.

That day, 20 February, was just the first of many cold windy days on that easterly trip. In hindsight it is good that I had no access to weather forecasts and did not know, storm after storm, what was coming next. Each season does take on a character and that mid-winter of 2003, once it got rolling, was a cold and windy brute.

Sipping and nibbling in the pleasant orange-yellow light of the tent, I let the morning pass. I started hatching a plan to advance a portion of my cache supplies farther east when the storm abated and I scribbled out the details of that strategy in my journal. By late morning tent life had lost some of its charm and I suited up for another stroll outdoors. On snowshoes I worked to make a bed of boughs for each dog and to set up the HF antenna for the first scheduled radio call. Then I toured the little grove of thick-trunked spruces, many of them probably at least three hundred years old and still only 30 or 40 feet tall. I found a small, crudely fashioned wood stove made from a fuel drum and slung from a low branch above snow level. It spoke of the past, and of other passing travellers. Sandy Lake was a natural highway offering 16 smooth miles of east–west travel across a rock-ribbed landscape.

Somewhere near that camp of mine, I knew, stood the remains of an old cabin where a piece of tent canvas had been signed and dated by many of the long-gone trappers. It was no day to go searching for it, and no one had ever told me exactly where it was. Years earlier I had pressed Richard and Lance about the precise location of this ruin, but they had not been very expansive. Only recently have I started to see how brash and intrusive I must have seemed twenty years ago, newly arrived in the country and eager to have everyone divulge all of their hard-won routes and landmarks. I see now that such easy acceptance and openness is not the way of the world, even as I recognize stirrings of that same secrecy within myself. When we live in a place we come upon things, and some of them are like the buried treasure of fable: old guns, tiny springs of water, grave sites, hidden cascades, or the skeleton of a bark canoe. We feel, rightly or wrongly, that we have *earned* the discovery of these things. Human nature plays into it, and so despite the pleadings of archaeologists and historians, many such places and objects get squirreled away in actual or figurative treasure boxes. They will someday pass, along with their keepers, back into the realm of mystery. Did that shred of signed tent canvas from that old cabin on Sandy Lake end up with one of the latter-day "locals"—and if so, is that a loss? Should all such objects wind up in distant museums? I am not convinced.

No one in the past hundred years has lived an entire lifetime out in the watershed of Sandy Lake—growing up, raising children, growing old. This country east of Great Slave is a land of newcomers and passers-by, and of short intense segments of people's lives. It is the land of summer wanderers, and of the prime two or three decades of a life—here and then gone. "Too remote," I wrote in my journal after returning to the tent that morning, "too lonely, and too goddamned Cold!"

So be it, I say. As this new millennium begins, this landscape has mostly been abandoned by our species. Humanity's attention is focused elsewhere. It is good that this country east to the Thelon, clear to Hudson Bay, remains wild and empty. Perhaps it can benefit from some formal protection, something low key and without a lot of bureaucratic paper-work, akin to the Wilderness Area designation in some provinces and in the United States. As such it will always attract some people. They will come, and in time depart.

By late afternoon I was again growing restless in the tent. For the third time that day I donned all my warm bulky gear and went out to prowl around the campsite, to visit the dogs, and just to stand for long moments listening to the gale. There was the evening round of dog-food prepara-tion to attend to, the hauling and heating of water scooped from the hole I had chopped in the lake ice. Always at evening on layover days, freed from the race to pitch camp and finish chores before dark, there comes a melancholy mood just at twilight. I have no explanation for it, but I know that I share it with others, for over the years I have come across many ref-erences to it. I could fill pages with quotes, like these opening lines from another poem by Haines, called "Foreboding": "Something immense and lonely / divides the earth at evening."[5] Or from old Joshua Slocum's book *Sailing Alone Around the World* (1899): "while I worked at the sails and rigging I thought only of onward and forward. It was when I anchored in the lonely places that a feeling of awe crept over me."[6]

Dogs fed, camp secured, and darkness falling, I crept into the tent again. Another simple delicious dinner of rice and moose meat washed down with a swig of cold lake water. I was content but for a nagging tin-gling pain in my feet. As I settled in for the night I had to acknowledge, unmistakably, that somewhere back up the trail I had managed to frostnip the forward part of the soles of both feet. For the past day and night I had felt an odd burning sensation there, and had been struggling more than usual to keep my feet warm. As with so many injuries and accidents, the underlying cause was sheer stubbornness. When I set out from home I had tried to hold in reserve, dry and ready, my very warmest set of moccasins and liners. For the first three days' travel I had worn my two alternate sets of footgear: the military-issue white "Mickey Mouse boots," and a prototype pair of leather-and-canvas moccasins donated to me by a young Yellowknife man who aspired to make a business based on them. Day by day, hour by hour, my feet had been losing the battle, and it must have been on the morning of day three that I had superficially frozen my two big toes and the soles of both feet. This was a small setback, not a show-stopper, and not without some humour. I imagined the product endorsement I could write for the young moccasin-maker: "J.L.: Thanks for the prototype mukluks for me to try out. I wore them for two full days on my winter solo to the Thelon River and I did not frostbite my feet until late on the second afternoon."

I would have to break out the heavy-duty moccasins in the morning. A little frostnip was only an embarrassment, but deep frostbite would be a disaster. This was no time to experiment.

It was the first radio-call night of the trip, and after gently warming the little transceiver on the rack of the camp stove, I was gratified by a strong clear conversation with Kristen. She reported minus 42 degrees in Yellowknife, clear and calm. We chatted briefly and confirmed a plan to talk again in six days. Aware of the need to conserve my radio's batteries, we said goodnight. Outside, it sounded as though the wind was dropping off. If it did the temperature would almost certainly drop with it. The dogs were well rested and I was determined to try to advance part of the cache supplies east to the far side of Whitefish Lake. Looking forward to a day of sledding without the chore of breaking camp, I fell asleep.

———

The morning of February 21st was beautiful—cold and clear. The wind had gentled and backed slightly into the northwest. I sorted supplies and dawdled through mid-morning. At about eleven I harnessed the dogs and we set out for Whitefish Lake.

All day the team flew; it was like nothing I had seen on any day of the southern trip. With a rest day just behind them, hardpacked snow, a lightly loaded sled, and clear weather, the dogs seemed resolved to underscore for me the abundant enthusiasm they had for what we were doing. It was an honest 20 miles to the tiny hunting shack on the northeast shore of Whitefish Lake, and we covered that distance in two hours and twelve minutes. I could tell that my race habits were creeping out of dormancy as I noted times and distances and miles per hour.

The shack was nothing more than a six-foot-square plywood-sheathed box, painted white for camouflage and fitted out with a sheet-metal heating stove, a shelf, and a couple of windows. After a brief stop, we turned west again. Four days' supply of dog food and stove fuel were now positioned on the east side of Whitefish. Lance had once warned me that Whitefish was a barrier along this route—big, open, and devoid of useful landmarks in even a moderate winter storm. Through the day the visibility improved—first the smoke-like remnants of the ground blizzard dissipated, then the sky turned to pastels of blue and yellow. By mid-afternoon we were travelling under a flawless dome of deep blue, with sharp horizons on all quadrants.

On the run west a brisk breeze was in my face. At minus 35 degrees on the thermometer, even a ten-mile-per-hour breeze adds to the nine-mile-per-hour forward speed of the team to make for a bitter wind-chill effect.[7] The sting of my nose should have set off a few alarm bells in my mind but I was oblivious, enraptured by the speed and beauty of that afternoon run, and only days later would I realize my folly. As the dogs whisked me home into that biting westerly breeze, the tips of several dogs' penises and the thinly furred flesh of Foxtail's flanks were nipped by frost. Ouch! I should have known better. All day we passed small bands of caribou, never more than forty or fifty in a group, prancing like storybook reindeer on the hardpacked snow. Often they would stand in a little cluster as we approached, confident in their ability to outrun anything on two or four legs. They would tense as we passed, splay their legs, and suddenly erupt into a gallop. Steam from their hot breath puffed from their flared nostrils, matched by puffs of snow at each hoof-fall as they ran flat-out with heads thrown back. Just as suddenly, and all in unison, they would slow to a smooth sidewinders gait, torsos swinging comically from side to side, before pausing to watch us from a few hundred yards.

That night I played with the GPS in the tent, and got a kick out of watching such authoritative precision flash up on the little screen: "sunrise 07:42, sunset 17:02, altitude 1168 feet above sea level." Skeptical as I was about this technology and its place on a dogsled trip, I could sense the allure of such wizardry. *No wonder people get such a charge out of these things,* I thought—and little wonder, too, that their outlook has been steadily, subversively altered. The entire realm of sky and caribou, dogs and wind, miles of travel, all reduced to tiny numbers on a portable screen, cute little icons and "precision" readouts ("precision" set off in quotes because I knew the sun would *not* rise, there at my camp, at 07:42, and that the altitude was a very rough approximation—give or take at least 200 feet. Yet who would dare question such **bold black letters,** delivered straight from Mission Control?).

Morning three at Sandy Lake, day six of the trip, and it was 40 below at dawn—in the jargon of the northern outback it was again officially capital-C Cold. Sandy Lake lay clear and white to the west. The previous day's trail led east through patchy spruce. A gibbous waning moon hung low in the south. Earlier a sudden gust of wind had worried me as it passed through the treetops just before dawn, like a sleeper's long exhalation in the hour before waking, but as I stood just outside the tent flap the air was calm. I was glad it was late February, for the sun had regained some strength and warmth. If the day stayed calm or nearly so, it would be good for travelling and we could look forward to soaking up some of that warmth. Beginning in late February a thermometer placed in direct sunshine will give ludicrously warm readings, like plus 20 degrees when the ambient temperature is still minus 30. Always a cheerful reminder that our old star still has some strength.

The deep cold would now be with us for many days. It heightened my sense of solitude and put me slightly on edge. As I crawled back into the warm tent, I reflected on how alone I truly was. In the summer of 1997, out on a flying contract with a solitary prospector, I rested one day on a hillside near Henik Lake, Nunavut—300 miles east of Sandy—and wrote: "This must be the geographical center of Solitude." As we moved east I was closing in again on that place and that state of mind.

On cold mornings the lowest temperature often occurs just after sunrise, because of a little-known meteorological nuance called the "albedo effect." This occurs as the sun first breaks the horizon, because its rays warm the upper layers of the atmosphere first. As the highest layer of air warms, it rises. This forces the air below to expand, and in doing so it cools. The surface temperature dips, slightly but measurably. (At home, Kristen and I jokingly refer to this as the "libido effect," although neither of us seems to be sure just how the libido is supposed to be affected.)

Packed up and moving, we began two days of travel which were the best and happiest of the trip. To my journal that night I exclaimed, "I am having, quite literally, the time of my life... Clear, absolutely clear, cold but nearly calm, maybe 3 to 5 knots of quartering tailwind from the northwest... The dogs made short work of 30 miles..." And so on. For a dog musher it does not get much better. We moved through scattered bands of caribou all day, the largest a group of about thirty-five animals. They all seemed to be drifting slowly north. Our heading was due east

Breakfast in the inner sanctum of the Hilleberg tent. I still have my "sleeping helmet" balaclava on.

and once we had passed Richard's shack I was on new terrain again, map reading and navigating mile by mile.

Just before reaching camp we drew close to a small band of caribou on the sloping shore of the northeast arm of Whitefish. Suddenly, as if on a dare from the others, a cow and her calf broke from the cluster and passed at a dead run just a few paces ahead of Ernie and Foxtail, my lead dogs. Then another animal crossed, not more than three feet from the lead dogs' noses, hell-bent on joining the other two on the south side of the trail. It looked for all the world like a game of chicken, with bets being laid by the group up on the hill. I laughed and gave a gruff "Haw!" command to the dogs as they veered to chase that third daredevil caribou.

That night I changed my dinnertime regimen and ate my supper inside the inner portion of the tent, instead of out in the vestibule. I wondered why it had taken me so long to arrive at such a substantial improvement in my routine. From that night on through the rest of the trip, and for the following two journeys, I stayed out in the vestibule only long enough to boil my one-pot meals, and to melt snow and heat water for the morning. Doing all that steamy work outside of the inner tent helped to reduce the steaming and subsequent icing of the interior tent fabric. With my cooking, melting, and heating done for the night, I carefully moved everything into the inner sanctum of the tent and enjoyed my food at a leisurely pace, sans hat, gloves, and steam. This was far more civilized than hunching out in the vestibule enveloped in steam and freezing fog, wolfing down my meal as quickly as I could.

A tiny clump of truly tiny trees, more like the stems of shrubs, provided a place to camp and a place to tie off the sled for our morning departure. The dogs seemed to have reached a new level of enthusiasm and energy, though, and on the morning of day seven we had another sobering near miss. As I was standing off to one side wrapping up the picket line, they yanked the snow hook. The sled shot forward, to be stopped and held only by the snub line around a spruce "trunk" less than two inches in diameter. That gave me pause. Out on the lake there were caribou for the dogs to chase, the wind was piping up to a brisk half-gale from the west, and *everything* I had was in or on that sled, including my big parka and fur cap. If the team had left me behind, they would have had it all.

After twenty-five years of mushing dogs I am still amazed by them, so I suppose I always will be. There they were, harnessed up after a windy night spent curled up on hardpacked snow at minus 40 degrees, leaping, lunging, barking, and screaming "Let's go! Go! Onward! Ahead! For God's sake what *is* the holdup here?!" I remember Joe Garnie at the Eagle Island checkpoint of the Iditarod, chomping on a cigar and pointing to a big shaggy wheel dog of his, saying "Now *that* is a dog. All he wants to do is fight, fuck, and go someplace."

The heartfelt joy that the dogs exude in the midst of a day of what some people would understandably see as hard labour, as drudgery or even slavery, is contagious. At our midday rest break on day six, in a beautiful bowl-like cove of the big esker north of Whitefish Lake, Edelweiss never did get around to lying down or resting. At eighteen months of age she was still a pup at heart, or at least a teenager. As I sipped my cocoa and soaked up the sunshine, she pranced and bounced and twisted and tried to get someone to play with her. Old Steve, who was just ahead of her alongside Murphy, thought he had better make sure she didn't have some other sort of play in mind, so he grudgingly stood up, caught a few passing sniffs as she twirled and pranced, gave her a quizzical look, and curled up to continue his nap.

In keeping with old Native and voyageur traditions, I carried a bottle of brightly coloured beads in the back pouch of my sled bag, to be left as offerings in exchange for safe passage, or as an acknowledgement of thanks. One night back home a friend who was visiting had asked whether I ever made any offerings on my travels. He suggested leaving little bits of tobacco and saying a few words. Skeptical, I told him I had not smoked for many years, that I did not intend to carry any tobacco, and that I had never understood why tobacco had assumed such metaphysical significance across the north. He considered my reply and suggested coloured beads as another choice. I thought about it, and decided to see how that felt. I suspected that it would strike me as an affectation, and I was wary. As I crossed Whitefish, one of the headwaters of the Thelon River, I dug out the little bottle of orange, blue, and yellow beads, held up a pinch of them to each of the four directions, and flung them high. I said aloud, "Thank you for this. This is wonderful." Fast dogs, bright sun, cold air, sled tracks...

As I moved east, I moved farther and farther from any vestige of humanity. Although I knew that Inuit villages lay along the coast of Hudson Bay, four hundred miles to the east, that knowledge did not allay the sensation that I was leaving everyone and everything behind me, mile by mile. I heard old Mr. Basic whining and worrying again—usually at about 4 a.m. (Was it a Napoleonic general, or Bonaparte himself, who observed that "there are no brave men at 4 o'clock in the morning"?) Mostly I managed to ignore my worries, secure in my caches and maps, my dogs and gear, the tent and stove and fuel. What did give me pause, again and again, was a profound respect for the old-timers. In my journal I wrote:

> I saw some caribou yesterday, yes, but how many of them could I have killed? Hunting on foot or by dogsled, with a single-shot rifle, in order to feed myself *and* the dogs, and thus to sustain our lives and our journey? I remember seeing one group of about a dozen as we turned north from the "Whitefish Hilton" (Richard's shack) and after glancing down at the map I looked up again—and they had utterly vanished. A matter of seconds, and I never saw them again, never came within range at all. And forget the rifle—how about a bow and some stone-tipped arrows?

Musing along these lines, I felt utterly disconnected from any ancient way of life on the land. I was out there, but how could I ever be there in the way that those long-gone people were? I concluded again that the answer would always be the same: *I could not.* I was a man of my culture, fitted out with the trappings of that culture, marching in lockstep to the mindset and pace and rhythm of that culture, even way out here. I could scatter beads, but I wouldn't be scattering any of those precious alkaline batteries that gave light to my headlamp and juice to the HF radio.

———————

There is an old saying, derived from a joke, used when things are expected to change: "waiting for the other shoe to drop." Like nearly every dogsled in the world in 2003, my sled was fitted with strips of slick high-density plastic on the underside of its runners. The runners on the sled I drove east were not wooden but fibreglass, with a foam core like a modern ski. Beneath the runner, attached with screws, was a thin aluminum rail which in cross-section looked like a woodworking dovetail. Mated to these undercut metal rails were plastic runner shoes or "sliders," pre-cut to the width of the runner and with a dovetail notch machined down their length. A single small machine screw secured the plastic shoe to the rail and runner at the forward end of the sled. Voila— the modern quick-change runner system patented by musher Tim White and standard on dogsleds for the past thirty years.

When I had flown east to set out my caches there had just been a snowfall and I had seen very little bare ground. I had set off from home with no spare runner sliders—none in the sled, and none at either one of my caches. By the time we reached the esker-threaded highlands between Whitefish Lake and the Thelon valley, hard on the heels of the windstorm that had blown through while we were at Sandy Lake, long stretches of high ground had been blown completely clean of snow. Oblivious to my impending fate, I was not hesitant to climb the sled up onto those bare windswept ridges and hilltops, in order to have a better view of the country and better clues for navigation. Because good dogs can easily pull a loaded sled over stretches of gravel and sand, and because *everyone* carries spare runner shoes for such situations, it is normally not a big calamity when a set of runner plastic wears through

At about 3 p.m. on the second of those glorious days eastbound from our storm camp on Sandy Lake, the trip changed. Just as we crested yet another gravelly ridge top I looked down to see tattered ribbons of orange plastic splayed out from the edge of the left runner. This was not good, for I realized with a sudden jolt that I had no spare sliders, and worse yet, on that sled I had not installed a layer of quarter-inch plastic to serve as a backup beneath the shoes. In other words I had seriously screwed up. To draw an automotive analogy, I had blown my tires and was left to run on the rims.

Apart from being embarrassed about such an amateurish mistake, I was deeply worried. Within minutes the plastic gave out on the right-hand runner also. Once both sliders were stripped off, the sudden deceleration of the sled that afternoon would have to be felt to be believed. I was riding on the aluminum rails, and there is no sled-runner material slower than bare aluminum. "With one shoe gone and one in tatters," I wrote that night, "the sled stuck in a snowdrift and I went forward to see just how bad things were. I leaned over and gave it a solid, hernia-worthy heave. Managed only to fart, and the sled didn't so much as budge. Geezus."

Mobility was the key to my journey east and to our safe return home. We had just lost our mobility. Something would have to be done.

The runner shoes gave out just as we descended from a long traverse of featureless tundra and within a mile or so we reached a usable campsite. A small grove of stunted spruce grew along a little ravine, crossways to the strengthening west wind. It looked like a good place to halt and consider my options. Ignoring larger questions I immersed myself in three or four hours of the familiar routine of making camp, feeding dogs, and eating supper. The wind continued to build from the west and I pitched camp with an eye toward being pinned down there for a long time. The tent was shoehorned between the crippled sled and the picket line for the dogs. After dinner I wrote the first four obvious choices in my journal:

1. remove aluminum rails here
2. run on rails to the cache (17.5 straight-line miles)
3. run empty sled to the cache, retrieve it and return to here (NO!)
4. get some sleep and take up with this problem in the morning.

Opting for number four, I closed the journal and turned in for the night.

———————

Morning, day eight, "QCR Lake," minus 33 degrees, calm, with high broken cloud. After a good sleep I wrote a more thorough consideration of my options in my journal. As usually happens, a collection of insights—some odd, some helpful—had come to me during the night. There is wisdom in the old maxim "sleep on it." I noted some choices ranging from workable to nearly unthinkable. The real danger was that without the plastic runner shoes, the countersunk heads of the stainless bolts spaced along the bottom of each runner would be damaged. These bolts pinned together the entire structure of the sled: load-carrying bed, runners, upright stanchions, rigging, bridle, and all. Were those bolts to fail, one by one, my little ship would fall apart quickly and dramatically. In the light of morning it seemed obvious that my best strategy was to carry on as far as the cache. Sliders or not, we could get

After running a short distance from camp without the plastic runner shoes I paused to careen the sled and remove the aluminum rails.

that far in less than a day. And, beginning immediately, I would have to make every possible effort to keep the sled on snow and ice, and *only* on snow and ice.

"Ironic," I wrote that morning, "that I spent half the day yesterday riding the brake to slow the team down, and now this!"

I did find comfort in one perspective, an outlook that I often preach to my children: "Listen, some people in the world have *real* problems. This, lest we forget, is not a real problem." The landscape in which I was immersed had claimed many lives over the years through starvation, disease, drowning...even a few gruesome murders. Looked at in that context, the runner-shoe glitch was, more than anything else, just inconvenient and embarrassing.

I packed up and headed east. It was a bright beautiful morning, the wind had dropped overnight, and our track had joined up with the big esker that would lead us right to the cache site. Within less than a mile it became plain that running on the aluminum rails was simply not an option, especially for 18 or 19 miles. I was running, pushing, and heaving on the back of the sled and the dogs were pulling their guts out. The runners squealed and squeaked over the cold, windblown snow. I stopped on a smooth stretch of lake, careened the sled and set about removing the rails with a brace and bit, screw by screw. With that done we resumed running, now on straight fibreglass (and slightly countersunk bolt-heads), and the going improved considerably.

The weather held all day, reaching a balmy minus 22 degrees or so in mid-afternoon. The cache was perfectly intact when we reached it and after four hours of work I had erected the wall tent, fuelled and lit the sheet-metal wood stove, and piled thick spruce boughs beneath my sleeping bags. As it turned out, I would spend the next four nights in that campsite.

The big wood-heated wall tent was a luxury, but I always found the transition from the nylon-tent-and-camp-stove system to the older, more traditional methods somewhat jarring. The only real advantage of the older method, at least in my situation, was the space it allowed for thorough drying of gear, and the fact that heat could be generated by a "limitless" resource—wood—instead of being rationed from the bottles of white gas. The radiant heat of a wood fire is deep and bone-warming. No other fuel or stove combination can match it. Morning and evening throughout my stay in the wall-tent camp, I searched for and dragged in firewood. The cluttered "indoor" space was filled with the pungent smells of drying dog harnesses, jackets, booties, and unwashed musher. The smaller, orderly space capsule of the sturdy nylon tent seemed appealing by comparison.

As I relaxed by the wood stove that evening, I decided to take a full day off from mushing on day nine. I woke overheated in my double sleeping bag sometime in the night, and realized that the weather must have changed. By morning it was minus 27 degrees and calm, with low grey clouds draped over the spruce grove and the esker. The Basic voice was happy, with warmth, light, a protected tent, fuel for the cutting, and heaps of food all in sight. The Lofty voice was struggling to adjust, now that the cache was reached. I was tired and the gloomy weather only dampened my spirits. This all felt familiar—it was the same heavy melancholy that had marked my layover on Nonacho Lake a year earlier. I suppose a pop psychologist would call it post-realization depression. The quest accomplished, the immediate goal achieved, I tried to work through my funk and busied myself with the usual chores: opening cache barrels, dividing dog food into daily portions and sacks, setting up the radio antenna, and cutting firewood.

Recalling the sting I felt in my nose a few days earlier, I took a thorough look at all the dogs. What I discovered was not encouraging: a few minor nicks and scrapes would heal, but what gave me real concern was the confirmation that four of the males had frostbitten penis tips, and Foxtail—a female—had frostbite on her flank. The flank I could easily protect with a dog jacket, but the penis tips did indeed qualify as a "real problem." Left untreated the tissue could easily become infected or refreeze or both. Painful and unpleasant, surely, but the critical threat was that the passage of urine could be blocked, and that would be deadly. I would have to make absolutely certain that those boys were protected from here on, all the way home. From past experience I had an inkling of what that would entail, and seeing the damage did not brighten my mood.

Next, I carefully examined my crippled sled and made some minor adjustments to its steel brake claws. The bald fibreglass runners would be all right, I concluded, although much slower than plastic. If I scrupulously avoided rocks and gravel, we could make it home without a catastrophic breakdown. "Surely," I wrote that night, "there exists an unbroken line of snow from here to the dog yard at home. All we have to do is stay on it."

In mid-afternoon I finished all the chores and set out on snowshoes east along the esker. After climbing steeply out of the trees to the bare crest of the ridge I was able to remove the snowshoes and walk. It was beautiful up there, looked at with the right slant of mind: gravel and sand, hardpacked snow, the frozen orange-yellow urine where a wolverine had marked a small boulder. In the utter calm of that grey afternoon my solitude felt like a weight on my shoulders. I tried to take a few photographs, which for a non-photographer is surely a symptom of mental unrest. Yearning for memories? Craving the cozy conviviality of the ritual post-journey slide show? A few miles out from camp my mood finally lightened. To the east I could see the broad sweep of the Thelon River valley. The prospect of setting foot on the river ice the next day was inspiring. The Thelon is a touchstone for me—a place so remote and pristine as to be always remarkable when my travels finally bring me within sight of it, whether flying over it or on the ground.

As I walked back along the esker ridge and approached my camp, I was struck again by the layers and layers of *stuff* that comprised my "outfit," and how such a mound of flotsam and jetsam would have astounded the old-timers. Surely they had camped where I was camped. The little grove of trees was a natural hideaway for a team of dogs and a hunter. I tried to imagine their days, and the fundamental *disconnectedness* of modern life crept into my thoughts like a tired refrain, dragging me down again. What really mattered out here? A good sled (which I now did not have), good dogs, an axe, a weapon, a tent, a fire, a cooking kettle, caribou-skin clothes and hides for bedding. Above all, skill and savvy—and patience, the more the better. Perhaps I never could get there, to that ancient rhythm, with my camera, my radio antenna, and my air-dropped barrels of jasmine rice and dog kibble. As I crossed the little lake where I had landed to put out the cache, I remembered those four muskox sauntering along in that bitter wind. Now I was back, as I had hoped I could be. But I was still a long way from being with them. Hearing my approach, the muffled lift and fall of the snowshoes, a dog howled. Even the team seemed a little down that day. *Not surprising*, I thought to myself, *if the tip of your pecker is frostbitten.* I set to work heating and soaking their evening meal. They watched my every move with weary, doleful gazes. Several of them did not finish their food. Only Edelweiss had her usual frisky happy attitude after feeding, as I moved down the picket line scratching everyone's ears and examining their paws.

Considering the realities, I knew that I would have to reconsider one of my goals for the trip east: to visit a grave on the east side of the upper Thelon. In the heyday of the white-fox fur-trade years, Scandinavian trappers Gene Olson (a Swede) and Emil Bode (a Dane) paddled east and established a pole-frame winter cabin along the upper Thelon River. Olson kept a daily diary, which was subsequently recovered by the RCMP. On a night in early December 1930 he made one final calm, terse entry, and that was that. Not until October of 1931 were the two corpses discovered by another pair of trappers who had come into the upper Thelon country that fall. Both of the bodies were in their bunk beds, and both had been murdered by a mysterious assailant wielding an axe. In January 1932 an RCMP patrol from Reliance reached the site by dogteam. The remains of Bode and Olson were laid in a rock-and-timber grave on a bald slope near the camp. The police investigation eventually focused on one prime suspect, another Swede named Carl or Otto "Blackie" Lanner, who was a former trapping partner of Olson. Lanner shot himself dead soon after the police interviewed him. Officially, the murders of Bode and Olson remain unsolved.

Since 1989 I have visited the grave and camp site now and then by float plane and canoe. I wanted to see it in winter, but with the runner-shoe debacle looming large in my mind, those extra 45 miles round-trip began to look daunting.

By dusk, the wind was up again, shaking the tent wall and rattling the stovepipes. To have such wind there, deep in the sheltered grove of snow-laden spruce, meant that another all-out gale was under way. Yet I was glad to hear the roaring of the wind that night. Each gust helped to dispel the sombre mood of the day. I drifted off to the sound of the storm, dreaming of the jar of homemade blueberry sauce that I had tucked away in one of the cache barrels, and of the hot greasy doughnuts I would dip into it come morning.

February 26th was a beauty. With luck every trip has a day like this. Something changes on that day, and with luck some goal is reached—a summit, a landmark, or some sort of turning point. After that day, you know you are going home or back or down. That day was it for me on that trip: clear and calm and 40 below zero at sunrise, an early start from camp, eastbound with the sled nearly empty; no agenda more specific than to travel toward the Thelon and have a look around. A moment from that morning remains fixed in my memory years later: the dogs were climbing fast up a perfectly firm slope, on packed snow dusted with a quarter-inch of fresh powder, each of their footfalls leaving only the precise print of a paw. Such power, such grace, such speed—every tugline tight, every gait smooth, and all utterly silent. I felt giddy with pleasure, and wondered whether by holding my breath I could stop time itself, like a photographer setting up a portrait: Yes. Right there. Perfect.

We meandered steadily through a little creek valley cut deep into the tundra, and descended into the softer snow of the Thelon valley. Once there, at midday, the way downriver tempted me. The Bode-Olson grave was only 12 miles away. But twelve times two is twenty-four, and we were already many miles from camp. The deep cold, the soft snow, and the looming end to daylight were all stacked against any more miles that day. Instead of pushing on, I decided to take a long pause. Unusual for me— perhaps I *was* learning something. I marked our arrival on the Thelon with another scattering of my coloured beads and some mumbled words of gratitude to the powers that are: wind, sun, the Barrens; snow, cold, and earth itself. God, or manifestations of God.

Rising in a place as wild and remote as any on earth, flowing 400 miles to tidewater below Baker Lake, along the way gathering strength and breadth from all the smaller watersheds of the north-central Barrens, the Thelon River is one of the North's arteries. Like the Back, the Kazan, the Hanbury, and the Dubawnt, it is a pristine and unsettled river right from start to finish—along its banks there is (as yet) no mine, no settlement, nary a camp or cabin in year-round use. With its game sanctuary to protect the heart of its path, the Thelon may just manage to remain pure and remote through the years and decades ahead.

It had been twenty-two years since I had left sled tracks on the Thelon. The country had not changed perceptibly, there where I stood, in those two decades—had not changed, in essence, since the retreat of the last glacial ice. As I stood there on the river ice, I was struck by how much my own perspective had changed in that time. Some basic tenets of my outlook were unshaken. I was still humbled and inspired by this vast northern wilderness. What had changed was my point of view. The Thelon was still a magical and powerful river, far from home and set apart. But "home" was now our little cluster of buildings 180 miles due west, instead of a thousand miles and a border-crossing away to the south.

The undercurrent of my thoughts was not altogether lofty as I paused to reflect and scatter beads on the river ice that afternoon. The dogs were restless and I was getting cold. It was time to turn west, after all those days of steady easting. "All right, come haw, let's go home…good dogs." With such a lightly loaded sled, and despite the rough-shod runners, the team scampered swiftly back up the long slope out of the river valley. I paused just once to gaze north, downriver, in the direction of the hilltop and the log-and-stone double grave of Bode and Olson. The Thelon valley westerly, which I remembered so vividly from my travels in 1981 as a green twenty-three-year-old, was kicking up a haze of blown snow, muddling the razor-sharp clarity that had been so striking in the morning. I shuddered. Hell of a spot to get axe-murdered by a lunatic, boys.

Somewhere in the final miles before reaching camp that night, or in the hour of chores upon arrival, I lost forever the little GPS receiver I had been carrying. Although I did not like using it for mile-by-mile navigation, I had pulled it out that afternoon in order to save the coordinates of a spot that I found intriguing. Alongside the narrow creek we were following upstream there was a striking little grove of thick timber. The GPS was cold and its small screen was just blank, but I knew it would still save a waypoint for me if I turned it on and waited a few minutes. Having done so, I pressed the Mark key with a cold fingertip, then punched Off and stuffed the little black box back down the front of my parka. I have not seen it since.

It may have been lost around camp, in twilight when I stripped to my fleece sweater and carried armloads of spruce-bough bedding to the dogs. After dark, in the tent, eager to match the waypoint to a place on the map, I realized it was gone. Its replacement value was several hundred dollars. Its loss—or rather the necessity of its replacement, for I used it in my flying work—would not be popular back home with my dear wife. "That cursed thing should never have come out of its place in the camera bag, or once out I should have stowed it back there," I wrote to myself.

The next day, the 27th of February, was the coldest of the trip. It was minus 43 degrees at dawn, with a light breeze from the north. My plan was for a final round of reorganizing, repacking, and preparation. I was tense. Cold of such depth should and does put any sensible warm-blooded creature on guard. The departure for home now loomed, and I knew that I had to take this next leg of the journey as seriously as any dog-driving I had ever done. The little spruce grove with its wall tent and trampled snow had begun to feel like an island in a vast ocean. It was time to weigh anchor. Out the door of the tent on that frigid morning, looking south, I could see only white snow and the blue-grey dome of sky. I wrote, "Mornings are hard sometimes. Hard to lie in a warm sleeping bag and find inspiration in the prospect of what is ahead: hours of heating the tent, stowing supplies, fussing over details, making decisions about the sled-load that will only be proven right or wrong in the unknown miles ahead. At least both the Basic and the Lofty voices will be singing in unison for a while: 'West! Home!'"

On every trip of the four there was this turn for home. Coming west from the Thelon valley had held that mix of relief and excitement the day before. It was as if only then did my *entire* self become committed to a clear, logical goal. No more sparring at weak moments between the "let's just go home" whiner and the "onward to adventure" brass band.

We would be backtracking. This is an unusual routing for an adventure trek nowadays, although nothing could be more traditional when it comes to the route for a journey. You go away, and then you turn around and go back home. Modern wilderness travellers, however, are not often going "away" and "home." Their preferences run to circle routes, or one-way journeys with an endpoint and an airlift. It is always exciting to see a piece of country for the first time, but I have always enjoyed the second look that a return over the outbound trail offers. I agree with Alaskan author Richard Nelson, who wrote in *The Island Within* that "There may be more to learn by climbing the same mountain a hundred times than by climbing a hundred different mountains."[8]

To a dog musher, of course, one obvious reward of the back trail is the trail itself. On the previous days' run back to camp from the river I had not said a word to the dogs for more than two hours. They knew where to go, and I was freed at last from, "Gee, gee over, that's right, straight ahead, good dogs, haw now, haw over..." et cetera, hour after hour, picking a route and announcing my decisions to the lead dogs.

I knew that the dogs would sense this turn toward home. Throughout our days at the wall-tent camp, immersed in the spruce grove in such deep cold, they had been quiet, almost sombre. Two of my stalwarts, Gulo and Riley, were on oral antibiotics for their frostbitten penis tips, which were now becoming painful and inflamed. Every dog in the team had at least one tender paw. Uneaten food was left on the snow at every feeding, and at 40-some below zero a poor appetite is a sure sign of some aches and pains. Still, they had been happy and lively on the day trip, and I was confident that the trail west would perk them up.

By noon the wind was up, gusting well above twenty-five knots, roaring out of the north-northwest. The thermometer showed minus 35 degrees, and I had to ruefully admit that I had again frosted the forward sole of my right foot and the tip of its big toe. Trying to eke my way through the day in the free-trial-period moccasins, trying to let my warmer footgear dry completely for the coming days, was not going to work. I shared a few morsels of caribou meat with the dogs, from some tenderloins that Roger and Miranda had given me back in Reliance. The wind continued to drone and gust, and I postponed making an outing to search for the lost GPS. I retreated to the tent, picked up the paperback serial-killer novel *The Alienist*, which I was reading in honour of Bode and Olson, and polished off the blueberry preserves. The cache and the sled load were ready for morning. At about three thirty, I initiated, and quickly abandoned, an attempt to hook up six dogs and go back up the trail to look for the GPS. Back in the tent I pulled out my journal and wrote, "Can anyone tell me how I am going to get four frostbitten dogs home 180 miles in such a wind?"

An hour later, a lull. This was, I thought, my last chance for that miserable $300 GPS. I hooked up six dogs, put young Ernie out in lead, and went back to the spot along the creek where I knew I had last used the damned thing. No luck. At least I could rest assured that I had looked, and that it wasn't lying back there in plain sight along the trail.

The radio "sked" was loud and clear that night. It was cold in Yellowknife, but not 43 below. I got a chuckle out of Kristen by telling her that I was getting pretty skinny, and that my bellybutton was starting to get a blister from rubbing against my backbone. I told her my plan for the next few days, and about the sled runners, and we confirmed the next radio call in six days. With that we signed off.

Another good sleep, another cold morning: minus 40 degrees with clear skies and some ice fog. West wind still blowing. The night muse had brought me a useful idea on how to protect the "Frozen Dick Foursome." I set to work with my knife, cutting the lower third of my caribou-hide sleeping pad into a dozen six-by-eight-inch rectangles. These would solve the problem I had been grappling with, namely this: I could protect the afflicted parts of all the dogs, using fleece belly guards and dog jackets, but for the males this only worked until the day's first urination. Boys being boys and dogs being dogs, this usually came within ten minutes of leaving camp, when a rock or shrub or mound of snow simply *had* to be marked in passing. In arctic winter temperatures, and wind chill into the minus triple digits, the instantaneous result was a hideous frozen clump of nylon, fleece, and urine over tender raw flesh.

On the day trip Gulo had been such a mess that I had been obliged to pour hot Tang from my water bottle onto his belly guard and flanks, just to thaw it all out and lift the cloth free of his tummy. I could protect the frostbitten parts, but I was stymied by the males' strong instinct to constantly piss-mark the trail.

The caribou-hide inserts solved the problem. All the way home to the Hoarfrost I simply inserted the thick fur pads beneath the dogs' cloth belly bands in the morning, checked them throughout the day, and inserted fresh ones the next day. The amazing insulation of the caribou hair kept everything from freezing, no matter how much marking and peeing went on, and my sleeping pad would provide enough inserts to get us all home. As it dwindled I could do without it, since I had other layers to put beneath my bed. I got a chuckle out of my announcement to the dogs, that "down where I grew up we had 'tick checks,' and on this trip, gentlemen, we will be having hourly 'dick checks.'"

I spent the morning dismantling the layover camp and hauling the tent, stove, and empty cache barrels out to the spot where I had landed the plane so many weeks earlier. Sometime in spring I would fly out and retrieve them. By noon we were under way. Everyone was revved up and pulling hard. I felt again as if we were leaving a protected harbour, turning into the fury of the open ocean. The wind was slashing at us from the northwest quarter, a gale from 40 degrees off our bow. I made sure that the most heavily furred dogs were running on the right side of the gangline, thus providing a little protection for their downwind partners. The hours passed and the miles fell away, all a blur of wind and snow seen from deep within the fur-circled hood of my parka. We stopped for a rest in the scant shelter of a few gnarled trees, and carried on for two more hours to the wide-open tundra campsite which I described in the first paragraphs of this book. That campsite remains one of a handful of places forever engraved in my memory—a blank white patch of windblown twilight, with no precise location and no defining landmarks.

Such is navigation on the winter Barrens. The sun, if visible, gives us a bearing for south if we have a clock. Drop an imaginary line straight down from the sun to the horizon. Point the hour hand of your watch at that spot on the horizon, or check the time on your digital watch and draw a clock face on the snow, with the hour hand toward the sun. Halfway between that hour hand and the twelve is south. (This method is described in Appendix C.) Knowing south, you then know all the other directions and any chosen heading can be held fairly well. The minutiae of hilltop, creek, and swale become only that—unimportant details. It is an old and satisfying way to move across a landscape. You don't ever know *precisely* where you are, but that is not vital. When it is time to camp, you have arrived home for the night.

I was home again in the Hilleberg with everything at hand. What a relief that was. Heat turned up or down with a flick of the stove knob, light from candle and pocket flashlight, no firewood to fuss with, no dog belly guards hung to dry, no spruce boughs or snow on the tent floor. It is difficult for a wood-smoke and canvas romantic like me to admit this, but the white-gas and mountain-tent approach is a delightfully tidy way to camp.

We had passed some fellow creatures that day, out there living their lives in the teeth of the wind. I had glimpsed at least some of them, even from the fur-rimmed porthole of my cinched-down parka hood. Dozens of caribou in herds of two to twenty, a tall Arctic hare, and a shuffling Keystone-cop flock of ptarmigan, scurrying to a rounded hilltop as we approached and passed. The sight of these creatures so obviously unfazed by the wind and cold leaves little room for self-indulgent heroism. To the hare and the caribou and the ptarmigan, this was just another February day. Another day in an eight-month winter. A little nippy and breezy, yes, but nothing out of the ordinary.

In the morning at that tundra camp, the three wolves came to visit, standing silent on the hilltop like apparitions in the deep cold. I began the book with the passage describing that night and morning, because over the years they still stand so clear as the very essence of my journeys. There was the wind, the solitude, the dogs, the tent, and the tundra; the deep awareness that although we were homeward bound we were still a long way out to sea.

After the wolves trotted away and I settled in to the tent again, it seemed as though the wind was rising. I tried in vain to greet that realization with a fatalistic Native-like shrug of the shoulders. Back in 1981 I learned a word from the Inuit of Eskimo Point (now Arviat) on Hudson Bay: *arjunimat* (though I spell it phonetically, and probably don't come close to pronouncing it properly), or "it can't be helped." It is a very useful word in the Far North, some days.

Staying put at such an exposed campsite was simply not an option. And if the wind did get up again, the process of getting packed and moving on would be miserable. Hobson would have been tickled pink. I muttered, "Well, shit." Yet even as I cursed it I knew full well that the wind was a defining element, perhaps *the* defining element, of the Barrens. Without it, where would we be? Knee-deep in fluffy snow, just like the year before, breaking trail on skis or snowshoes, and certainly only a few dozen miles out from home. It was better to have the wind-blast. The dogs and I were in solid agreement on that, even as we yearned for a respite.

Wind or no wind, we had to move. Thankfully, once the decision to move is made, there is commitment, both mental and material. "Booting up" a ten-dog team—forty paws at minus 40—is no small effort. In deep cold and strong wind, it is literally a pain. With that accomplished there is a strong incentive to gain some mileage. So it was that morning. As numbing fingers slip that first cloth bootie onto that first dog's paw, the die is cast—we ain't sittin' out here today, boys and girls. At the very least we're going to find someplace better to hide.

Soon the tent was down, the dogs were barking and straining at their tuglines, and the hours of routine packing, filling Thermos and water bottles, and tying down the sled load were done. It was a good day. Those wolves in the morning, more caribou, less wind, bright sun, here and there some vestiges of our eastbound tracks marking the way like old wagon ruts on the prairies. In late afternoon, we arrived at Richard's little hunting shack, perched on the brow of the esker overlooking Whitefish Lake. I emptied the entire sled load onto the snow in front of the shack, and as usual it made a thought-provoking pile. With the sled empty, the dogs whisked me over to a tiny stand of spruce a half-mile east. There I cut deadwood and piled it into the sled. The dogs pulled the load back to the shack. I tied them out, fed them, and moved in for the night. With the frozen fleece belly guards strung on a line overhead, dripping you-know-what onto the hot wood stove, I sat in Richard's rickety lawn chair and boiled up my dinner of meat and rice.

I tried to relax and settle in, but a mood of vague disorientation made it difficult. This is a side effect of cold-weather camping that comes with a return, even overnight, to any semblance of real warmth. After travelling and living in deep cold for days or weeks, coming into a warm building— even one barely bigger than a phone booth—is disconcerting. It is like arriving in a place where some basic law of physics has been repealed. Thus my evening passed with comical moments of sheer amazement: "What? Soft butter? Rolled-up shirtsleeves? Dripping windowpanes? A cup of tea after dinner?" The world of deep cold is an absolute world. It is solid, predictable, and utterly sterile. This actually makes some things easier. Everything is black and white when it comes to temperature. If something is not being purposely, actively *heated*, then it is frozen solid. Period.

Sitting in the warm shack that night writing and thinking, I was fully, deeply at ease for the first time since leaving home. I took stock of my physical condition. My hands, I noted, were a mess. My fingertips ached at night from too many flirtations with frostbite. One battered finger, the middle one on my right hand, had a pair of deep cuts from reaching into the sled and meeting up with the teeth of the bowsaw. The cuts went down through the layers of superficial frostbite and into the blistered remnants of a second-degree burn from the door of the wood stove out at the cache tent. I was skinny and my face was startling when I caught sight of it in a little mirror on the wall.

Throughout the evening I stepped outside every now and then, to stand for a moment as nature demands. Even back at home I have always counted this necessity as one of the unsung blessings of having no indoor plumbing: solitary moments of darkness and starlight, whisper of wind, pool of glow spilling out from the window. Dogs all quiet, staked out on two parallel picket lines alongside the building. Everything around me and within me was thawing out a little, softening like the gear and food spread around inside that tiny cubicle of heat. For days I had been locked to the straightforward struggle of cold and the trail. That evening my mind gentled and wandered to my little daughters and my wife. How good it would be to hug those girls again and to hold Kristen.

To my journal I wrote: "My concern about the sled runners, the dogs' feet and privates, and the weather is waning now. We made a good crossing of that 'blank stretch' between the cache and here, about 65 miles. Runners are—so far, touch wood—still hanging in there, and I am trying to be *very* careful. Even stopping the team and easing the sled by hand through the worst of the rock-jams."

Despite all the luxury I slept poorly that night, for the first time since leaving home. I am well over six feet tall and I was wedged into the six-foot space between the door and the southwest wall of the shack. The unaccustomed warmth and the hard plywood floor conspired to make it a long night. Sunday the second of March dawned with a vivid red sunrise at 7:10 a.m., some thin cirrus and cirrostratus clouds, a light north wind, and minus 38 degrees. I had decided that we would lay over for the day, and then, weather permitting, make a steady march for home. I puttered around the shack all day, doing the usual rest-day chores that writer and adventurer Colin Fletcher so aptly calls "administrative details." To wit:

1. hung dog booties, belly guards, and caribou-hide "diapers" over the wood stove to dry;
2. fed dogs twice;
3. brought Schooner and Foxtail indoors for a while, one at a time;
4. applied warm Povidone-iodine salve to dogs' frostbitten places. Riley and Gulo, the worst victims, both improving on twice-daily Amoxicillin 500 mg. Gave those pills out;

5. checked and clipped dogs' toenails (some getting long and at risk of breakage);
6. sorted dry dog booties and burned those that had holes (20%);
7. mended one mitten and my woollen nose/cheek protector;
8. finished reading the serial-killer novel;
9. wrote a letter to Richard, who with his trapping partner Lance built this little hut, and who now lives in Illinois, just a few miles from my boyhood home;
10. fixed myself a fancy brunch of bacon, cornmeal hotcakes, and granola;
11. cut firewood;
12. shot up roll #2 of slide film, including some self-timed shots of dogs and myself and the hut. Changed film and dried and warmed the camera [to no avail—the camera was plagued by moisture and ice, and only about ten of my 108 photos from the trip were usable];
13. made some new necklines;
14. wrote a letter to my parents;
15. organized the sled load and tied it up for the night.

In early afternoon I took a walk back to the spot where I had cut firewood the day before at the foot of the esker. I retrieved the axe that I had left there by mistake and then climbed to the gravelly crest of the esker itself. The northwest wind was beginning to stir again and the loose surface snow was starting to blow—a sign that the wind is approaching twenty knots. As I strolled along I was thinking about that wind and trying to imagine how to write about it. What a punch such dense cold air can pack when it is moving fast, and what a demonic, obsessive force it can become after days of struggle. Out on the Barrens the wind moves over the land like an ever-shifting river, with a steady current and its own invisible eddies, pools, and rapids. I remembered a line from climber Thomas Hornbein, near dusk on the summit of Everest in 1963: "the immense roaring silence of the wind."[9] Yes, I thought, that is it. The wind roars across the tundra, but the noise is like compressed Silence. Lost in such thoughts, I caught sight of the little shack in the distance, an off-white speck on a pure white expanse. I was struck by how the *inhuman* vastness of a place is underscored by such a puny fleck of human presence. The little square box perched on the ridge, a line of dark curled-up forms barely visible alongside it, the wide sky above, the snow stretching to every horizon, and the wind flowing over it all. For two weeks straight I had been immersed in solitude. I could tell I was *there* by the flow of my thoughts. Yet it was startling at times just how disjointed my mental ramblings could be and how quickly they could shift planes: at the end of that lofty contemplative stroll I burst through the door of the little shack and caught a whiff of the pecker protectors hung to dry over the hot wood stove. I exclaimed out loud, "Geezuz! Aren't these fuckin' things dry *yet*? I am so *sick* of the smell of burned dog piss!" Basic indeed.

That evening solitude hit me again with a resounding thud. When my chores were done I was still hours from sleep. Darkness enveloped the world and a weight of loneliness and foreboding settled around my shoulders. I knew it well and carried the weight of it. In my journal I wrote, "We humans instinctively prefer to face the onset of night in the company of others. I wonder if other animals do too. I am tonight about a hundred miles from home, by the route we are on, and at least 80 miles from another creature of my own kind." The wind was up again, rattling the stovepipe with an incessant *ping-ping-ping*. I invited two more dogs in for separate audiences—first Jasmine, then Steve. They each seemed happy to lap up a bowl of clean cold water. After a thwarted attempt to pee on the wood stove (eliciting a loud "No!" from me, for obvious reasons), Steve curled up at my feet on the dwindling pad of caribou hide. I stroked his muzzle and the thick white fur of his mane. He flashed up a happy grin, telling me plainly that he was at that moment the most contented dog in the northern third of North America, if not on the entire planet.

I wrote letters, listened to the wind, and wondered about the morning. The stars were showing when I stepped out to put Steve back on the picket line, but the wind was in a steady crescendo. Finally I slept. At three in the morning I could tell that the wind was getting truly vicious and I lay there listening to it, hour after hour, until the first hint of dawn.

I was tired of wind. Again and again to my journal I complained childishly about it. My petulance was embarrassing—what the hell did I expect from the central Barrens in February, if not wind? A *calm* day was a rarity, not the other way around. Out here wind was the rule, and the ruler. I had read somewhere that Baker Lake, a few hundred miles northeast down the Thelon, was the most consistently windy settlement in all of Canada—*the windiest place in the second-largest country in the world.* Whether it was true or not, I could certainly buy that claim. So far we had had ten out of fifteen days with a wind from the west or northwest at over fifteen knots, and three of those with steady winds above twenty-five knots. The wind had begun to seem like a ferocious, cunning adversary, and I was beginning to falter.

Daylight, and we had to leave. It was 32 below zero, and the dogs had no real protection there. I had put jackets on them all, but I knew that those would not be enough. Once again our only choice was to get down

Three of the infamous Frozen Foursome, sporting their protective gear: Murphy and Riley in wheel (closest to the sled), Gulo the black dog, and Jasmine curled up beside him. Note the wind-driven snow stuck to Gulo's face.

from there. I set to work organizing, feeding dogs, packing gear, closing down the hut, harnessing, and putting on belly guards and caribou-hide inserts. With almost no overland travel ahead until we reached the west end of Sandy Lake, I decided I could safely skip the dog booties. On stretches of glare ice the booties are more a liability than an asset, since they render the dogs' toenails useless and a slip can quite easily lead to a shoulder injury.

When I finally tugged the slip knot free from the footing of the hut, the team charged down to Whitefish Lake in a blasting release of pent-up eagerness. It was obvious that they were delighted to run pell-mell into that bitter wind, after a night spent huddling on the picket line in the blast of it. I was tense, but the tension quickly gave way to sheer exhilaration. It was a dramatic day to be out moving. With a solid team and a three-lane set of our old runner tracks (from our run out and back to the hut from Sandy Lake, and from our passage east), even the notorious north end of Whitefish was navigable. The dogs whisked me across the lake ice at a steady lope without once losing the trail. The blowing snow made the whole passage dreamlike, as if we were moving through a bowl of milk. At times I briefly lost sight of all but the sled and the two wheel dogs. Memories of Iditarod runs along the Bering Sea and Norton Sound, of Golovin, Topkok, and Elim, kept me daydreaming as we made our way west. By early afternoon, we reached the old campsite and the intermediate cache at Sandy Lake. I paused to take a final resupply out of those barrels, and the dogs napped in the shelter of the little grove of ancient spruce. I ate some nuts, drank some Tang and hot cocoa, and we carried on. Departing from that cache I had three nights of supplies in the sled, along with extra fat and stove fuel in case of a delay.

All day the sun shone above the ground storm. Twice I glimpsed caribou. One group, three antlerless bulls, stood like ghosts alongside the trail, dimly visible through the smoky haze of snow, their white neck manes glowing in the diffused sunshine. Beyond the Sandy Lake cache the sled tracks were twelve days old. Still perfectly plain, carved in bas-relief by the wind, they led us west. It is always amazing to me that, given the right conditions, a single brief passage of a sled and a team of dogs, or a snowmobile, can leave such a long-lasting track on an open expanse of windswept snow. That day it was good that we were backtracking, for in such conditions I would not have ventured navigation without help from an old trail. The lead dogs, Steve and Ernie, stuck to the old runner marks down the length of Sandy Lake and late that afternoon I tucked our campsite into the fold of a steep bluff on the lake's north shore. We had come about 35 miles from Richard's shack on Whitefish.

The nights on the esker top and the night we had spent right out on the tundra east of there made every camp thereafter look sheltered. The wind was still ferocious but a few spruces made a hollowed nook and the snow was fluffy and soft around the bases of their thick trunks. The dogs seemed relieved to be in the deep snow and the shelter of a few trees. They were frisking and playing with each other as they dug out their beds for the night. I snowshoed around the camp, doing chores, feeding the team, and setting up the radio antenna for the third and final scheduled call. By dusk I was in my little haven. The tent fly still snapped and rustled and the candle flame bounced with the subtle shifts of air. I pulled out my journal and wrote:

The dogs continue to amaze me. None of the setbacks on this trip have been shortcomings on their part. They remain a solid team. I have not seen a slack tugline since we left Hoarfrost. I know that only sounds like more bullshit musher bravado, but it's the truth...

My world is so narrow on these stormy passages. Hours slip by as I focus on trying to catch glimpses of our old sled tracks. The parka ruff, cinched down tight, becomes stiff from my frozen breath. I peer out through a drafty circle trimmed in frosted wolverine fur, and see only the sled, the team, and a tiny round world of wind-blown snow, hour after hour. It takes most of the fun out of this!

I was drowsy in the warmth, with supper done and the long day behind me. I was thinking of a phrase Joe Runyan used in his book *Winning Strategies for Distance Mushers*, as he described a group of teams threading their way down the Yukon River in the early years of the Yukon Quest race: "You had to be at the top of your game."[10] That was how the day had felt for me. It had been a culmination of years of learning, and with the dogs performing so exquisitely it had all worked out. We were going to get home—windstorms, flayed runners, frozen private parts and all.

I talked with both Kristen and Roger on the radio. How odd to sit in the tent and suddenly begin a conversation with those familiar yet completely disembodied voices, to chat amiably about the weather and goings-on in Yellowknife and Reliance, and then, so casually, "Well, okay. then, Sandy Lake out." Click. Alone and silent again, digesting the news. "No mention of the World at large or an invasion of Iraq," I noted to my journal, "so either World War Three has not begun, or they decided not to ruin my evening with the news."

Tuesday 4 March, day sixteen, 34 below zero, and a vivid red sunrise through an opaque haze of ice crystals and blowing snow. Some cirrus and patchy cirro-stratus clouds. North wind blowing at 15–20 knots.

As I closed in on home, my confidence bolstered by the prospect that we would make it in one piece, a new voice was piping up inside my head. Perhaps, it said, these trips are all too short. Perhaps only now was the trip really *beginning,* now that I was immersed in the rhythm of travel, and the fatalistic acceptance of each day's weather. Had this all been just a shakedown cruise?

I concluded, after some pondering that morning, that it was only the Basic voice, singing a slightly different tune this time. Instead of whining about heading *out* it was now bemoaning the prospect of heading back *in.* The self-absorbed simplicity of trail life—if only it could just go on and on, looking out only for myself and these loyal dogs, cache to cache, meal after meal, storm by storm...never a bill to pay, the plane to fly, a chainsaw's pull-cord to repair, letters to write and emails to answer, children to raise and teach and gradually fledge out into that huge, crazy, insatiable world where madmen hurled bombs, astronauts burned up on re-entry, seemingly intelligent people stared for hours every day at computer screens, leaders threatened war or promised peace...It was all over *there,* that morning, just beyond those steep rock slopes west of Sandy Lake. Little wonder that a part of me yearned to stay out on the trail. Life would be so utterly simple out there—at least until the white gas or the dog kibble ran out.

At 8 a.m. I flicked on the HF radio again in hope of getting a weather report from Roger in Reliance. Above a crackle of static we were able to hear each other well. The wind was dying down nicely there, he told me, and he was laying plans to drive east by snowmobile toward us, "just to have a look around."

Powerful high-pressure systems were dominating the weather map, and powerful highs and lows continued to be the theme of my mental life. Perhaps my reluctance to go home contributed to my miseries that day. The light morning breeze again built rapidly to another northwesterly gale. It was warmer though, above minus 30 degrees by evening, and I was overheating as I jogged behind the sled on the steepest uphills. Vehement profanity, poor visibility, difficulties with my navigating, the constant concerns with the feet and flanks and swaddled parts of various dogs in the team, more battering and damage to the long-suffering sled runners. It was a day better summarized than drawn out in a narrative here.

Around 4:45 that afternoon Roger and I must have passed quite close to each other. By then the visibility had improved to something close to a mile, the best it had been all day. Still it is not surprising that we missed spotting each other. I was absorbed in the uncertainties of my navigation, and had by that time begun to think about finding a place to hole up for the night. Roger was following, as best he could, my outbound sled tracks from two weeks earlier. I had abandoned that old trail in mid-afternoon in order to avoid its descent into the little bowl of soft snow along Ingstad Creek. My other landmarks along that stretch, the old police shack and the lone tamarack tree near it, eluded me again that day. I was headed west, keeping course by sun and pocket watch, and not overly concerned with my precise location. The steady thrumming of the wind would easily have drowned out the sound of a snowmobile engine at any distance over a few hundred yards.

At around 5 p.m. Roger had turned for home. A few minutes later I pulled up into what I dubbed our "krummholz camp," for the clump of stunted spruce stems that were its only feature. A rocky defile led southwest out of what appeared to be a small lake. I was often uncertain as to what, in all that whiteness, was land and what was snow-covered ice. I left the dogs in pairs on the gangline again that night. It was warmer than it had been for well over a week, about minus 29 degrees at dusk. As darkness deepened, a brilliant collage of the northern lights began to take over the sky. ("A beautiful sight," I noted nonchalantly in my journal. I thought of a line by Annie Dillard from her book *The Writing Life*: "It was very grand. But you get used to it.")[11] I closed my evening notes with, "I should just get some sleep and put this day behind me. Too much cursing and exasperation. I have one night of dog food left now—tomorrow's route-finding and weather will be crucial."

I slept. At four in the morning I was awakened briefly by the crisp close crackle of a jetliner passing directly overhead. I lay there thinking how odd a juxtaposition we made: down below, one man and ten dogs, tucked into a ravine in a hollow of snow; up above, a few hundred people in their world of coiffeurs and perfumes, sipping drinks, watching movies, hurtling along at 600 miles an hour. Over the past several days I had heard several jets overhead while I struggled along in the wind. It always made me smile to imagine suddenly closing that six-mile gap with some sort of bionic leap, to burst into the jet's passenger cabin, an apparition of fur and frost in an enormous greasy parka, whisker-stubble thick with frost and frozen snot, eyes peering wildly out from a wind-burned face, to swipe a cup of hot coffee from the cart of a startled flight attendant.

Morning, and dead calm, perfectly clear, and minus 36 degrees. I was up before dawn, and I could tell that the clock was ticking—in my head if nowhere else. We were burning precious fuel whether we were moving

Krummholz camp, final camp of the east trip, at dawn on day seventeen.

or not. A dogteam is like a diesel truck in winter—it is never shut down. Even while the driver sleeps, the engine idles and fuel is consumed. After everything the dogs had done for me on that trip, I was even more determined than usual to get them home without asking them to miss even a single meal. The puzzle of the day's navigation intrigued me. The GPS unit was now a 150 miles to the east, lost in some snowdrift. Had I not lost it, it would have come out of its case the evening before, to be warmed gently on the rack of the Coleman stove, and—bingo!—its screen would have flashed up a readout of my position, give or take a few hundred feet. Instead I carefully studied the 1:250,000-scale topographic map (itself a product of high-tech imagery, lest I forget), factored in my best estimates of yesterday's speeds, headings, and distances, and made a little box of pencilled lines. The dogs and I had to be somewhere within that box, bounded on three sides by distinct landmarks: north, Artillery Lake; west, the valley running out of Burbanks Lake; south, the eskers and wooded swales of Ingstad Creek. All I had to do was continue west, and I would surely hit a trail, either my own or someone else's.

Everything seemed to be sorting itself out. My impatience and petulance of the day before had been erased by the good long sleep. The dogs seemed solid and content, ready to march forever into that wind as long as I kept up the feedings and the care. In a minor housekeeping improvement, I had rigged a small clothesline over the Coleman stove, by using some tie-loops sewn into each end of the tent, and I crowed to my journal that it was "a smashing success...truly dry mittens and face guards!"

One other note in my journal, written as I took stock of my gear with an eye toward the next winter's trip north, bears repeating here. It was a lesson every modern traveller in deep cold has learned: "Caribou skins, wool, goose down, leather, canvas, wolverine fur. When all is said and done these are the materials that we utterly maladapted (but clever) humans depend upon in this deep dry cold. The synthetics are all stiff and ungainly. We cannot improve on the old standbys."

I watched the sunrise that morning while squatting outside the tent on other business, and once again I pulled out the camera to try for a photo of the camp just after dawn. The Nikon had a severe case of frostbite, and I was wildly varying the shutter speeds in hopes of salvaging a few usable frames. Never an avid photographer, I was trying to force myself to use the camera on that trip. I found it as distracting and somehow disorienting as ever, as if by taking a photograph the present ceased to be *now* and instantly became a preserved part of *then*. This leap from present to past tense, compounded by cold fingers and my impatience with finicky machinery, dooms my efforts at photography.

And then we went home.

It was, after seventeen days, almost that simple, and quite unexpected. Not more than fifteen minutes out of camp I hit a fresh snow-machine trail—Roger's from the day before, angling in from the northeast. He must have been afield looking for me, I surmised, and I chuckled at the thought of the two of us, neighbours and friends, blundering around in the windstorm, the only human inhabitants of a space the size of Montana or the Maritimes, and not catching sight of each other. Once on that trail, which soon joined other trails and my old outbound trail, I knew I would go all the way home without camping again. It was 50 miles or so to Hoarfrost. With an early start, a calm day, and a good team those miles would be a pleasure.

For as long as I live I will remember one moment from that day. Just above Cloudberry Lakes we topped the hill west of Barrenland Lake— and suddenly the landscape ahead was no longer white. Every fold and wrinkle of the hills to the west was coloured a rich dark green. It was treeline, as sharp and distinct as I have ever seen or felt it. I could not see Great Slave Lake, but I could see the intimations of its basin in the slope of the country below us. Trees again. We were leaving the Barrens. The dogs were wild with excitement, as if they too knew what that hilltop and that dark green meant. Down there in the timber was where we belonged. For two solid weeks the tundra had done its best to prove that to us day after day. I stood there for several long minutes, utterly convinced that I lived where I wanted to live.

One result of these four trips, this winter compass rose, has been that personal affirmation: that considering all the options, we do live in the right spot. The big lake, the timber, the river. Yes, the tundra is nearby, but at home we have shelter from the wind, wood for heat, and, in summer, a deep-water freighting port linked to the lines of supply upon which we depend. Standing on the snow hook there to keep the dogs from going home without me, I surveyed the scene with a heartfelt smile. Home sweet home. I clicked off a photo, and down the hill we went. The familiar descent of Pike's Portage, the day bright and clear and calm at last, a stop at Reliance for coffee and a visit with Roger and Miranda and their two little children. In all the rest of those miles that day, I saw one lone raven. And Noel's dog, still barking, still tied up at the tent frame on Harry Lake. No sign of Noel.

At dusk we crossed McLeod Bay for home. Roger zoomed ahead with a portion of my sled load, as much to get out of the house, I gathered, as for any other reason. A sliver of the new moon hung over the pale immensity of the lake ice. I met Roger again a few miles out from our homestead, and then he was away for home again. The dogs pulled me up into the snowed-in yard by the barn. I opened up the house, fed the team, and made a call on the HF radio to Kristen. Two upstairs windows shattered as the cold-soaked structure of our log house warmed up. It had been minus 46 degrees on the recording thermometer sometime while I had been away, likely on the morning of 28 February, the day we started west from the far cache.

That night I dug out the collected poems of William Stafford and found the one called "So Long." For several days I had been trying to recall it precisely:

At least at night, a streetlight
is better than a star.
And better good shoes on a
long walk, than a good friend.

Often in winter with my old
cap I slip away into the gloom
like a happy fish, at home
with all I touch, at the level of love.

No one can surface till far,
far on, and all that we'll have
to love may be what's near
in the cold, even then.[12]

The ten o'clock CBC news came on: the impending invasion of Iraq; a suicide bombing in Israel; an retaliatory attack by gunships. I turned off the radio. What, I asked the window, am I to do with such *news*, in a cold cabin on a dark March night in the Northwest Territories?

It was 44 below zero outside the next morning. The dogs were silent, curled up on thick straw in their wooden houses. Pulling out my journal by force of habit, I wrote:

It has been a good journey. Hard and lonely at times, cold and windy nearly always. What I have affirmed again is the vastness and emptiness of the wilderness, its absolute apathy toward humanity, and its gifts of clarity and crystalline beauty. The joy of watching huskies run, the pleasure of hardpacked snow and fast sledding.

As I did chores last night and tended the dogs, I had the tired, wrung-out, lightheaded feeling which comes when a race or a hard run is over. Today I feel strong and happy but at the same time more fragile and precarious than usual. My face and fingertips are frostnipped, and over the next few weeks all that skin will peel again, for at least the 25th time in the last 25 years.

I must admit, looking at the trip objectively, that old Mother Nature would be awarded the TKO in this bout. She never knocked us out cold, as my dream before the trip seemed to portend, but I was on the ropes. The sled-runner debacle never did play out to its nastiest conclusion—i.e., the fibreglass runners failing and the bolt-heads shearing off—but it was only a matter of miles. The weather dictated our days out on the brink of the Thelon valley, but even if it had been beautiful I would have been hampered by my mistake with the sled.

The other problem was the dogs, and specifically old Riley and his comrade Gulo, with their gruesome penis-tip frostbite. That had potential for misery and tragedy and a musher with my experience should have seen it coming on that fast day trip between Sandy and Whitefish. Once the damage was done, the need to protect those dogs added a new set of chores to each day's efforts. Now they are healing up.

Mobility equals survival, here in the Far North. The ability to cover distance relatively quickly, with efficient use of strength and supplies, has over the ages often been the difference between life and death, or between an uneventful journey and a desperate struggle for survival. The downward spiral of weakening dogs, diminished strength for hunting and travel, ever-worsening odds against reaching a cache or an outpost, is a familiar arctic theme. There is the old story about asking the Inuit elder how far away the mountains on the horizon are, to which he answers: "Good dogs, mountains close. No good dogs, mountains far away."

———————

Weeks later on the third of April I flew east to retrieve my leftover cache supplies and containers from Sandy Lake and the Thelon esker. I made two flights alone in the little plane, out and back. Altogether it took me five hours.

A bush-pilot friend of mine once remarked that, although he had flown thousands of hours all across the Far North, "it's all been like watching a movie." The swift passage from our homestead to the Thelon valley that day was like watching "Solo Trip East" in fast forward. Landmarks and campsites passed in familiar procession, each conjuring a flash of memories and emotions, each quickly replaced by the next. There was the campsite where the dogs had nearly run off without me; there were all the confusing little gullies and ponds east of Whitefish; here was the long east–west esker and the hilly stretch where the sled runners gave out.

I landed at the far cache. I was struck immediately by how familiar the place felt, compared to my first landing there in February. It felt as if I had lived there for an entire winter. There was my little line of trees set out as markers on the ice, the cache barrels and folded tent bundle all drifted over at the base of a spruce tree, and my sled tracks—a month or more old but plain as if made that day—criss-crossing east and west out of the campsite. I stuffed the gear into the plane, taxied in a tight circle, gunned the engine and climbed for home.

I was carrying radio-telemetry tracking equipment that day—two wing-strut-mounted antennae and a scanning receiver. I had been on a flying job for the territorial government wildlife department a week earlier, and had offered to scan for signals from radio-collared wolves on my flight east. Partly to get better reception, and partly just for the view, I climbed to 10,500 feet above sea level (about 9,000 feet above the landscape) on the westbound leg. Suddenly, unexpectedly, there came through the headset the steady *beep-beep-beep* of a signal from a radio-collared wolf. I banked in a circle and recorded my location along with the radio frequency of the signal.[13]

As I banked the plane around, nearly two miles high, I realized that from that altitude I would be able to see my entire route at once. I finished my note-taking on the wolf location and continued the turn. There was the thin line of trees marking the valley of Sandy Lake; there was Richard's esker where his hut stood on Whitefish. As the turn brought my view east I could see the eskers leading down to the timbered valley of the Thelon. The plane's nose swung back west. Far out on the horizon was McLeod Bay, and a dark wedge of forest leading northeast up to Artillery Lake.

So there it was, all at a glance: my winter trip. A little deflating to see it all in a single turn, and to cover the entire distance from home to the far cache in an hour and nine minutes. Such routes always look so simple from the air. Farther west I looked down on the traverse from Sandy Lake to Barrenland Lake, where I had been thoroughly confused several times. I thought ruefully, *Oh, I see now—you cross to there, follow that lake, cross over that drainage, pick up the ridge, and you're there. Piece of cake!*

Sixty miles out from home I began a gradual descent, easing down through smooth air at 120 knots. I could see the Snowdrift River winding southwest from its headwaters at Sandy Lake. To the south of the river the country was all forested, and the entire horizon was deep spruce green. I studied the view and picked out the two lakes which, by their aspect, had to be Noman and the north arm of Nonacho—last year's farthest south.

Year by year, journey by journey, the land was all starting to take on a new character. "The movie" my friend had referred to was giving way to something deeper, even when seen from the airplane. That was what I had hoped for. Still descending, I cranked into a steep bank to gaze north. I could see Cook Lake on the upper Hoarfrost. Beyond it, the land clear out to the far horizon was pure white, without so much as a fleck of sheltering green. North. Well, well. *That* would give me something to think about all summer.

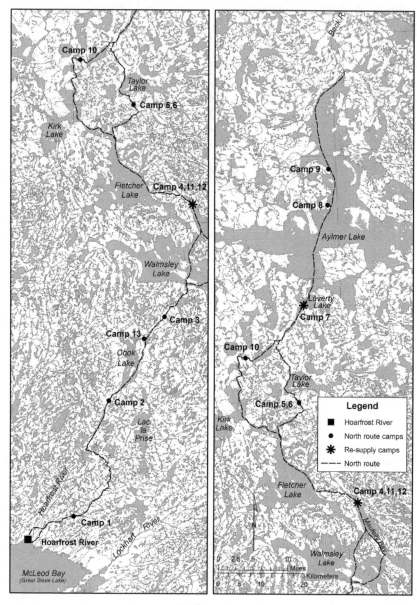

North 2004

North

Fourteen days, 17 February–1 March 2004
Hoarfrost River to Back River headwaters, and return: about 310 miles
Ten dogs, two resupply caches

North.

The word has been a mantra for me since I was a boy. For years my life was a steady migration, a wandering path but always north. From Illinois and Wisconsin, it was Montana, then Minnesota, Ontario, Alaska, Manitoba...camps and cabins and towns passed through—Missoula, Ely, Atikokan, Churchill, Eskimo Point, Anchorage, Nome, Leaf Rapids, Yellowknife...like a bird circling to land, descending, and finally flaring to touch down...Hoarfrost River, Northwest Territories, 1987.

On that final day of my trip east in 2003, I had realized that my incessant yearning and northing did have a tangible limit. Gazing down into the tree-green basin of McLeod Bay, body and dogteam and sled all battered and bruised by the tundra's wind and cold, I had felt a deep relief. I was at heart a forest creature, gladdened at the prospect of a return to the trees. Home sweet home, boys: let's buck up some deadwood and light a *really big* fire!

My dogs, too, had on that east journey reminded me of their limits and their aptitudes. They are Alaskan huskies, if they need to be designated as a breed. They are most definitely not Polar huskies. Alaskans are bred for speed, endurance, and all-around resilience; not for days of tractor-paced hauling and overnights on windswept tundra or ice pack. They are most in their element where little patches of spruce timber offer protected campsites, with long stretches of fast running between sheltered oases. The taiga–tundra edge is their natural habitat. Mine too, it seems.

Knowing all of this as I considered the compass rose of my four winter journeys, the northern leg always loomed as the biggest challenge. I had been working up to it year by year, south and then east. As the days of mid-winter 2004 gradually lengthened it was time to face the music. To the north, well beyond treeline again, the cold and the wind were waiting. This time around I was determined to meet them with more finesse, perhaps even with a touch of panache.

Oddly though, years later as I begin to draft the first longhand version of this chapter, it is hot—up to nearly 30 degrees already, likely hotter in the direct sun on our south-facing sand beach. It is 11 a.m. and I have already been into the lake for the first of several cooling dips, spaced at three-hour intervals through the day. There is nothing unusual about summer heat here. What is unusual, and almost incredible, is that summer has not even officially begun. It is only the middle of June. The summer solstice is still a week away. Two years ago, the year of the north journey I am about to describe, we ran dogs and landed the airplane *on the ice* in front of the homestead until 20 June—a week later than today. What is going on here?

What is going on, obviously, is serious upheaval. The buzzwords are all familiar: *climate change, global warming, greenhouse gases.* I do not discount any of this, and I do not want to sound flippant. There is already plenty of denial and delusional finger-pointing emanating from the fans of the carbon-puking status quo. But we must remember that Nature will be Nature, that she is infinitely complex, and as the saying goes she will certainly be last up to bat. By that I mean to remind myself: the earth warms and the earth cools, and it is always either warming up or cooling down. Change is the constant. Although at times we humans talk and act as if we know so much, even the most brilliant of our thinkers and forecasters will if pressed admit that we are essentially ignorant of how these changes will all play out. It is all so complex, so vast, so subtle . . . and we have been around for such a very short time.

A thousand years ago the Vikings grazed their sheep on Greenland slopes. Four hundred years later those green slopes were buried beneath the ice cap. Now, perhaps, they are going to support a few sheep again. Or not. In 2004 McLeod Bay—the bay I just swam in—set a new record for *late* ice out, and in 2006 it set a new record for *early* ice out. In 2009 it flirted with another late-ice record. Of what use are "records" only fifty or a hundred, or for that matter five thousand, years old? What does seem clear now is that all bets are off. We are relative newcomers to this planet we call home, and we deceive ourselves when we so glibly choose to use the word *normal* in any sentence describing weather, or nature, or earth. End of digression. Another dip to cool down, and north to the tundra.

The winter of 2004 was an "old-time winter," in the words of my Chipewyan friend Tom Lockhart. December and January passed in a twilight blur of 40-below days and nights. At the Hoarfrost River homestead it was also the winter of the passing travellers. In early January we got word that several dogteam expeditions would be visiting us. First there was Will Steger, a well-known Arctic adventurer and spokesman. Will and I had worked and travelled together for four winters, from 1979 to 1982, and in 1980 he and I made a long dogteam trek from Churchill up the coast of Hudson Bay to Baker Lake. By the close of the next decade, Will had led dogteam expeditions to both poles, and across the ice cap of Greenland. In 2004, he was back at it, as the senior figure-head and leader of Arctic Transect, a team comprising five men and a woman along with thirty dogs on an ambitious six-month journey from Yellowknife to Baffin Island. One of their goals was to document and spotlight the effects of the changing arctic climate.

Will and his "Transectites" arrived at our home on 18 January and stayed with us for three nights. He and I had not seen each other for many years so his stopover was like a mid-winter holiday around our place. It was a pleasure to have our home enlivened by new voices. Our two young daughters were enchanted by these friendly people and their big furry dogs. The expedition was up to the current standard for such journeys—there were daily Internet dispatches to thousands of grade-school classes, much buzz, photogenic sponsor logos on clothing and gear, and a steady stream of communication. A satellite dish and computer wires blossomed on the snowy yard, and our little log "writing cabin" was festooned with enough high-tech wizardry to rival the *Starship Enterprise*. A gas-powered generator the size of a shoe box purred away morning and night, powering the uploads and downloads.

I talked briefly with Will about the solo trips I'd been making, and about the coming trip north. We talked about dogs and gear and about the next leg of his trip, east toward the Thelon. We talked about our lives and old times and good friends, some gone. On the first night Will produced a bottle of tequila, and he was soon cutting the rug in a twirling dance with four-year-old Liv.

After four days they were gone. In June they reached their destination on Baffin Island. Watching them go I was struck by how our two lives, mine and Will's, with huskies and winter and the North as common threads, had diverged and evolved in the two decades since we had travelled together. He is now an eloquent and well-recognized advocate for the Arctic and Antarctic regions, and he works to publicize their peril in a rapidly changing and warming world. The expedition's four-day stopover at our homestead was like being on the set of a film documentary, with pressing deadlines for new footage and commentary to be met morning and night. My own path had been less flamboyant, but similarly unconventional by any normal standard. I had raced dogs, learned to fly airplanes, moved to Canada, and along with Kristen built a home, found ways to make a living, and started down the road of a marriage and a family. I had made a connection to this one place out of all the vast North. I have never seen the poles and I suppose I never will. Like all reunions, ours on McLeod Bay made us both think about choices made and paths not taken.

Two weeks after Will's group dwindled out of sight over the ice toward Reliance, more dogteams appeared from the southeast—wave two of the winter's guest expeditions. This was the Arctic Quest, four Minnesota women driving two big teams. They too were eastbound from Yellowknife to Baker Lake and the west coast of Hudson Bay. They settled in to our guest cabin and stayed for four nights. We had never met any of them before, but we shared some common roots in northern Minnesota and at camps and outdoor schools there. Again the place hummed with new energy, new faces, and fresh conversation. Their approach was less flashy and high-tech than the Transect team, but they too were combining their adventure with altruism. They were raising Outward Bound scholarship funds and keeping steady contact with sponsors and schoolchildren.

In the first 225 miles out from Yellowknife they had weathered some bitter cold and some wind. They struck me as quietly competent, and they seemed appropriately cautious as they faced the next leg of their journey east onto the Barrens. I suppose the fact that this was an all-woman group would seem remarkable to some. Since Kristen has long been associated with the world of all-woman expeditions, and since many of the top mushers and champions over the course of my racing career were women, the gender of the group did not strike us as unusual. As their visit ended we stood by as they harnessed their dogs, then wished them all well and watched as they dwindled into specks across the bay. Peace and quiet settled back around us. By then it was 10 February, and time for me to get on with my own winter journey.

———————

In the two previous years, Kristen and the girls had been away when I departed, and still away when I returned home. For the north and west trips in 2004 and 2005 I had the luxury of their presence at home right up to my departure, and their welcome the moment I returned. This made my departures from home more pleasant, and more difficult: pleasant in that I had the company of my family through the process; difficult because I had to find a way to focus on the tasks of preparation amidst all the diversions of home-school, mealtimes, chores, and bedtime stories.

As I prepared for departure I found that I was again struggling with motivations. With two trips behind me this mental struggle was becoming familiar. I knew that my waffling would pass. I trusted the time ahead, out and away, over the boulders. I knew that out on the trail there would come some moments. Year by year I realized that the lasting reward for these journeys would be that small collection of powerful yet fleeting moments. Those moments awaited me *out there,* after the fuel bottles were all filled and the dog kibble was measured out and the sled gone over and the rip in the wool trousers sewn.

At dusk on the evening of 17 February, I kissed Kristen and the girls goodbye. I shook hands with our friend Ken Frew, who was living in our spare cabin and helping us out that winter.[1] The caches were in place, spaced 70 and 110 miles north, and the first 30 miles of trail were as familiar to me as a city dweller's backyard. My departure that evening felt almost nonchalant, and Kristen told me after the trip, "This year it really felt like you were just going up north on a long training run." While that was a little deflating, I knew what she meant. I was setting out over familiar terrain. It felt good, as it always does, to be finished getting ready, to yank free the slipknot on the snubline, call to the lead dogs Steve and Foxtail, and *go.*

The night was clear and cold, about minus 35 degrees. I travelled for only 11 miles, up the first steep climbs northeast away from the big lake, roughly paralleling the tumultuous lower Hoarfrost. I had ten dogs and enough supplies for six nights—more than ample to reach the first cache. I had picked the dogs with last year's lessons firmly in mind. Riley and Gulo—the two most hard-bitten veterans of the infamous "March of the Frozen Peckers"—were not with me, nor was Edelweiss, the little female. Instead I had B.J., a solid old female lead dog, and another female called Minnie, a big fluffy bear of a dog. Both B.J. and Minnie were spayed. As Iditarod master Rick Swenson once remarked, "those spayed females are the perfect dog—nothing hanging out in the wind to freeze, and they never come into heat." Also in the team was Fipke, an older male dog with a thick coat and a knack for taking good care of himself in deep cold. Fipke was named in honour of Chuck Fipke, one of the two geologists who, in about 1990, sparked the decade-long diamond rush in northern Canada. With such sturdy, heavily furred dogs I was fielding the closest resemblance I could to a team of Steger's massive Polar huskies—dogs with roots in Greenland and the High Arctic. Will and others had built the bloodlines of their teams with an eye not on cruising speed but on durability and brute strength combined with a bombproof resilience in extreme cold. My Alaskans, by contrast, could hold a brisk nine-mile-per-hour trot instead of a tractor slog. They could cope with wind and cold so long as the musher did his or her part to help them.

In a conversation with Will during his stay with us, he had remarked, "Doing expeditions is a good way to slow time down." I knew what he meant, and as we snaked up through the hills that first night with a million stars and a slender arc of northern lights bright above us, I could feel that deceleration. My solitude struck me powerfully after the bustle of the homestead and the eager chatter of my daughters.

I made camp in the dark. My main headlamp's batteries were almost dead in the cold, but I was unwilling to commit any fresh ones so early in the game, so my camp-pitching was done with my pocket flashlight clamped in my mouth. My father had sent that light to me as a gift, early in the evolution of the LED flashlights, and I valued it because of that. With drool freezing around its lanyard and my jaw aching from clenching it in my teeth, I got the dogs staked out and the tent pitched. It was a good reminder of the niceties of making camp *before* darkness fell. By 11 p.m. I was back home in the Hilleberg, and the trip had started.

––––––––––

My goal, if pressed to name one, was the Back River headwaters north of Aylmer Lake. The Back is one of the three major rivers of the north-central Barrens, along with the Thelon and the Coppermine. I had placed my two caches with a slightly different strategy than in previous years. I hoped to use the most distant cache, on Laverty Lake south of Aylmer, as a resupply while continuing north rather than as a turnaround point. Likewise for the cache on Maufelly Bay of Walmsley Lake, where I had built a little plywood hut back in 1988. That hut would be my main dry-out and refit stopover. It also marked an abrupt transition from familiar to new terrain. I had been north of there, to the southwest side of Aylmer Lake, only once before by dogteam, and it had been a brief trip in spring-time a decade earlier.

There is such joy in travelling with dogs over a familiar route. They know precisely where to go, even if it has been years since they have passed that way. Every boulder, turn, and tree is locked in their memory after a single journey. The musher can just stand on the runners and give the leaders their heads while the miles slide by. Every now and then I might think they have forgotten some small detail of the path, and I start to speak up to correct them, only to realize that nine times out of ten they have it right and I have it wrong. Humbling.

On day two, the first full day of the trip north, that was all I had to do: just ride the runners and let the lead dogs do their job. I could stand on the runners and look around, face backwards if I felt like it, even pour a cup of cocoa if the trail was smooth. (Try that while driving a snowmobile!) The weather was good, with overcast skies, some light snow late in the day, and a weak headwind out of the northeast. It was cold but not bitterly so. We paused briefly at midday and the dogs took a nap. I sat back on the sled and thought about racing.

For twelve years straight, it was on that network of trails northeast of our homestead that Kristen and I and dozens of Iditarod dogs had ground out the training miles in preparation for the long races. Time and mileage were our taskmasters. On long-run days in the dark weeks of December we would not even see the homestead in daylight. Just a faint glow lit the southeast sky when we pulled out of the yard before dawn, and sundown was hours past when we returned. Always in those seasons there was that fascination, not to say obsession, with speed. After all, pared to the essence, every race comes down to speed. As I let the dogs enjoy their nap on that first day, lounging and reminiscing with a warm mug in my hand, I was glad for those years of hard racing and for the lessons taught by such maniacal perseverance. I was glad too for this opportunity to move past that chapter of my life, while I could still stand on the sled runners and run these old trails with a new perspective.

Still, whenever I reach down to pull the snow hook or yank the slip-knot from a hitching post, I almost always check my watch. *So be it*, I thought. I kind of like that old Iditarod habit.

This stretch of trail was packed with memories. I realized again how much it is our memories that infuse a piece of country with its character. I thought of Haines' profound and simple sentence: "The land lives in its people." Yes, because the people who live on the land each carry their memories; as they travel and camp, again and again, the land comes alive for each of them. When that thread of personal and collective memory falters or breaks, when it is not refreshed by the echoes of day-to-day connection and physical presence, our relationship to the land begins to falter and fade.

On they came, my own echoes, as the dogs pulled me along—a late canoe trip that ended in a full-scale blizzard, a 52-below morning on a training run, a caribou hunt by boat when Annika was a baby and Liv was not yet born. Our trail rejoined the Hoarfrost 27 miles out from home, and I stashed the skis at our old 1993 "fish camp," figuring that from there on I would not need them. We were steadily crossing over to the tundra beyond the trees. By late afternoon we were just below Cook Lake, along the east bank of the upper Hoarfrost. A light snow began to fall. There was open water at a narrows in the river there and a grove of small spruce—two campsite accoutrements not to be ignored. Tired and relaxed, well north of home, we stopped for the night.

It is a pleasure to camp alongside moving water in the heart of winter. The sound of flowing water brings thoughts of summer, of waves and rapids and waterfalls, and it breaks the silence of the winter night. Winter in the Far North is stern and rigid—no flow, no lilt, no wavelets sparkling in a breeze. Deathly still on many days, and on many others only Hornbein's "roaring silence" of the wind. That night I had the steady gurgle of the Hoarfrost only a few yards from the tent and I slept to the tune of the river. Time continued to slow. The weather continued its benign pattern and day three ended at minus 30 degrees under clearing skies. All of the dogs howled several times during the night, and then stopped—as they almost always do—in uncanny perfect unison, as if watching the wand in a conductor's hand. The howling ended, and in a beautiful segue the burble of the rapids filled back in behind it.

That morning as I broke camp and snowshoed our departure path along the east bank of the open river, I heard another sound—the distinctive *whock-whock-whock* of a helicopter hammering in from the west. The machine closed on us rapidly to within a mile or so, but I never saw it and the proximity of noises in winter can be difficult to gauge. The chopper's approach reminded me that I was on the eastern edge of a long swath of diamond-exploration activity. I would be skirting that edge throughout the trip. Just 20 miles northeast of my second night's camp was the DeBeers outpost called Kennady Lake, where at least five dozen people were living and working that winter.[2] I wondered whether this would be the year in which I encountered other humans on my journey.

Out of camp and under way, we moved north up the river. The dogs made short work of the nine-mile length of Cook Lake. At the northeast end of the lake I paused to bolster my socks and change my insoles. Sheepishly remembering my frosted feet of the journey's start the year before, I broke out a pair of magic-powder heat packets and stuffed one into the toe of each sock. The trees were almost gone and the familiar backyard feeling was fading quickly behind us. We were 43 miles out from home on the evening of day three, and instead of hundreds of trips through that stretch of country—as I could claim farther down—I could think of only about a dozen.

Again that night we camped alongside the river, at the second-to-last open water on the winter Hoarfrost. Here the rapids were more rambunctious, splashing and steaming in the cold air, coating shoreline boulders and stunted shrubs with a thick rime of the river's namesake frost. Again I enjoyed the luxury of that steady sound in the darkness, as I lay awake after blowing out the candle. I thought of another remark Will had made one morning before dawn, sitting at the table with us on his January visit: "I just love those big icecaps, Greenland and Antarctica. Just that white expanse." He had then added one of his trademark snippets of Catholic-school analogy, which had stuck in my mind: "Crossing an ice cap is like skiing the rosary."

What had he meant? Not being Catholic, I have only a vague Lutheran notion of the rosary, but my impression is of a mantra, "om mani padme hum," hour after hour, on and on, leading one into an altered, medita-tive state. I remembered a night I spent with Will at Christmas about 1980 at his cabin north of Ely, Minnesota. He had suggested we go for a walk after dinner. It was clear and cold and the stars were out. We were alone, miles from town. Will carried a tape player—in those days a big, expensive reel-to-reel unit with good-quality sound—and as we walked on the ice of Pickett Lake in the darkness we listened to Gregorian chants. I was twenty-two years old, and the ambience Will was seeking was more or less lost on me, just as the ice-cap and rosary remark would have been. Now, in middle age, I begin to understand: winter, darkness, cold, auster-ity...and deep in its heart this *thrum,* this repetitive subtle chant, leading us along. That night the cold river, gurgling in the darkness just outside the tent, seemed to be the voice of endlessness, of patience, of eternal truth and ephemeral existence all blurred together. Rosary beads sliding along their looped strings, to softly murmured prayers.

A dog barked and the spell was broken. It was a quick short bark, an alarm: a fox was likely nearby, or a wolf or wolverine. None of the other dogs joined in, and silence, except for the river, returned. *We are not alone out here,* I thought. I drifted off.

The next day, day four, came up minus 33 degrees, with a cloudy sky and no wind. My thoughts turned immediately to those other two dogteam expeditions, Will's group and the four women from Outward Bound, somewhere off to the east. We were many miles apart now, and that dis-tance was increasing by the day. Still I found a pleasant vague connection in the notion that my dogs were among a big pack of sixty-one huskies staked out on the central Barrens that morning, and that there were ten other people somewhere out there with me; people I knew, although I could not see them or talk to them. Throughout that north trip I held to that notion of solidarity, and it was pleasant knowing that all those oth-ers were harnessing up dogs, feeling the cold and the wind, and watching some local variation of the very same clouds and sky.

That morning my notes ran the gamut from the mundane and practical to the sentimental:

Dogs eating unpredictably so far—they aren't gobbling their evening chow. I am carrying bowls this trip, and I watered them with broth yesterday. I will try that again today.

Small crack on sled bottom—watch those rocks. BUILD SOME NEW SLEDS YOU IDIOT! White gas is warmth, which is wealth in my world, especially now as we leave *all* the trees behind.

I am dumbstruck, almost literally, by the huge measure of support Kristen has given these trips. On this one she threw herself into assisting with my preparations, and thanks to her I have several key items of equipment to save my sorry ass in the days ahead: the removable fleece neck gusset on the parka, new duffles in my mukluks, and new fleece wristlets. When I walked up to kiss her goodbye the other night she stood by the leaders, happy and calm, cheery as ever. I knew—and she knew—that the house was dishevelled, the day's water had not been hauled, the wood supply was scanty, and the barn and workshop were both a mess. Makeshift lights and railings and shelves and cupboards festoon our home, some of them coming up on seven years as "only temporary." And yet she stood there, all smiles, and wished me well. What a woman.

Haven't looked at a map yet, as we cross the 50-mile mark out from home. The route so far is intimately familiar to me, and full of memories, faces, and past outings. A wonderful easiness of mind comes with that familiarity.

That mix of tones fills all of my journals for the trips. The sudden shifts of emphasis and theme give a glimpse into the heart of dog mushing and the arctic winter. It is impossible to live *constantly* in that breathless, lofty, awestruck mood which deep solitude and pristine wilderness can at times impart. (And who would want to?) Mundane realities constantly intrude, and in no season does reality deliver such a punch as in deep winter. Pitching and breaking camp, melting snow for water, tending to cold toes and fingers, troublesome zippers or snaps or stove pumps... rips in clothing, frozen dog shit to be chipped off the sled runners. Rocks and thin ice to avoid, hollows filled with bottomless powder snow, all in an austere landscape mostly devoid of other living things.

And then along comes one of those moments—a sudden appreciation of it all: sky and wind, freedom of movement, every part of one's body actually *warm*, the dogs leaping and barking with sheer joy and exuberance. All of it so very fleeting, gone in a flash. But the thought comes: *Ah, so that's why we came out here!*

Fleeting too, the very lives of the dogs and, without much of a leap of reasoning, all lives. On the trip north I pondered the career of my stalwart lead dog B.J. (for Banjo Junior, after her grandmother). She had become such a dependable leader, such a joy to work with, as she neared "old age" at ten years. I had not brought her south or east, but she came north for what would turn out to be her last big trip. What she lacked in speed I did not miss—I wanted her wisdom and her solid stature, that thick fur with no low-slung parts dangling in the breeze. Such patience, such calm acceptance in those pale blue eyes, yet I could not ignore the telltale quiver in her hindquarters after any prolonged stretch of fast running. I knew she would soon be retiring from lead, and within a year or two from runs of any real distance. And unless she set some new longevity record for our kennel, within five years she would be dead. All those miles, all those races and days and nights on the trail, a decade of running—B.J. always up there at the front, steady and dependable. *If only a dog could live a lifespan something similar to our own*, I thought to myself that day, *mushing would be so much simpler*—"That's my leader B.J.," he said, nodding his bald head and pointing with his cane. "I've had her for forty-seven years now..."

The day led north, onto Walmsley Lake, past the last open rapids on the upper Hoarfrost. For 20 feet or so there the dogs pussyfooted and the sled wobbled, a scant few inches from the steaming rush of the river. A short distance upstream from the rapids, we passed the site of another old RCMP patrol shack, this one just a heap of boards lying beneath deep drifts of snow. The dogs were strong and I enjoyed the ride, despite a pesky cold wind and intermittent haze. We picked our way across the broad and confusing expanse of Walmsley, threading blind channels studded with barren islands, confusing and almost indiscernible. We stopped for a break at the narrows where Maufelly Bay joins the main lake.[3]

By mid-afternoon we had arrived at the little hut on the north end of Maufelly Bay, 77 miles out from home. Our Maufelly Bay shack is not much to write home about: just an eight-by-twelve-foot box of plywood sheathing, with two-by-four stud walls and fibreglass insulation, all capped with a weatherproof roof. Its south wall frames a big double-pane window, and there are two bunks, a shelf, and a flimsy sheet-metal wood stove—the type known in the Yukon as a "hippie killer."[4] Back in 1988, I built the hut using leftover building supplies from Roger's new house in Reliance. Roger and I had picked out the site together one summer day, on a caribou-scouting flight in my old Piper Cub, and we both had visions of travelling to it often. As the years pass, though, I am always surprised and chagrined at how rarely the place gets used. My plan on the north trip was to stop over there on both the outbound and homebound legs, as I had done with my cache at Sandy Lake the year before.

The hut sits on a narrow peninsula at the foot of a big esker. It is a dramatic location for such a humble little structure, especially in summer and autumn. Like Richard's shack on Whitefish Lake the site offers a great view down a big sweep of the lake (important for wolf hunters like Richard and Roger), but that same impressive exposure offers no windbreak for a resting dogteam. Thus my first project after our arrival that afternoon was to dig a long trench in the huge snowdrift at the base of the slope. I then strung the dogs' picket line down the trench. I had once flown up to the site in late summer with a posthole digger and set a few stout spruce posts in the ground, thinking that I could anchor my picket line to them. They stood five feet tall, and I have yet to see the tops of those posts in winter. This pattern prevails across the Barrens: the esker tops are blown clean and the hollows beneath and alongside them are filled with deep soft snow.

As the dog food soaked that night and I waited to feed the team, I realized with a start that for the moment I had absolutely nothing to do. My shelter—the hut—was up and already warm inside. I could cook and eat in there whenever I was ready. I found the lee west wall of the building, dropped to my haunches, and rested there. The last pinks and blues faded from the sky and the first stars appeared. The earth rolled into another night. *How seldom I simply watch this happen,* I thought. In the year since last year's solo, my father had died. We had always been good friends, and I was able to be with him as his life ended. Once years ago we had spent some pleasant August days and nights at the hut on Walmsley. I thought of him and of his talent for relaxation—a talent that I never fully inherited. "Ah, what luxury," he would intone, tilting back in a big chair at home, or on a log beside a fire at the close (or even the start) of a day in camp. *Luxury indeed*, I thought that night—a warm hut, dogs sheltered in their trench, and nothing to do but sit and think and watch the sky. Perhaps at forty-six I could still learn this trick from my old man.

Coming in from the cold and living in a heated room overnight was as disorienting as ever. Compared to Richard's little shack on Whitefish, the Maufelly Bay hut was the Ritz. I spent the evening reading and writing by candlelight, brought Foxtail in for some companionship, and at bedtime stretched out on the double-wide bunk. As I lay there an odd notion of guilty pleasure crept over me. *What am I doing here?* I thought. *This is only night four—I haven't earned such ease and luxury yet. I should be out*

The hut at Maufelly Bay. The dogs are picketed in their snow trench. Note the sharp line of overcast cloud in the distance.

there somewhere. Not easy, this legacy of Scandinavian Lutheran guilt. Finally I fell into a deep, warm sleep, well-deserved or not.

Morning, day five, brought a brisk east-southeast wind and a clear sky. It was minus 30 degrees. I felt like a sailor, moored there in the hut; the space cramped but efficient, shelves on the walls and clothing hung on nails, tiny bright portholes to port and starboard—a little ship in a cold white sea. I remembered a quote I have always liked: "A ship in harbor is safe, but that is not what ships are built for."[5] The weather wasn't shouting, "Don't move!" but neither was it inspiring me to hit the trail with a blast of enthusiasm. I eased through the morning chores and gradually made up my mind to pack up and get moving north again. My gear was all delightfully dry, thanks to the cabin's space and its wood-fire heat, and it was only the Basic voice, joined perhaps by my dear father, urging me to settle in and spend another night in luxury. There I would be: warm, dry, and—I knew—bored stiff and fidgety by mid-afternoon. No, it was better to go.

That day all of my familiar landmarks fell behind us, and by day's end we had climbed out of the watershed of the Hoarfrost River. In late morning a light southerly breeze puffed up from behind us as the dogs trotted swiftly up the broad expanse of Fletcher Lake. On the open stretch of Fletcher the light and the sky began to change as a deck of overcast cloud moved in. For an hour or so we moved through an opaque, cold dreamscape, everything everywhere a soft bluish-white.

———————

At the north end of Fletcher is another big esker system. On canoe trips in the early 1990s I had camped there with large groups and our big freighter canoes. It was in late July 1991, camped at the toe of that big esker on Fletcher, that I had first seen a pair of geologists taking a sample of esker sand. The process seemed odd to me that day: a small float plane landed and taxied in, the pilot hopped out and heeled the plane up on the beach, and two passengers appeared. We chatted, making small talk as they sifted and scooped about sixty pounds of pebbly sand into a big cotton sack. That day I could never have guessed that over the next decade I would get to know all of those fellows (they worked for DeBeers) or that I would myself spend thousands of hours of my bush-flying career ferrying such geologists and their minions, loading sandbags into airplanes, and even helping them sift their samples.

The search for diamonds in this part of the world is a matter of following tiny clues, some of them literally microscopic, scattered over a vast landscape. If conditions are just right, gem-quality diamonds can form in a "pipe" of a rock called kimberlite. The kimberlite pipe erupts as molten lava under pressure, from far down in the earth's crust. Eskers, as I have said, are the ancient bas-relief riverbeds of glacial meltwater. If the glacier has passed over and lopped off the top of a pipe of diamond-bearing kimberlite, the flowing ice and meltwater will spread the tiny clues of that occurrence outward across the terrain, down-ice from the pipe. Indicator minerals—minerals strongly associated with the formation of diamonds, but more numerous than the elusive gems themselves—are spread along those under-glacier riverbeds.[6] The relative concentration of them in a sample of sand will be highest near their source. So goes the detective game, one sack of sand at a time, and that game has made a fortune for small airlines, helicopter companies, camp builders, sample takers, and laboratories. In the peak of the diamond rush between 1991 and 1997, a swath of the north-central Barrens 400 miles across and stretching from Great Slave Lake north to the Arctic Ocean was intensively sampled, shovel scoop by shovel scoop. All of that frantic activity resulted in the establishment of four mines producing gem-quality diamonds. One of them has already slid into bankruptcy, but some other promising sites are still gearing up for production.

As the dogs scampered past the esker at the north end of Fletcher, into the uppermost reaches of the Hoarfrost drainage, I was glad to see every-

The team advancing slowly through the boulder field above our night-six campsite.

thing there still pristine and vacant—no prospectors, no mine. Looking for kimberlite formations, and finding the rare ones that contain marketable gem-quality diamonds, is like searching for a few dizzyingly valuable needles in the world's largest haystack. Thus do some of us who have made a part of our living from this frantic search for diamonds console ourselves: "It will never lead to anything but a few scoops of sand from a hillside and a paycheque in my pocket." Even the sand-scooping geologists usually chuckle at the far-fetched odds of the search.

—————

That night I camped alongside a small pond just south of Taylor Lake. I named it Boulder Field Lake after our tortuous passage down the slope of the Hoarfrost-Lockhart divide. That hillside looked deceptively white and smooth as we started down, but inches beneath the fresh snow it was strewn with big chair- and table-sized boulders, and some whoppers the size of grand pianos and small cars. The dogs picked their way through the minefield of crevasses, with me out ahead of them on snowshoes. *We will have to look for another route on the way home*, I thought, but once we were into the boulders it seemed better to continue downhill than to turn back. Luckily no one was injured and the heavy sled came through undamaged.

I was getting out there again. We had left the home watershed behind, and the familiar trails leading up it, and the little bastion of coziness at Maufelly Bay. From my journal:

My world has narrowed to the contents of my sled, these ten dogs, my clothing and the things I always carry in my pockets—matches, knife, pliers, cord…Strip all of it away and I would die almost instantly. The cold and the vastness together would do me in. My caches are miles apart. I creep carefully, cautiously, from one to the next. An odd sensation like vertigo sweeps over me at times, in my mind and the pit of my stomach, and I have to breathe deeply and muster my resolve. The feeling is similar to an unnerving sensation I sometimes conjure up when I am flying the Husky: suddenly I see myself all alone—the plane and its engine have vanished. It is just me up there, strapped into my tiny chair, suspended a mile or more above the earth.

My lead dog Steve had been favouring his right wrist since our mid-day break just north of Fletcher. In camp that night I heated some Algavyl salve and rubbed it in, then wrapped his wrist and lower leg with a neo-prene brace. The pungent smell of the liniment flooded my mind with memories of the Iditarod and the Yukon Quest races. I imagine it did the same for Steve, B.J., and Murphy, who were the only race veterans in that team of ten dogs. Since we were not racing, I was free to treat Steve with aspirin, and I gave him a coated 325-milligram tablet. By the next morning he was still favouring the wrist slightly, but he was putting a little weight on it again.

Taken together, Steve's bum wrist and the weather seemed to call for a rest day. It was day six of the trip and we were about a hundred miles out from home. In my journal I recorded the morning weather, and although it looked harmless enough when written down there was something about it I did not trust: minus 20 degrees, very light snow, visibility four or five miles, the sky overcast at about 400 feet, and a light breeze from the east. I had no barometer, but I guessed that the pressure was rapidly falling. Something was going to happen.

It was a pleasant sensation, that minus 20 degrees. Considering the magnitude of the difference between 20 below and 40 below (the spread of 20 degrees Celsius being about 35 degrees Fahrenheit) it is easy to imagine how pleasant it could feel. The range was analogous, for example, to a pair of summer afternoons: one a balmy 23 degrees, the other a chilly 3 degrees. A swim, anyone? Lunch on the deck?

It had snowed steadily through the night, and soft flakes were piled five inches thick over everything in camp. As I padded around just enjoying the mild morning, the dogs raised a chorus of howls, their heads thrown back, voices quavering in and out of harmony. They had heard something—a high-flying airplane or some distant wolves. Perhaps we were closing in on some bands of caribou and their accompanying packs of predators. We had seen none so far, and they had to be somewhere. In landscapes drawn to the scale of Canada's north, though, a few thousand—or for that matter a million—caribou "somewhere" leaves a lot of terrain open for possibility.

I was postponing my decision about travelling that day, while I doled out the dogs' morning ration and made my own breakfast. I noted in my journal that a person's reaction to the sight and smell of a quarter-pound of cooking bacon could provide a very accurate measure of both the outside temperature and one's level of physical exertion. In the relatively mild air that morning my daily ration of pig fat suddenly looked like an enormous helping—but down it went, and quickly.

At last a rising wind nudged me into a firm decision. A gust from the east settled into a steady blow of about twenty knots. The sun was dimly visible through the overcast, but it was not a day for route-finding north toward the next cache. Decision made, I went for a walk on snowshoes, tracing a wide arc north of camp. Found some muskox droppings on a rocky ridge along the south shore of Taylor Lake and played hide-and-seek with a red fox, but those were the only signs of activity in the neighbourhood that morning. I returned to camp and set up the HF antenna for an evening radio call. The dogs were happily dozing, and the wind was whipping the fresh snow into a true ground storm.

There is comfort in a stormy day, and even alone on the edge of the Barrens a contented mood of resignation and rest accompanies the first sign of a blizzard—if camp is made, the dogs are secure and sheltered, and there is ample food and fuel. That camp south of Taylor Lake had all of those, and the storm day we passed there was entirely pleasant. After my morning walk I was happy to burrow into the tent and take up with Colin Fletcher's book *River*, his account of a long solo trip down the length of the Colorado, which he made at the age of sixty-seven. Inspired by Fletcher's musings on the true source of the Colorado, and with time on my hands, I spent well over an hour poring over the 1:50,000-scale maps I had brought. As accurately as I could, I traced the precise boundary of my home watershed, the Hoarfrost River. A few surprises came out of that project. The first had to do with the De Beers diamond project at Kennady Lake, which will soon become a mine. I had understood that the development there lay within the upper Hoarfrost drainage, since it is only a dozen miles or so to the west of Walmsley Lake. In fact, by the maps it looked like it was a part of the watershed of a smaller unnamed river that flows into McLeod Bay about 15 miles west of our homestead.[7]

This was a relief to me, although in truth I have never been overly concerned about the water-quality effects of a relatively small diamond mine. Perhaps I should be, given the historical track record of Big Mining around the world. Any large project, along with the housing of hundreds of workers, will of course have impacts. Maybe I have just been won over, but the crushing of kimberlite and the sifting out of gems can be painted as pretty innocuous when compared to the infamous tar sands or the legacy of toxic leftovers at the Giant gold mine in and under Yellowknife.

The other interesting result of my watershed tracing was that, according to the detailed chart of the northwest corner of Fletcher, the lake might in fact drain in two directions, down both the Hoarfrost *and* the Lockhart rivers. Its flow south down the Hoarfrost is obvious, but on the map a tiny line indicating a drainage also connects Fletcher with Kirk Lake. From Kirk the water flows north to Aylmer and down the Lockhart. I decided I would try to look at that connection on my homeward journey. I have always found watersheds interesting. Rivers, lakes, and oceans form the most fundamental connections and passageways on this watery planet. My imagination has always been fired by the notion that, for instance, a downstream journey in a capable boat could take me from our beach on McLeod Bay all the way to the Arctic Ocean, and from there—depending on which direction I turned at the mouth of the Mackenzie River—out through the Bering Strait to the North Pacific, or through the Northwest Passage to Baffin Island, Greenland, and the Atlantic. And from there...well, the world. Whether I ever make that journey or not, I still find it thrilling to know that it *could* be done.

By early evening the wind was battering the tent. I felt as though I was sitting inside a big folded rug while an energetic housekeeper beat the dust out of it. I suited up and went out into the storm for evening chores, and as the daylight faded I erected a little wall of snow blocks to help protect the three dogs who were not getting shelter from the small spruce grove. Something nearby—or some strong smell carried on the gale—suddenly sent the entire team into a frenzy, all howling and bellowing and staring east into the twilight. Wolf? Wolverine? Windigo? I detected nothing. We humans with our poor noses miss so much of the world. I put jackets on Ernie and Foxtail and decided that everyone else would be okay without them. I preferred the prospect of having some perfectly dry dog jackets stowed in the arsenal for the days ahead.

I tried to contact Kristen on the HF radio, since this was night six of the trip, but one channel, 5760 kHz, was overpowered by a syncopated drumbeat beamed out from some hip Third World transmitter. On the other, 5031, it sounded as if every Inuk in Nunavut was talking at once in rapid-fire Inuktitut. Through all the chatter I could hear Kristen on that channel. After several attempts we managed to confirm that I was near Taylor Lake and that all was well with me and also at home, and we gave up.

———————

Anyone who likes a long bus or train ride would know how it feels to ride out a storm in a small tent. At first the prospect of all those waking hours of self-absorbed, task-free relaxation is exciting. By the end of a day or two, though, one begins to hope that the ride will soon end, so the real work can resume. (If the ride goes on long enough, though, say three days and nights, I can attest that one begins to feel like the state of limbo might be a reasonable way to live out one's life: "This is Wynyard, and we will have forty-five minutes here for your lunch stop. Remember your bus number.")

Overnight the real work did resume, in the form of clear cold weather. I woke to only a slight rustling of the tent fly, and a nip on the end of my nose protruding from the frosty hood of my sleeping bags. A quick trip outside showed a blue sky and 38 degrees below zero. The wind was holding easterly, but steadily dropping. The camp showed all the signs of having weathered a blizzard: huge drifts on the downwind side of the sled, the tent, and the dogs' snow-block wall, with hollows scoured right down to bare rock and moss on the upwind side of every object. The dogs were frisky and eager as I spoke to them. It would be a real chore to dig out and pack up, but once that team was in harness their wagging tails promised me a fast ride north.

From my journal: "Again I feel the shift in my life's pattern that these trips represent. They are the end of an era—the self-perception as lean and hungry young man, giving way to a different m.o., a different set of priorities. Today I will move north, but I will not *push*."

In that frame of mind I set to work on getting under way. The cold slowed my efforts, as deep cold always does: extra minutes here and there, warming up fingers and doing tasks with mitts on that would be much more quickly done bare-handed. I took extra time to bootie all the dogs, in an effort to prevent ice balls and fissures between their pads. The only place where a dog truly perspires, I have been told, is in the soft folds of skin between the footpads. Running in deep cold, through fresh powdery snow, can lead to little cracks and cuts deep in those narrow pockets of tender skin. For a day or two these are tiny things, like hangnails or mosquito bites, but on a long race or a long trip the tiny cuts cannot heal. They can begin to crack and fester, leaving the dog with sore feet. Booties prevent this, but having stated that I must immediately add that booties reign supreme as the single biggest pain in the neck within the entire métier of dog mushing. Modern dog booties are made from tough synthetic cloth and fitted with soft Velcro wrist straps. They are durable and effective. They are also finicky things to put on a team of dogs, with cold clumsy fingers, one bootie at a time, four booties per dog.

Flynn, an extremely shy dog, adamantly refuses to wear booties, or to have anyone so much as touch his paws, so he is always a good foil to any argument in favour of putting booties on the entire team. Because he is so shy, I would never choose Flynn to sire a litter of pups, and long ago we brought him to the veterinarian to be neutered. That morning in camp, as I laboured for thirty minutes in a half-crouch to put booties on the rest of the team, I promised Flynn that if he came through the trip with good feet, bootie-free from start to finish, I would personally sew his balls back on and make him the main stud for a new breeding program. (His feet did, in fact, come through in good shape, but I didn't hold up my end of our bargain.)

That day we crossed into the high country, or that is how it felt. The terrain was all new to me, and I carefully followed a route I had plotted on the 1:50,000-scale maps. Rock ridges interspersed with small interconnected ponds and frozen creeks led us north to the resupply cache on Laverty Lake. It was a sunny cold day and even at midday there was a bite to the prevailing easterly breeze. On three of the steepest climbs I had to snowshoe ahead of the dogs to make a trail. The team was a joy to work with, following in my broken trail so that I did not have to backtrack to the sled and urge them forward in the soft snow.

Laverty Lake is a narrow trough running southwest–northeast, with high rock ridges on its west shore. On my flight to place the caches I had landed on a patch of bare ice near the brow of a rock island at the lake's north end. We reached the cache in mid-afternoon. I realized that by the time I dug out and opened the barrels and reorganized the sled load to fit the new supplies, it would be nearly time to camp. There was no real shelter at the cache site, but I figured (mistakenly, as it turned out) the weather would hold calm and cold for the night, so I camped. As always it was pure pleasure to make camp without wearing snowshoes. Snowshoes are ingenious tools, but their ability to invoke sheer frustration is almost

Resupply cache camp at Laverty Lake. Wind-polished ice shows black in the background.

incredible. All is well on smooth, uniform snow cover, with a straight-ahead route to follow. When one is twisting and turning through heavy brush, leading an energetic husky to or from its place on the picket line, an enormous tennis racket dangling from each leg on a flimsy rubber harness, things get interesting. I recall a trip with a group of university students, when I heard a loud curse in the dusk: "I *hate* snowshoes!" I looked over in time to see one of the students launching his snowshoes from deep in an alder thicket. He forged ahead waist-deep in the powdery snow, determined to finish the evening chores with only his mukluks on his feet. Five minutes later I noticed that he had quietly strapped the snowshoes on again.

The pleasure of making camp on open tundra or ice is obvious: one just walks naturally back and forth around the campsite, the tent is staked out with little aluminum pins, and life is easy. Easy yet uneasy, since one cannot help but recall the *reason* why the snow is packed as hard as a boardwalk—strong winds and plenty of them.

That night I knew we were stepping out of our home element again, the dogs and I. We hunkered down at the rocky tip of the little island. All around the tent were patches of wind-polished black lake ice and elaborately hard-sculpted drifts called sastrugi. As the sun slipped below the horizon, its light threw the high rocks just west of camp into dark silhouette, and washed pink the altocumulus clouds above the ridge. A thin sliver of moon hung in the west with an evening star (Venus? Jupiter?) close and bright beside it. A clear cold night seemed to be a sure bet. I pulled the sack of dog jackets out and put a jacket on each dog. Just as I finished doing that a light wind came up out of the northeast, and just as I crawled into the tent I noticed some haze and stratus cloud building in from the south. *Here we go*, I thought, *we're about to get hit.* As the unexpected wind came up, we suddenly seemed far too exposed, but at that hour of evening with the camp all set up, there was not a thing to be done about it.

This was North, I thought that night as I ate. Mile by mile, each camp a little higher up the curve toward the pole, the land was being whittled down to its essence. The sparrows, loons, phalaropes, and jaegers of summer were far south and long gone, grizzlies and ground squirrels all fast asleep. For miles in every direction now there was only wind, rock, and ice. A meagre handful of creatures—hare, fox, wolf, wolverine, raven, ptarmigan, muskox, caribou—continued to roam and somehow find a living, but often there was no sign of them for miles and days at a time.

I slept well, so I must have been tired. Instead of cold clear weather, the dawn brought minus 24 degrees with wind pummeling the tent. A quick glance out the vestibule "hatch" showed the dogs all curled up, noses beneath tails. They seemed oblivious to the storm, but they were completely exposed to the east wind and there was no loose snow to drift over them like a soft blanket. That camp felt alpine to me, a high camp on a ridge where a climbing party would position themselves for a bid at the summit. For us the "summit" of the trip would be that big esker alongside the headwaters of the Back River. There the river was just a trickle over stones, flowing north by northwest out of Sussex Lake. If we could make it there I would be happy to turn south. The wide-open sprawl of Aylmer Lake lay between the cache camp and that goal, and now this shift in the weather loomed as a fresh twist in the plot.

Before leaving home, I had made a request to the dispatchers at Air Tindi in Yellowknife, the air charter company where I then worked as a pilot. While I was out on the trail they saved the faxes of the daily weather maps called graphical area forecasts, so that I could look at them after my trip. On the map for 24 February at 1800 UTC, or midday, I can see the symbol for an "occluded front" lying in a ruler-straight line all the way from the Yukon–Alaska border to the northwestern corner of Saskatchewan. An occluded front is an ambivalent sort of weather system—"a cold front, closely following a warm front, finally overtakes the warm front and lifts the warm air mass off the ground," writes meteorologist Paul Lehr, in his book *Weather*.[8] Of course the "cold" and "warm" of these fronts are relative to latitude and the time of year. What this thousand-mile-long occlusion brought to us over the next few days was a potpourri of unsettled winter mildness—some cloud and wind, some sunshine, some snow, but no definite change or decisive storm.

I did not know what was depicted on the weather maps that morning. I could only go by what I could see. It looked as though we were going to get hammered, and it looked as though the dogs would be better off on the lee side of the island's bald rock outcrop. I put on all my layers and went outside. I strung out the gangline and shifted all the dogs back onto it, then staked the empty picket line over on the sheltered side of the rock. I led the dogs in pairs over to the new set-up. This put them much farther from the tent than I liked, but they were in a protected nook of deep fluffy snow. That done and their breakfast doled out, I turned back into the tent. I was frustrated by the change in weather and the prospect of another storm day so soon after the last one. We *could* travel in such weather, I knew, but we were on unfamiliar terrain and we were perched right on top of our supply cache. To venture north in a windstorm would only be plain stubbornness, and I had learned to be leery of my lifelong inclination to stubborn perseverance. I took my cue from the dogs and curled up, brewed a pot of real coffee, and spent an hour musing happily over all the intricacies of an old 1:500,000 aeronautical chart called Upper Back River, then another hour perusing some boat-building sketches. The morning hours passed.

Just before noon the wind dropped off suddenly and—for a moment—completely. Amazed, I threw on my parka and scurried out to have a look around. Sure enough—the visibility had come up to an honest four miles, and the sun seemed to be teasing from behind a thin screen of cloud. I stood there for nearly ten minutes, mulling over my choices. Was this a change, or just a lull? *Perhaps it is just a "sucker hole,"* I thought, as pilots call those enticing breaks in cloud that can lure us onward into deteriorating weather. I walked over to the dogs and tried a soft squeak through my pursed lips. Every head popped instantly up. This was a test I had often used when running long races—a way of asking the dogs just how well rested they were. Their instant response to my squeak told me that they were just as eager to get going as I was.

Two hours later we were under way, north to the outlet of Laverty Lake and over a short downhill portage onto the ice of Aylmer. Haze shrouded the dark headlands there. We sped along with a quartering tailwind, the team galloping flat-out. Dramatic spears of lenticular cloud hung in the western sky, and directly above us a sharply defined cloud-edge arced from northeast to southwest. I checked and rechecked the map, matching vague landforms to the lines printed there. Aylmer is an enormous lake and there were no sharp horizons once we moved onto its main expanse— only the shapes of promontories and stretches of rocky tundra rising into sight, passing alongside, and falling behind us.

It was easy to forget just how hard the dogs were working, since they seemed delighted to make it look easy. When I had finished packing at the Laverty Lake camp, I had lashed down the load and tugged the sled over to where the dogs had been repositioned. In the soft snow it had taken every bit of my strength to move that sled. Yet even with my own 200-pound weight added to the total load, they were still whisking me along as if we were out for a sprint on McLeod Bay. At about four forty-five, I found what shelter I could and tucked in on the flank of a wide cove, with not a tree or shrub to be seen. Camp making was pleasant and swift in the mild weather, and on the wind-packed snow I did not need snowshoes. The dogs' appetites had fallen off with the rising temperatures, and I fed them sparingly. In deep cold their metabolism becomes so efficient that it is always tricky to adjust the diet when the cold eases. Fat, which is a major part of their caloric intake, is the most important ingredient to adjust. When mild weather follows after deep cold, I have seen entire teams refuse to touch their dinner if the food is too rich in fat.

That night in the tent I played with the GPS again, first pinpointing my position at 64° 08.85′ N X 108° 32.14′ W, then flashing up various other tidbits of information: 92 miles to home, 19 to Sandhill Bay at the north tip of Aylmer, 210 north to Bathurst Inlet on the Arctic Ocean, 375 to Baker Lake, 1,420 to Spooner Wisconsin…As usual I found it

> nothing short of miraculous that a little box the size of a deck of playing cards can tell me, in about 20 seconds, my location, the approximate time of sunset and sunrise at this place, the distance to all these other points on earth, and so on. Yes, a little box and many billions of dollars in satellite hardware, research funds, rocket fuel, NASA itself since 1970-something…What can I say to this portable bundle of tricks and all the effort and careers that it represents? Well, thanks—I suppose—to the U.S. government, to some 1980s visionaries deep in the Pentagon and NASA, and to all those taxpay-ers…We're much obliged, whether or not we care to admit it!

The mild weather held, and it changed everything, but I remained deeply distrustful of it. After all, a year earlier out on the edge of the Thelon val-ley, the temperature had briefly moderated—and two days later it was minus 43 degrees with a northwesterly gale. We were still moving *away* from home and away from treeline. I was uneasy. My uneasiness was akin to the foreboding a lone sailor would feel on a notoriously stormy passage, when out of sheer luck he or she happens to approach it on a pleasant day. Later that evening it occurred to me that in such balmy weather I might take a stroll around camp before going to bed, or even drag my sleeping bags outside and sleep under the sky. But I did not— the most I could manage was a peek from the open flap of the tent vestibule, just enough to confirm that the sky was overcast and the breeze was southerly. "Could it be," I asked my journal, "that before a long dark sleep alone in the cold—way out here—I just don't want another reminder of how empty and vast a place this is? I have my little cocoon, my stove, candle, and journal, not to mention the goddamned GPS and its little TV screen, to cushion me from that thought-provoking immensity just beyond the tent flap—the darkness and the sky and all that they imply."

The night was minus 23 degrees and by morning an almost incredible minus 18. The south-southwest wind continued all night, almost a chinook, as such sudden mid-winter floods of warm air are called in the northern Rockies. As I lay in my bedding in the tent and listened to that wind, I had in mind an image of a big broad weather system, loaded with moisture, pushing inland a thousand miles from the North Pacific. The weather map for 6 a.m. on day nine shows, in the perfect clarity of hindsight, nothing of the sort. Only that long occluded front, still stretched from the Yukon to Manitoba, and to the west and south of it a pair of "quasi-stationary" highs that are labelled "weakening." In short, more of the same—no storm brewing, no basis for that feeling of impending tumult that coloured my mood at the start of the day.

There being no clear signal from anywhere that I should stay where I was, I packed up and we set off northward. By shortly before ten we were under way and the dogs were eager and happy as they towed me up Aylmer Lake. At five past one that afternoon we left the tip of Sandhill Bay and climbed a gentle sloping shore, still northbound. As we topped out on the broad hilltop I put my foot to the sled brake and stopped the team. The sun shone from a sky that was pure blue above us and cloudy on every horizon except due north. This was the summit for that year's journey, and I took my time as I did summit rituals: took a couple of photographs, had a lingering 360-degree look around, and scattered some coloured beads on the snow.

A tall esker dominated the skyline to the northeast. I knew that on its west slope was a wolf den, because in springtime over the years I had often seen a pack of white wolves there, resting at their den's entrance. These sightings were all from the air, as part of the flying I have done for the Northwest Territories' wildlife department.[9] At the foot of that massive esker trickled the uppermost waters of the Back River. The river was showing me that day its most prevalent form: ice.

Reaching the watershed divide between the Lockhart and the Back that day was a completely private triumph, which I suppose only I can ever understand. I stood there as happy and fulfilled as a mountaineer atop a peak, although the sunlit landscape around me was more prairie or desert than alpine. My pause on that bald hilltop held the epitome of what I had hoped these journeys could be. We had come to that place, the dogs and I, in good form, under our own power, and in solitude. The moment was a culmination but it snuck up on me quietly, as culminations often do. The dogs were wonderfully quiet and patient as I sat atop the sled load and poured a cup of cocoa from my Thermos. I looked north and east down the Back River, imagining its 600 miles of steadily increasing volume and strength, its rapids, cascades, and enormous lakes, all flowing to the Arctic Ocean at Chantrey Inlet. I had come to an edge. From here north lay Nunavut, the home territory of the Inuit, a place distinct from the taiga and forest to the south. I told myself that someday, if time and fate and life's uncertainties allowed I would travel down the Back by canoe, as Kristen had in the summer of 1988.

The dogs had finished their naps and they were standing again, restless and ready to run. I stowed the camera and the Thermos and pulled out my sunglasses for the first time that year. It was time to start south, toward the sun instead of away from it. First, though, we made a short stop on the frozen bed of the river. There I paused again to chip some river ice and store it away in a plastic bag. I snapped one last photo, with all the dogs screaming to go (all except Minnie, who makes it her strict policy never to waste an ounce of energy on such enthusiasm). We climbed the hill and turned into the sunshine.

By late afternoon we were well down the coast of Aylmer again, retracing our trail. A damp east-southeast wind had me chilled. At about 3 p.m. a thick wall of dark cloud blotted out the sun, and my visceral dread of being caught out on the enormous expanse of Aylmer Lake welled up again. We camped only four miles north of our previous night's camp— an odd proximity considering the 35 miles we had travelled that day. As I settled in, dozy and fed, I mused at random to my journal about Steve's gimpy right wrist, which continued to bother him each evening, and about my camps above treeline, with their pared-down ambience of simplicity:

A flat summit photo. Turnaround point for the trip north, at the headwaters of the Back River above Aylmer Lake.

dogs, sled, tent, whiteness. As backdrop to these musings was the profound satisfaction of that day, of our turning point reached and the trail home lying before us.

———————

Feb. 26 a.m., Day 10, west shore Aylmer Lake, –17°, overcast, visibility > 3 mi., light SW wind, sunrise 07:16, sunset 17:17, a total gain of seven minutes in 24 hours, in this same spot.

The tent is quiet, except for the hissing of dear Mr. Coleman, busily converting naphtha (old energy of sun) into carbon, both di-and mon-oxide, water vapor, Heat, and who-knows-what other emissions.

I feel as though Aylmer Lake has a deep power, like an old guardian spirit-of-place, and that this Power has issued an edict: 'Let them pass.' This mild calm weather is such an aberration that it feels like a gift. Much obliged.

Lacking the blow-by-blow struggle of the past two years, my journal of the trip north wanders in and out of focus, like the snapshots of a carefree

photographer with an unlimited supply of film and spare time. I had
an odd sense of our passage being watched and *allowed* by the force that
might have quickly and decisively put a stop to it. I felt like a ship ghosting
around the Horn on a gentle swell under sunny skies, not quite trusting
my good luck, just waiting and watching. A corny Hollywood scenario had
taken shape in my mind: a military-style "weather control room," a wall
filled with television monitors, and a grumpy old officer in charge:

> YOUNG PRIVATE: "Sir, it's that goofy fellow with the dogteam
> again, going north toward Aylmer Lake..."
> GRUMPY OLD OFFICER: "Oh Christ, not again—same dogs as last
> year?...Okay. Well, suspend normal operations until he's clear of
> the zone..."
> [Later]
> YOUNG PRIVATE: "Sir? He's off Aylmer now, southbound."
> GRUMPY OLD OFFICER: "All right then, resume mid-winter
> operations."
> [A huge switch is thrown back to "ON," and monitors show imme-
> diate transition to whiteout, digital temperature numbers blinking
> rapidly downward. Fade.]

I suspected that my mind would start to wander even farther from
the here and now as we edged closer to home and back onto familiar terrain. Even on day ten, still picking our way down the southwestern side of
Aylmer, thoughts of the summer's flying work began to crowd in—dollars and hours, customers and contracts. I pushed them away and yanked
my head up, breaking my blank stare at the sled's brushbow that over the
years has become my mental "screensaver" when daydreaming. Here I
was again—the big lake, these ten dogs, this incredibly light and fluffy
snow where I had expected only wind-blasted hard pack.

Caribou! At last, after all the miles with nothing but occasional tracks,
I came up on a band of a half-dozen just as we approached the portage
to Laverty Lake. They stood still and watched us pass, our distance from
them briefly closing to less than 150 yards. By evening we were navigating in completely new terrain again, heading west from the lake south
of Laverty after a brief pause at the cache. Big flakes of snow were falling
as I made camp. The spindly stand of midget spruce towered like coastal
redwoods after the treeless terrain of the past three days. I was tired and
out of sorts that night, my mood soured by a stupid logistical screw-up
at the cache. I had grabbed what I thought was a full 4.7-litre jug of stove
fuel, and miles later realized that the jug was only half full. I knew that it

would be adequate if we did not get pinned down by weather, and I knew I had more fuel waiting at the hut on Maufelly Bay, but I had wanted that comforting reserve.

The weather map for the morning of 29 February shows the huge occluded front finally beginning to dissipate. Nothing else dramatic is depicted on that day's forecast. There is a low-pressure centre north of Great Bear Lake, moving up toward the Arctic Coast, and a big *H* showing high-pressure air far to the west in the south-central Yukon. When I woke that next morning, day eleven, the thermometer showed minus 13 degrees. "I am astounded," I wrote. "A 30-degree (Celsius!) leap from a year ago—the difference between a hot day in summer and a lake skimmed over with ice!"

In such easy weather my sleeps were utterly relaxed and my dreams became, if possible, less meaningful than ever. I noted in my journal one silly dream after another, such as the one where I met several complete strangers in some big city, and offered to buy them all lunch. From such goofy images I would awake, somewhat dazed, to the familiar scene inside the tent, half-lit by dawn. On the level of reality, though, the lake just southwest of Laverty had gripped me. It was a place of palpable power, such as one sometimes finds in wild landscapes. A certain slant of light, an island with a steep prow of granite, some perfectly placed clumps of small spruce. Often a single such place will leap out during a day's travel and remain in my mind long after the other details of that entire day, or even that entire trip, are gone.

For twenty years or more I travelled the wilderness with a cabin-builder's squint. In those years I could not paddle the length of a remote lake without spotting at least one enticing location for an outpost cabin—a simple log or frame structure with a couple of bunks, a chair, a window and a porch. It was the same in winter, on dogteam trips and even on long races, although in the cold my imagined cabin sites were biased by the likelihood of nearby firewood and a sheltered, south-facing aspect. Now, older and a little weary after the decades of building that have gone on at our homestead, the outpost camp builder within me is much less eager. These years I find myself hoping that our civilization and our various levels of government will always at least *allow* dreamers of a certain age and stage in life to pursue that timeless frontier desire; allow it either officially or by laissez-faire or by plain ignorance. For I have learned first-hand that when it comes to connecting with a place, nothing compares to scratching that old itch. In a country as vast as Canada I say, "Let them try, the young and the restless, or the older and world-weary." In the end, surprisingly few such places will actually come to fruition.

The trade-off of having a cabin site "marring" an otherwise pristine lake, or riverbank, or ridgeline, is that someone, somewhere, will have made a strong connection to that place. These sweat-and-blood connections to *specific* places are, in my view, vital to our relationship with the non-human world. They are utterly different from "last year we entered the Park at entry point 14B, camped at designated campsites 37 and 19—19 is really nice, you know, on that rocky point—and exited the park at 22A." "Wilderness camping" has come to that already in many places, as I suppose it must. Surely we can sidestep such a dismal fate here. Sometimes I still think about that nameless lake just southwest of Laverty, and I know it for what it is—just a beauty, on the right day, in the right light. It will probably be years, or lifetimes, before I ever pass that way again. It is filed away among countless other such lovely places in my mind's eye; a place like the face of an attractive woman encountered on a busy street corner—noticed, intrigued, smiled at, passed by...and never seen again.

It was day eleven. We were off Aylmer and back into "the lake and portage, hill and creek, warp and weave of the country," as I wrote that morning. I had no idea what a magical day lay ahead, on the 30-some miles between my campsite and our late-afternoon arrival at the hut on Maufelly Bay. I had known the night before that I was cranky and tense: the weather seemed unsettled and I was tired. Perhaps, as often happens, I could sense a fall of the barometer. Come morning I wasted no time getting up and moving from that campsite. It was 29 February. The run began with a wild dodge-'em descent of a frozen creek bed studded with big boulders. One of the sled's metal brake claws caught in a rock and instantly broke off. I was able to hook down just past that boulder, and I gingerly scampered back to retrieve some of the damaged brake parts. It was a dicey manoeuvre to step off the sled and walk back up the trail so early in the day's run, but the dogs obliged by not running off without me.

Some days just blindside a person. Once we hit the next stretch of that drainage, everything turned to pure magic. We ascended a shallow valley on hard opaque ice dusted with an inch or two of fresh snow. The day was mild and the sun soon broke through puffy cumulus clouds. The dogs were clearly enjoying our passage through this new route; at every brief delay even Minnie was barking impatiently. I went up once to untangle Eagle's hind leg from his tugline, and his thick white tail pounded against my calf—*whop! whop! whop!*—while he literally quivered with eagerness. In the dog world, nothing spells happiness, willingness, and "count me in come hell or high water" like a wagging tail. I often wish that one of the Humane Society detractors of working dogs could stand on the runners behind a team of huskies on such a morning. The sense of fulfillment, of life's essence for the moment attained, is palpable. I often wonder how the most vocal and professional critics of dog mushing would spin such a moment, were they to be transplanted into it and at the same time grasp all that leads up to it. In that fantasy of mine I hope, probably naively, that they would not try to spin it at all, and that as they watched the team run a smile would slowly spread across their faces.

Soon we had reached Kirk Lake (named for one of the RCMP constables stationed at the old Reliance detachment), and the meandering creek opened out into a broad expanse of ice. A few caribou watched our passage across Kirk, and about four miles on we climbed gently out of a southwest bay toward Fletcher and the headwaters of the Hoarfrost. This was the spot where I had seen the little drainage marked on the map, showing that, at least in the mapmaker's opinion, Fletcher Lake drains both north and south. From what I could see that day it might be true, but probably only in rare periods of very high water. At 2 p.m. I paused on the northwest arm of Fletcher Lake. The sun was bright and the only wind was a breath of a breeze from the *south*, of all places. I sat there a long time, aware that such a day—in February, on the west-central Barrens—was a priceless gift. I had donned the snowshoes for only one short stretch of trail-making all morning, and soon we would rejoin our outbound track down the Hoarfrost and its lakes. The dogs snoozed contentedly in the sunshine, and I sat there with my little logbook open, pencil in hand. After a few minutes I folded it up and put it away, having written nothing. I thought of a passage from John Balzar's *Yukon Alone*, a book about the Yukon Quest race: "I ask myself, Are there words strong enough to convey the play of sunlight angling on all this vast, empty snowscape? Or words for the collision of the sun's marmalade rays against the white reflections of the snow? ... If there are such words I have not learned them."[10]

Late in the afternoon after crossing the two-mile neck of land between Fletcher Lake and Maufelly Bay, we arrived at the hut on Walmsley. The poetry of the day shifted to the prosaic tasks of digging a snow trench for the dogs, fooling with the stovepipe of the wood stove, and offloading gear from my sled. I intended to layover for a day at the hut, even though a part of me now was like a horse that has caught a whiff of the barn. It would be a challenge to avoid getting lost in thoughts of the future, as the steadily more-familiar miles rolled out downstream to the homestead.

At dawn I sat and peered out at the world through the building's wide south window. Puffy eyes, cotton mouth, a dull headache. This is common upon returning to a bed in a heated space after days spent sleeping in a tent in the cold. Outside it was 25 below, clear and calm. The wind had been gusting fitfully during the night, but nothing came of it. The day stretched ahead and I mused to my journal about time. That morning I found myself again in the contrary stance of the backcountry pragmatist:

> Time. It is all nice and fuzzy, that: "Go out in the wilderness and just let Time flow" or "let Time have no meaning" stuff, but in travelling between supply caches, or climbing a mountain, or paddling a long river in a short summer, Time takes on fundamental importance—it cannot be ignored. It is the approach of dusk at day's end, the looming onset of winter in mid-September, the final sack of feed rationed out to a hungry team. Like it or not, folks, the clock is ticking, even "way out here" in la-la land. Today, though, sitting just 75 miles from home, I am long on time. I can rest, and walk, and watch the day go by. Muir and Thoreau would be happy for me.

As I had done a year earlier at Richard's little hut on Whitefish, I rested and puttered and walked while the sun traced its arc through the southern sky, climbing a smidgen higher and taking a few minutes longer than it had the day before. I have passed many days at that little hut, and I have seen it in each month of the year, so my afternoon stroll felt like a tour around a familiar city block. Up on the esker top, fresh muskox tracks— a lone bull. Then down to the cove where we had once built a makeshift shelter for some big cedar-strip canoes we had stored there. More tracks, north along the flanks of the big esker, showed the comings and goings of all the usual cast of characters: fox, ptarmigan, and wolverine. I paused and sat down, looking northeast up the little chain of lakes which leads north from Maufelly Bay. What *is* it, I found myself asking, trying to delve deeper into my impressions of the day. Why was I here again, alone, after all these years? What the hell was I looking for, or hoping for, or expecting? Same esker, cold day, some tracks, a little breeze. Tonight the cramped, candlelit hut and its unpainted plywood walls, the lichen and moss on the doorsill growing thick after so many years.

Nothing came clear. I walked back to the dogs and the hut. The east wind was rising and I spent an hour or so digging out the dogs' north– south shelter trench. Almost as soon as I finished, the wind dropped off again. I did the evening chores and had another long sit against the west wall of the hut, watching the light fade from the sky and listening to the pings and clicks of the lake ice as it adjusted to the falling temperature.

After dinner I got through to Kristen on the radio, and she surprised me with her report that cloudy weather had prevailed at home through the past week, only 50 to 100 straight-line miles south of my travels. It was good to hear that all was well at home, but I felt a twinge of melancholy after switching off the radio. I felt stymied in my stilted, purposeful attempts to drive my thoughts deeper. I turned in for the night and read by candlelight until sleep came.

At four thirty in the morning something finally crystallized. It came to me as a single word: *interregnum*. It seems simplistic now, but for some reason, as I lay half awake in the pre-dawn darkness of the little hut, the word hit me with the strength of a revelation. In it there seemed to lie a new perspective, some way to make more sense out of my musings of the afternoon walk the day before. Here, in this odd word, was something I could latch onto. The *American Heritage Dictionary* defines *interregnum* as "1. The interval of time between the end of a sovereign's reign and the accession of a successor. 2. A period of temporary suspension of the usual functions of government or control. 3. A gap in continuity. [Latin: *inter–* + *regnum*, reign.]"

I was reading Fletcher's book *River* on that trip north. As he describes the mating flight of a cloud of mayflies, he muses on the scientific name for them: *Ephemeridae*. These insects, in their twenty-four hours as adults, do nothing but fly, mate, and die. "If you live only a day or two as an adult, you've got to get things moving," writes Fletcher. He finishes with this: "I stopped, turned, looked once more across the river at the rock wall, black behind its slanting sunbeam screen. A few tiny insects still danced their brief dance. But against the time scale of the background rock, was there really much difference between twenty-four hours and three score years and ten? Was there any difference at all?"[11] I had drifted off to sleep with his words in mind, mixed in with the austere, basically dreary impressions of my cold afternoon walk along the esker, and—oddly enough—some fleeting thoughts about my friend Tony Foliot, the self-proclaimed "Snow King."

Every winter, on the ice of Yellowknife Bay, Tony and a handful of helpers build an enormous snow castle—a huge multi-room snow-and-ice palace with a large theatre, big arched doorways, ice-plate windows, and a wide pavilion. Tourists and locals all stop and visit, and special events are scheduled at the castle in conjunction with the winter carnival. Every spring the entire elaborate structure melts away to nothing. (It is first physically knocked apart—liability issues, of course.) As I closed the book and blew out my candle, I had been thinking of Tony and his snow castle in light of our own brief stay (now twenty-seven years, as this goes off to press) at the mouth of the Hoarfrost River. I paraphrased Fletcher: "What difference is there, against the backdrop of a landscape scoured by Ice Age after Ice Age, between a castle made of snow and a little cluster of buildings made of logs?"

Interregnum. Tony's snow castle. My middle years, and our life—so focused and self-absorbed at times—at the little homestead down on McLeod Bay. I wrote that morning: "Cold is king. Winter *is* this country. Ice and snow set the limits and write the rules here. A brief window between glaciers is our life here, and everything is really just temporary and suspended, to be flattened at the start of the reign of the next King."

I dozed again until the first faint daylight brightened the hut's frosted windows, then swung my legs out of the bunk, stoked the wood stove and started to dress. A step out onto the little porch showed clear sky above and a solid wall of cloud to the south. Minus 27 degrees with a lively east wind. The dogs were all asleep, curled up and drifted over in their trench, and no one stirred at the sound of my footsteps on the porch. The wind had a nasty bite to it. *Interregnum all right,* I thought as I slammed the door behind me, *and that bitter wind is the crown prince, flexing his muscles, keeping in practice, just biding his time.*

Just before dismantling the radio that morning I had a second brief talk with Kristen, her voice happy and full of life. Afterwards I climbed up on the roof to take down the radio antenna and the stovepipe extension, jumped down and continued the process of boarding up the little building. Nailed a big shutter of plywood over the south window and smaller pieces over the little east and west portholes. I made a mental note to come repair the big window (cracked years earlier by an errant framing nail). After all, one of the great joys and contrasts of a cabin in winter, as compared to a tent, is the chance to sit in a warm place and look out at the world through a window. "Window glass must rank as one of the great unsung achievements of the human race," I told my journal.

Swept the floor, stored my leftover food and dog food on the bunk (presuming the grizzlies to be fast asleep in winter), and stacked fresh kindling by the stove. As I prepared to close the hut, I thought again how a land dotted with little shacks like that would be a dream come true for mushers, researchers, canoeists, and pilots. All on the honour system, all owned and maintained by everyone. I held the familiar thread of this thinking on to its familiar endpoint: such altruistic anarchy is probably hopeless in this day and age, under the current *regnum* of Canada's north.

Such a "system" would be ruined at the very moment it officially became a "system," either policed to death by zealous government overseers in Ottawa and Yellowknife, or driven to a dismal state of entropy, à la that miserable shack on the north end of Nonacho Lake.

The dogs were threatening to pull the hut right off its foundations by the time I loosed the snubline and we shot down onto the ice. The little brown square faded quickly to a dot over my left shoulder. I would see it again in just over a month, when at the end of a long day of route-finding it would loom up out of an April blizzard at a distance of a few hundred yards. I would be guiding two paying guests by then, and the hut would be in its glory—a safe haven in a storm.

With all my gear dry and the fuel supply topped up, I was looking forward to the day's trek. It would be a pleasure to camp in the tent again. Tent life in winter is at its finest when interspersed with overnight stops at heated shelters, big enough to throw down a sleeping bag, hang up a parka, and sit by a hot stove. Such periodic stops make a huge difference in the maintenance of dry sleeping bags and clothing, which then make the nights of tenting much more pleasant. Our stopovers at the Maufelly Bay hut both north- and southbound made me appreciate a fact often forgotten. In the days of the old, pre-airplane North, when *everything* moved at the speed of paddle stroke and dog trot, most travellers moved at a predictable pace along well-established routes. Overnight stops were often taken at trading posts, trapper's cabins, roadhouses, or traditional campsites, where some modicum of hospitality and support—dried fish for the dogs, a hot bowl of beans and meat for the musher—was the standard. In winter it was unusual to cover more than 40 miles in most parts of North America's boreal forest and taiga without arriving at a "fort," a post, a line cabin, or a Native encampment. That network of trails and stopover places is virtually gone now. The back country is, like the apt title of Dan O'Neill's 2006 book about the Yukon River, *A Land Gone Lonesome*. Gone is the delicious anticipation of a light in the window at the end of a long day. As for the prospect of a dogteam traveller stopping unannounced at the site of a modern mine, with its full-time security patrols and surveillance cameras, I can imagine all too well the ensuing Orwellian nightmare.

I took a new route down Walmsley that day, and it gave me a chance to do some careful map reading and navigation. The passage was pleasant and uneventful in a way that I was beginning to take for granted on that trip. The snow was surprisingly soft and fluffy, amazing in a part of the country where I had never seen anything but carved sastrugi hard as oak.

In mid-afternoon we crossed the trails of two caribou, fresh in the powder, but I never saw them and the dogs did not seem to think the scent was fresh. As we moved south on the overland route between Walmsley and Cook Lakes, the snow changed perceptibly. The wind had evidently blown much harder there in recent days than it had farther north. This realization fed into a larger theme that was emerging for me those days— that being our tendency to view "the weather" in big, definite blocks: windy here, warm there, snowy or rainy there. We all tend to forget that weather is intimately and fundamentally *local*. There is no weather *here*— no matter where *here* is—that is precisely the same as at any other *here,* even only a few hundred feet away. All is change, subtle shifts, microcosm, and nearly imperceptible gradations. To find the snow becoming *more* wind-packed as we moved south toward the treeline that day was a good reminder not to rely on any broad preconceived notions.

The flip side of this minute local variation is represented by the weather maps churned out every six hours by the computers of Environment Canada. Those are miraculous accomplishments considering their scale and pace—and their accuracy. For 29 February, the day we travelled south from Walmsley, the map shows a big *H* centred over Great Bear Lake, drifting south-southeast at five knots. The isobars of equal air pressure are widely spaced around it, like contour lines on a map of a broad hilltop. The notation in the vast area dominated by the high is simply SKC, for sky clear. It is the kind of weather map that puts a smile on a pilot's face. For me and the dogs, cruising into the sunshine that afternoon, that big dome of high-pressure air meant blue skies, light winds, and cold air.

Once we rejoined the Hoarfrost north of Cook Lake I was back on familiar terrain. The trip had again come into the home stretch, but I was not feeling nearly so battered and desperate as in the previous two years. We were in the groove, moving in rhythm, the dogs and I—no one was suffering and the gear was all holding up. Like Will had said, we were "mushing the rosary" that afternoon. The journey had become its own world, and its self-absorbed theme of packing up and moving on had generated that long-bus-ride state of mind that wanted to go on forever. We camped that night alongside the rapids at the Hoarfrost just above Cook Lake. A stand of ancient thick-trunked spruce, along with a few birch and tamarack, line the steep bank where the snow edge drops straight off into the black surge of the river. After many nights of melting snow for our water, I could creep cautiously to that black-and-white edge and dip sweet-tasting water straight from the river into the cooking pots. The dogs were tired and seemed happy. They knew where we were, and where we were headed, and I think they liked the sight of that little clump of forest.

I sat up late that night in the tent, writing, reading, and figuring. The GPS was in its glory again that evening, and my notes start with a laundry list of numbers: coordinates in degrees and minutes out to a ludicrous three places beyond the decimal; distances to various other locations; projected times of sunrise and sunset. I was fascinated with the subtle daily changes of sunrise and sunset times—not the precise times so much as the trends as we moved north and south, east and west, and every day closer to the spring equinox.

From my journal: "Good to be on the Hoarfrost again—I am ready for company, companionship, hugs from the girls and all the pleasures of reunion. Solitude can be rich, but I have to admit that it is ultimately unfulfilling. It is a state of mind best appreciated as a contrast to everyday life, or as a small dose of a day within the daily round."

It was Saturday night, and it was the Saturday of the start of the Iditarod race. I thought of the race, and the mushers I knew who would be on the trail to Nome. I recalled a long night in 1992, about halfway to Nome on the race trail between Cripple and Ruby, when I had thought I might not see morning. While cooking broth for my team at a trailside stop in late afternoon, my mind fogged by lack of sleep, I had carelessly sipped some water which had been tainted by raw beaver meat. (Beaver meat is one of the all-time favourite race snacks of long-distance sled dogs, so irresistible to the dogs and so packed with calories that mushers call it "the crack cocaine of the Iditarod trail.") Less than two hours later I was trembling in my sleeping bag beside the trail, in a wretched state of exhausted delirium. Foul liquids spewed at frequent intervals from both ends of my digestive tract. The night was cold and—this being the race trail—other dogteams and mushers were passing me one at a time as the hours wore on. I would hear the soft *chuff-chuff-chuff* of an approaching team, and now and then someone would pause and shout, "Are you all right?"

"Yeah. I think so. Thanks."

The night passed, and I lived. It was a close call, probably with salmonella poisoning or something slightly less deadly. Thinking back to it from my snug tent twelve years later, I wrote: "The race was more difficult, in almost every way, than what the dogs and I are doing now. The lack of sleep, in particular, pushes mushers and dogs into a bizarre state of mind. Now, in deference to all those friends and comrades who are starting down the Iditarod Trail—who will not enjoy a solid sleep for the next 10 or 15 nights—I think I'll turn in!"

In the dark at 5 a.m., I laid awake a while thinking about the long view, the view which geologists must master. Like astronomers, they grapple with expanses of time far beyond the day-to-day realm of our brief human lives. As a bush pilot, I work with geologists often and I marvel at this perspective on time that they carry in their heads. Yet they are themselves human, and just as caught up in human affairs and moments as the rest of us. Who, I wondered, could possibly hold in sharp focus the span of a *million* years, while watching a four-year-old girl eat her breakfast, bright sunlight streaming in on her smiling face? We can look down the row of a few generations into the future, if we try hard, but beyond that it all fades into mist or flows out of sight beneath ice, like the river that morning above Cook Lake. Looking *upstream* from ourselves seems a little easier, for we can muster names and faces, and put our ancestors in specific places and into the context of the recorded events of human history. But a million years, ten million, a billion, for God's sake! Who are these people, I wondered, who can so glibly talk (and even train their minds to think) in such terms? Any serious effort to think about the span of a million years leaves me stupefied and short of breath. Little wonder that some people find solace in the belief that the Bible records all of history, that it is about six thousand years in total, and that everyone's father and mother can be traced by "begats" right back to good old Adam and Eve.

I rolled over and snuggled the cold tip of my nose into the musty warm dampness of the sleeping bag hood. Still sleep would not come back. Maybe we would be home tomorrow. Maybe our beautiful star would burn a thousand or a million years longer. Finally sleep washed back over me.

Morning, 1 March again. A year ago on this date we had been out on the Barrens, having a visit from the wolves at 40 below zero. Two years back we were alongside the Snowdrift, setting off for the cache at Noman. This time around it was the upper Hoarfrost, the moon setting in the northwest, the river chuckling and gurgling in the dawn. "It is about 37 below. The big four-oh has missed us again," I wrote. "We might make the whole trip without seeing it!" Sky clear, dogs quiet, about 50 miles to home sweet home. At seven forty sunlight struck the campsite. I was out dipping water from the river, crouched gingerly on the lip of the cornice alongside the rapids. I paused to watch the sun light up the world. The dogs were all curled up—all except Steve. As soon as I came out from the tent that day Steve stood, stretched, and fixed me with a stare as if to say, "Well, what's the plan—are we going to just sit here all damned morning?"

"What a dog," I wrote when I came in from the cold with the water. What a dog indeed. If a musher is lucky, he or she is endowed with just a few dogs like Steve in an entire lifetime on the sled runners.

By mid-morning Steve had his wish and we were under way and moving south. We came onto Cook Lake by making an overland hop, a shortcut to the lake's northeast arm. I was immediately surprised to find the lake's surface there windblown and hard, and as the dogs sped along with such good footing I began to wonder if the trip might end without another night on the trail. I tucked that thought away—we were still 44 miles out and heading south into the forest, where there would likely be nothing left of our outbound track.

Early afternoon. Still moving quickly and steadily south. By then we were on the wide stretch of the Hoarfrost below Cook Lake. Delicate brushstrokes of cirrostratus had appeared in the sky, smooth undulations suggesting powerful winds aloft. A dense haze of ice crystals closed briefly around us, instantly reducing visibility to less than a mile, then lifting and vanishing as quickly as it had come. Something was changing. I stopped briefly at our old autumn fishing camp, where in September 1993 my friend Mitch and I had worked for a month, netting and hanging fish for dog food. We had built the cache from spruce poles and perched it 12 feet high on the thickest poles that the scrawny taiga forest offered. Unfortunately, we had at that time not yet appreciated the rot-resistant superiority of tamarack (*Larix laricina*) over any of the species of spruce. A decade later all four of the cache's support poles rotted through at their base, and it only took a big storm to bring the entire structure crashing down to the tundra. The little peak-roofed cache itself somehow survived the fall, and now it sits on the knoll like a troll's log cabin.

I paused to pick up the skis I had jettisoned there on my way north, and as we left I looked at my watch. It was only two forty in the afternoon. *Wow*, I thought, *they just might bring us all the way in*. On training runs up and back to that site in years past, it was traditionally a three-hour run, 27 miles, back home from the fish camp. It would all depend on the trail ahead, or the lack of one.

I tried all that day to stay focused on the here and now of my journey, but as we came down the Hoarfrost toward home I could not. Those miles, so much a part of our backyard, held such an array of remembered events and images that I kept slipping into reverie. Canoe trips, fish netting, friends around campfires, training runs in darkness, our children as infants and toddlers...That little thread of trail cuts a huge swath through my life. The million-year view still eluded me, but I had been stubborn and lucky enough to have been granted my own long view, from decades lived with a commitment to this one little watershed. Beginning with my arrival as a naive immigrant, my life and viewpoint had slowly evolved, and was still evolving. Now I had lived here longer than I had lived anywhere else, and the landscape was becoming a montage, a scrapbook turning its pages around each fold of the hills.

As we climbed over the quarter-mile portage between Louison and Hatchet Lakes the lowering sun was layering rich late-afternoon light on everything it touched. I watched it play on Dandy's shimmer of thick cream-coloured fur, pulsing over the ripples of hard muscle in his hindquarters. His head was down and his tugline was, as usual, taut as a bowstring. He was in his glory, plowing through the soft snow. The moon was up, there was wind from the north, and the sun was a perfect gold circle in the west-southwest. The temperature was starting down. Suddenly, I looked up from my admiration of Dandy to see a huge red-tailed transcontinental jet, a 747 or an Airbus or something of that size, sparkling in the sun directly overhead. By some quirk of high-altitude physics, it left not even a wisp of contrail that afternoon, and it looked as if it was suspended there. A second or two passed before its roar came down to us, crackling sharply as sounds do in frigid air. *Next stop: Tokyo,* I thought. A few minutes later another huge liner appeared on precisely the same track, its paint scheme exactly the same. A moment or two looking ahead at the dogs and the narrow trail, watching Dandy and Minnie forge ahead in their element, and when I looked up again the jets were out of sight.

I remembered a passage from another Colin Fletcher book, *The Man Who Walked Through Time,* about his solo walk through the Grand Canyon. On a quiet day deep in the canyon he was suddenly buzzed by two low-level fighter jets, and in retrospect he wrote, "I knew exactly what I should have been feeling. I should have been deploring with self-righteous fervor what these two pilots had done...They had shattered the silence. My silence. Yes, I should have been deploring all right. Instead all I could feel was admiration. Admiration for their skill, their damned-fool daring, and their courage. And that, whether I liked it or not, was no disturbance. Rather the reverse, in fact."[12]

The contrast of Dandy's haunches, trembling with the effort of his work, and the two jets hanging seven miles above us, roaring toward Asia, left me once again in agreement with Mr. Fletcher. I was not offended, and although I have no infatuation with airline travel I was not feeling cynical. *What a world we live in,* was all I could think that afternoon.

By the time those two jets were nearing the airspace over Anchorage we had reached the northeast tip of Windy Lake, only 16 miles from home. It was just past five in the afternoon. Decision time: if we were going to make camp in daylight it was time to pull over and get started. The snow on the lakes ahead was going to be soft. I had tried the skis, in an effort to take my weight off the sled runners, but my latest version of mukluk-friendly ski bindings had proven to be just another in a long string of failures. If we carried on through the evening the dogs and the sled would be plowing, and I would be jogging. Obviously no one had been up this way in well over a week, and probably not since our outbound trip. (Once home, I learned that Kristen had laid plans to come northeast the next day, to lay a trail for our return. What a welcome sight that would have been! But we were coming down those final miles sooner than she expected.)

I decided to put the question to the dogs, at least in jest. "Well, ladies and gentlemen, what'll it be? Four hours slogging to a hot meal and wooden houses full of straw, or another camp-out and home tomorrow?" Steve, Ernie, B.J., and Dandy seemed firmly in the "Go" faction. Fipke, Flynn, and Minnie—all three of them plump and decked out with coats like muskox wool—seemed to be voting "Camp." Jasmine, Foxtail, and Schooner were, as near as I could tell, ambivalent and abstaining from the vote. I was on the fence myself. The moon would be up and it would be a cold clear evening. The lure of those lights in the windows at home, those faces and that warm bed, partly dispelled the unpleasant prospect of trudging down Windy, Long, Pistol, Brinkley, and Dietz Lakes. If the homestead had been dark and cold, as in the past two years' returns, we would have made camp. But there was warmth and light down there, a bed and a wife and children...

"All right gang, let's do it."

Minnie was not a poster husky for sled-dog enthusiasm at that moment. At the sound of my voice everyone else rose and leaned dutifully into the traces. As I shouldered the sled into a lurching start Minnie grudgingly came to her feet, dragging on her neckline to make her point clear to everyone. A few dozen yards down the lake, her tugline was tight. "Working for these wages," I chuckled to myself, imagining her thoughts, "and now he wants overtime. Criminy sake... where's my hotline to the SPCA?"

The trip ended as it had begun, in darkness on the most familiar trails of all. My headlamp with its alkaline D cells was useless in the minus-35-degree cold. After a momentary trial on Pistol Lake, I realized I would have to save it for a brief flash of assistance in an emergency. I stuffed the battery pack deep in the pocket of my innermost sweater, to give the batteries a fighting chance should I need them, and carried on by moonlight.

I will not forget that last descent, after crossing the river below Lacy Falls and climbing the hill north of home. By then the moon was high and bright, the trail was like a luge run, and the dogs knew full well that supper and straw-filled doghouses were mere minutes away. Our home is cradled in a bowl beneath a towering rock bluff, and that night the moonlight filled the bowl to the brim. The team tore down a series of swooping S-curves, and then we were in sight of the house and the glow of its lights. The dogs in the yard set up a loud ruckus as I hooked down alongside the cabin. It was 9:30 p.m. Four-year-old Liv was already sound asleep and eight-year-old Annika nearly so.

I could not tell precisely what Kristen thought of our unexpected arrival at that hour, but she quickly rose to the occasion as best she could. Ken walked over from the guest cabin, thinking there must be a dogfight or a loose dog causing all the commotion. He obliged my request to snap a few photos, shook my hand, and ambled away into the night. Kristen and Annika helped me put the team back in the yard and fed them a rich stew of fish, rice, fat, and kibble. We walked back up to the house and by eleven o'clock the entire place was dark. We were Home.

That year, with the household in full swing, it took only a day or so for me to shift gears and take up with our winter routines. The trip quickly faded into the demands of everyday life. There was wood to cut, a broken sled to repair, water to haul, and the chainsaw to sharpen. Home-school, laundry, kitchen tasks and dog chores filled the days from before dawn until after dusk. Very soon—much sooner than in the past two years—my simple and selfish life on the trail was a distant memory.

For forty-eight hours straight, beginning the morning after our return home, the wind screamed brutally out of the west-northwest. The temperature dropped to nearly minus 40 degrees, driving the wind chill to some absurd figure. The old man I had imagined in the Weather Control Centre had clearly got the news: the wandering fool and his skinny dogs were off the Barrens. He had given the word and someone had thrown the lever back to "normal." I watched our windmill furl and sway in the 30-knot gusts, generating more power than we could possibly use, and I was glad we were not hunkered down on the blank white shoreline of Aylmer Lake. By dumb luck or mysterious fate, we had been granted quite a reprieve, a little interregnum of our own.

One more year. Ever since I had conceived this cycle of four journeys, the trip north had loomed as the most obvious and intimidating test of our mettle. Instead, by sheer dumb luck, it had been a pleasant and con-templative two-week outing, long on introspection and short on despera-tion. All that was left now to complete the circle of the compass was a journey west, out across the big lake and back.

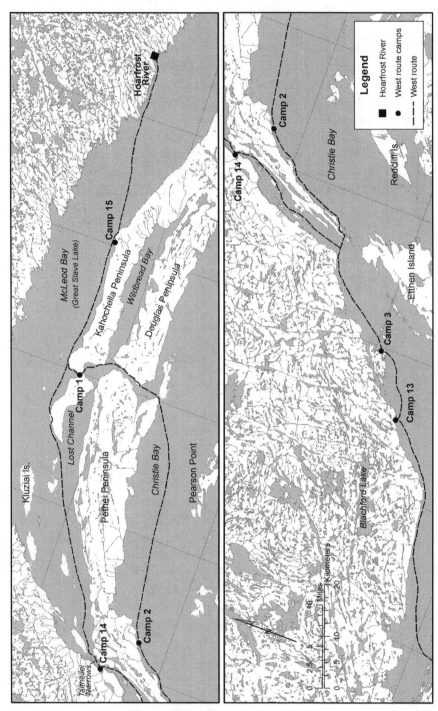

West 2005

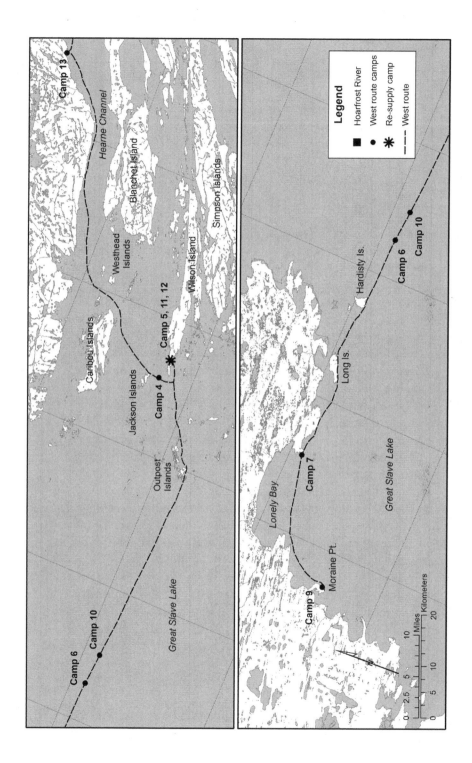

West

Sixteen days, 11–26 March 2005
Hoarfrost River to west shore of Great Slave Lake, and return: about 510 miles
Eleven dogs, one resupply cache

March 11th, Day 1. Shelter Bay portage. Nearly midnight. –28°,
clear, wind from east, gusting and eddying here in the lee of the big
headlands.

Back out on the trail. The going, the setting off—it's always the
hard part. This year, of course, the trip is tinged by the awareness
that this is it—this will complete the cycle. The compass has swung
around to its fourth and final cardinal point.

Pulled the hook in late afternoon, after goodbyes at home.
Came 5¹/₂ hours non-stop and arrived here in full darkness at
about 8:30 p.m. We are 40 miles out.

A wolf is howling from very close to camp. The dogs have
answered twice, and have settled down to sleep again now. Every
few minutes the wolf howls again. My boys (and two spayed girls
this time out) are too tired to keep up their end of the conversation. Me too...

I was glad to be away again. It had not been easy. On the home front
my departures became more difficult year by year. They were less frantic
and more matter of fact on one level, but they were fraught with increasing layers of complexity relative to our family life, my paid work, and our
various schedules. A block of time set aside for the long solo trips had
gradually become a part of our winter routine, part of the annual round
much as the running of the Iditarod had been for us a decade earlier. Year
by year the packing up, the setting out, the run, and the return. And—
like the Iditarod—the commitment to these four long trips could, I had
written earlier that winter, "all appear silly and quixotic, and certainly
unprofitable, when held up in a purely practical light. Kind of like my
whole life..."

This west trip had run up against so many other conflicts on the
Hoarfrost River dance card that it became, on the calendar, the latest of

the four journeys. It would even lap over into spring, past the equinox, although in the Northwest Territories it is far-fetched to claim that spring actually begins on the 21st of March. In the second half of February we had hosted a two-week course with students and professors from Alberta. Then, to make sure the trip west took place, I had turned down a lucrative and appealing stint of flying work. That decision had cost Kristen and me some money and some sleepless nights.[1]

It all boiled down to this: it was the night of March 11th and I was on my way west. The resupply cache was in place 150 miles out on Wilson Island, and I had a solid team of eleven dogs to drive. As I drifted off to sleep just past midnight at that first campsite, I was confident that our decision would prove out. Some things in life are not measured in dollars, and no one ever claimed that life in the outback was the road to monetary wealth. We had more guiding and homestead work ahead in April, and we would take our chances on what came along for paid work beyond that.

My journey west was not to be precisely 270 degrees true, due west, just as the other trips had not been strictly north, south, or east. A course held straight west from the Hoarfrost would first have traced a chord across the arc of McLeod Bay, then climbed steeply into broken hill-and-lake country north of Taltheilei Narrows. Within about 50 miles I would have been off the ice, climbing into terrain similar to what I had traversed on my trip south three years earlier. Across the west-central portion of arctic and subarctic North America, it is a fact of climate and ecosystems that to go west is in many ways the same as going south. The divide between tundra and forest, the tree line, crosses the continent in a giant V, with the apex of the V far south along the shores of James Bay in Ontario, and the tips along the seacoasts of the Yukon and northern Labrador. Even with almost no change in latitude, a long journey west and southwest is a dramatic step away from our home on the edge of the tundra.

Great Slave Lake is the fifth-largest lake in North America. Only ten lakes in the world are bigger. Like its siblings Great Bear, Huron, Michigan, and Superior, it can without hyperbole live up to the label "freshwater sea." Its odd name does not refer to slavery—although around our homestead there have been occasional remarks about such a derivation during days of hard labour. The *slave* derives from the language of the Slavey people, an Athapascan Dene band whose territory includes the lake's southwest shore and its outflow down the Mackenzie River. Two hundred years ago it was literally "The Great Lake of the Slaveys," then in French "Grand Lac des Esclaves" and now, unfortunately, it is "Great Slave." If any place name in North America could benefit from a change, surely the big lake is one of them.[2]

View from the cockpit of the Aviat Husky, westbound to set the resupply cache at Wilson Island. Tip of Wilson is in centre of frame, in the distance.

The lake's shape is often likened to a flying goose, wings lifted in mid-flight and only the silhouette of the head and body outlined. The goose is eastbound and about 275 miles from beak to tail. From full round belly west-southwest, to scrawny neck east-northeast, the lake's character varies dramatically. At the neck and head Great Slave forms three parallel fjord-like bays, pushed up against the rocky margin of the taiga: Christie, Wildbread, and McLeod. In its wide basin to the south and southwest, 200 miles from the Hoarfrost River, it is an immense expanse of brown shallow water bordered by low shorelines of poplar, pine, and alder. That goose-belly of the lake stretching west and south from the Simpson Islands, across to the lake's outflow down the Mackenzie River, was all unfamiliar to me as I headed toward it with my dogs.

The first night's non-stop run of 40 miles was a far cry from our axe-blazed snowshoe climb up the McDonald Fault, four years earlier. For the dogs and me, it was clear from the beginning that the route west would be a trip of *running,* with few of the pauses for navigation and trail-breaking that broke up the miles of the other journeys. As we set off on that March evening the snow-covered lake ice was in perfect condition for sledding, and the dogs were fit and strong after two weeks on the trail with the university students. That long gallop into twilight and darkness was a dramatic send-off. The lake surface was stippled with hard snowdrifts and the dogs were insanely eager. I could not let my attention stray for an instant until we had covered the first 20 miles. The sky was clear, and as darkness fell Orion stepped into view over the thousand-foot rise of the Kahochella Peninsula. A gusty east wind pushed us from behind. The sled skittered and fishtailed on big patches of bare ice at Sentinel Point, and I hung on like a skater in a dog-powered version of crack the whip.

Sadly, I lost several small treasures to the wind on that first night's run—little bits of paper surreptitiously tucked into my beaver-fur mitten just before I left the dog yard at home. They were farewell notes from Annika and Liv, ages nine and six, which they had hidden there as a surprise. As I lifted my mitts out of the sled bag a few minutes after leaving home, I just glimpsed the little folded-up notes as they were carried away on the wind. In a split second they were gone forever down the lake.

Three hours out, as full darkness came on, I could almost hear the dogs muttering, "Huh? What's this all about?" Ernie winded himself, a victim of his own insatiable eagerness, and he "hit the wall" aerobically at almost precisely 26 miles—a marathon's distance down the bay. I paused to shift him back out of lead. Steve, older and slightly wiser, stepped up to lead us the rest of the way to camp. Ernie wobbled along in the team for a few minutes before finding his stride again. Stolid Fipke, at age nine, was the crusty old-timer of the dogteam. He finished the evening looking a little shell-shocked by the five-and-a-half-hour blitz.

At Shelter Bay we climbed off the ice and camped smack dab on the southbound portage trail. In a place where I might expect overnight traffic this is something I would not consider doing, for obvious reasons, but on that night it was an appealing option. The packed trail greatly eased the effort of making camp in the dark. Someone on a wide-tracked snowmobile towing a toboggan had recently gone over the portage. A few days before my departure, I had flown past and spotted a snowmobile heading north from Wildbread Bay, so I knew that the portage trail was broken open for us.

I had a niggle of concern about starting with such a long and fast run, non-stop to the first good camping spot on that south shore. I hoped I hadn't taken too much out of the dogs. As I ladled out their supper, I was happy to see that they all devoured it. If a dog is overly tired or footsore or lame, a lack of appetite is one of the obvious clues. On long races even the most eager eaters can turn finicky. This in turn leads to some comical scenes at checkpoints, with sleepy, half-frozen mushers laying out exorbitant buffets for tired dogs: lamb strips, chunks of warmed turkey skin, cubes of beaver tail, ground caribou meat, glycogen powders, broths

baited with a few drops of anise...the list goes on. After many years of
that kind of competitive menu-making, I still get a real thrill when the
dogs just attack a big helping of simple chow without coercion or coaxing.

Dawn came remarkably early—we were nearly a month later than my
previous solos, so this trip would be blessed with abundant daylight. The
sky was clear, the air was calm, and the temperature was 34 degrees below
zero. The tent was already brightly lit at 7 a.m. With the stove going I
wrote for a few minutes, ate the usual skillet of bacon followed by a bowl
of granola, hot milk, and raisins, and went out to give the dogs their
breakfast. We were on the trail early, climbing due south into the sun.
I paused to photograph the striking natural silhouette of a human face,
visible from just the right angle in the cliffs alongside the portage. The
team, barking and hammering at their tuglines, nearly pulled away on
me as I struggled to stow the camera back inside my big parka.

The mile-long portage south from Shelter Bay is one of the only breaks
in the precipitous south shore of McLeod Bay, and it must have been fre-
quently used in the era of canoe travel. Nowadays it sees very little summer traffic, because the overland crossing is too long and rugged for the
hauling of a big outboard motor, fuel, gear, and an aluminum runabout.
Around Gibraltar Point ten miles to the west, and cutting back east again
to Lost Channel, boaters come to a spruce-pole skidway or "corduroy
road" that has been in place for many decades. There is no mechanization
there, but small boats and motors can be dragged across by people power
from Wildbread Bay into McLeod Bay. In recent years even this skidway
at Lost Channel is falling out of use, since many of the locals now own
cruising boats so large that portaging them overland is out of the question. In order to travel from Lutsel K'e to McLeod Bay, these bigger ves-
sels must go west around Utsingi Point, then up through the narrows at
Taltheilei, adding 50 miles to the voyage.

Coming down off the portage, the track we were following continued
south and led into the upper reaches of a narrows called The Gap. I knew
this was a treacherous passage. A steady deep current flows through this
strait—the water of Wildbread Bay flowing south to join the immense
depths of Christie Bay. One telltale warning of questionable ice is this:
beware of any area that is noticeably slow to freeze over in autumn and,
conversely, quick to thaw come spring. This happens in The Gap, as it
does at Taltheilei Narrows, Utsingi Point, the narrows at Reliance, and the
mouth of some incoming creeks and rivers. I had never driven a dogteam
down The Gap. I knew that a recent week of mild weather had already

Kaltag (left) and Ernie (right) screamed their impatience as I paused to snap their portrait in The Gap.

started to erode the winter ice. Even with that week-old snow-machine track to guide me, I was nervous. It was no day for a swim.

The trail angled across to the east shore and hugged the alders there for a mile, never more than a few feet off the land. The lead dogs, Ernie and Kaltag, stuck to the trail and only once tried to cut a corner. I called them back with a sharp and somewhat nervous-sounding "Haw!" Little by little my fears eased. After all, it was a gorgeous morning to be out—sunny, cold, and crystal clear. Spring and open water were still at least a month away, even there in the narrows. By noon we had emerged from the south throat of The Gap and the trail scooted diagonally across to the west shore. Again I took its cue—whoever had made the trail was no passing tourist but someone with a lifelong knowledge of the danger spots in that passage. Opposite Fortress Island we drew up alongside a wall of smooth chocolate-brown rock, swirled and convoluted by unimaginable pressures, strikingly different from any of the rock formations around home. For the thousandth time in my life I wished I knew more about geology. Somewhere in that area, I had heard, is a world-famous showing of two-billion-year-old fossilized blue-green algae called stromatolites.[3] A rock hound and lifelong denizen of the East Arm, Dave Smith, had some-how hoisted a two-ton chunk of this rock onto his freighting barge one summer. He had then propped it up alongside his house in Yellowknife, where it sits for all to see.

Christie Bay opened out before us. To underscore the size of that part of the lake, to the southwest the horizon was simply ice and sky—no land in sight. Christie is a bigger bay than McLeod, and similarly named for an early-1800s British, Scottish, or Métis functionary of the fur trade. On its southeast shore is the settlement of Lutsel K'e, which until the 1990s was named Snowdrift. There the Snowdrift River, which I had travelled on the trip south three years earlier, flows into Great Slave Lake. I con-tinued to follow the snowmobile track south onto the open bay. I knew it was headed straight into Lutsel K'e, and I was not. I would have to turn the team west off the trail at some point, and I spent the next half-mile trying to make some calculations: our rapid progress southwest on the good trail, versus our slower speed on a direct course west once I decided to make the turn. Suddenly the trail-maker appeared in person, rapidly closing on us from the direction of Lutsel K'e. It was Alfred Lockhart astride his bright red snow machine, towing a load lashed tightly to a long oak toboggan. He zoomed up to us in such a flash that he must have been making nearly 50 miles an hour. Denizens of the North seem to utilize only two throttle settings when at the helm of either a motorboat or a snowmobile: Off and Wide Open.

Alfred smiled and waved, and my lead dogs leaped to one side of the track as he roared past just a few inches from them. He stopped alongside my sled and I kicked the snow hook in. The dogs took turns shying and barking as we made our way through a brief chat. Stilted though it looks on the printed page, as near as I recall the dialogue proceeded as follows:

"Hey Alfred. Nice trail."

"Yeah. I figured it was you. Where you goin'?"

"West. I'm out on my winter trip again. I've got a cache at Wilson Island."

"Wilson Island. You gotta watch the ice aroun' there—bad currents there."

"Okay, good. I will. You headin' to McLeod Bay again?"

"Yeah. I got some wolverine traps up on the north shore. I got a tent up there this winter. Lotsa caribou close to there now."

"Was that you that drove up through The Gap a few days ago in that warm weather?"

"Yeah, I did. Slushy, boy. I just drive *really* fast through that part. I just give 'er!"

"Well it seems like it's all good today. We just came down through there. We camped at Shelter Bay last night. Heard a wolf there."

"Yeah. I left a caribou there. It had those little white dots in the meat. When you comin' back?"

"About two weeks. But I'll go up through Taltheilei on my way home I think."

"Yeah. Well. Okay. Long trip. Well. See you!"

"Wait, Alfred. Lemme take your picture—you mind?"

"Oh, I don' care. Sure."

"Okay. Here, just a sec. Okay, now smile and say 'Bikini!'"

I almost burst out laughing at the perplexed expression that flashed across Alfred's handsome dark face as he softly muttered "bikini." I could almost hear him thinking, *What a strange duck this one is.* I waved as he hit the starter on the snow machine and roared away, throttle pegged: Wide Open. The sound of the engine faded and was muffled further as I buttoned the flap of my thick hat under my chin.

Mental gears switched back into S for Solitude. *Well. Brief interlude of pleasant chit-chat. So. Where were we?* Back to my decision about where to abandon the hardpacked trail. The dogs settled into their steady pace again. I decided to stay on Alfred's track for another mile or two.

I thought about Alfred. It was Alfred I had seen on Charlton Bay on the final day of my trip south, three years earlier. Then too he had been alone, heading out and far from town—competent, confident, all smiles.

I had seen him at other times, in town and up on caribou-survey jobs around the diamond mines, but never did he look so self-possessed, sharp, and at ease as when he was out in winter, hunting and trapping. One of a dying breed: a clichéd phrase, that one, and fraught with patronizing undertones, but it applies. Little by little, funeral by funeral, the North is losing that generation. Whether anyone wants to admit this or not, the Alfreds are an endangered species. The next generation of northern Natives is not making its forays out on the land in the savvy, low-key way that puts such a smile on Alfred's face. The attention of the next generation of his people—born in the mid-1970s and beyond—is quite plainly elsewhere: employment, technology, and consumption. Trips into the backcountry are fewer and less wide-ranging, and old routes are being forgotten. There is much hand-wringing—and much spending—being devoted to addressing, reversing, or simply discussing this obvious and unavoidable demographic shift. The plain fact remaining is that there are not many Alfreds left. Forty years from now there will be none.

———————

Jerking myself out of such musings, on a sudden impulse I called a sharp "Gee!" to the dogs. Without a moment's hesitation Ernie and Kaltag left Alfred's trail and turned west onto unbroken snow. I smiled. What dogs! I would miss this annual outing alone with them, and I was convinced that they would miss it too. Out ahead of us were only snow, ice, and sky. To our right rose the sloping south side of the Pethei Peninsula and to the left the darkly forested shoreline around Lutsel K'e. *No town visit for us today*, I thought.

The snow was firm enough to give us a seven-mile-an-hour cruising speed. It would be a 35- or 40-mile day if the conditions stayed so perfect. Miles. Hours. A lunch stop in bright sunshine. I could tell it was March and not February—the thermometer sitting in direct sunshine read plus 4 degrees, and when shifted into shade a mere two inches away it showed minus 11. I was still enjoying some bison jerky left with us by the Steger expedition a year earlier. Packed in my lunch bag with other goodies I was surprised and delighted to discover a note Kristen had tucked there. Surprised because I had thought that all the farewell notes had been plucked away by the wind the night before.

"Dear husband—your final compass-point trip. Please ENJOY every moment—good and bad, challenging, mundane. Remember what Oscar said to his horse Spook on the narrow trail: 'Now we wouldn't want to get bored, would we Spook?'[4] I love you—I am proud of what you are doing. I look forward to your safe return..."

I sat there and smiled, reading and rereading her note. Worries about missing that big chunk of paid work slid back into proper perspective. I looked at the dogs and decided we would sit there until Dandy woke up from his nap. A lone raven gave us a slow fly-by and landed on the ice just south of the sled, where it repeated a three-caw pattern, over and over. Five minutes passed. Dandy opened his eyes, stood up, peed non-stop for at least twenty seconds, and then looked directly at me. A question was written all over his face: "Well? Are we leaving soon, or shall I go back to sleep?"

"Okay, Dandolph, we'll call it a lunch." I hooked up harness toggles, pulled the aluminum picket out of the packed snow at the front of the team, kicked the snow hook free, and softly said "All right." Beautiful, silent acceleration as every tugline came tight. It wasn't at all like putting thumb to throttle—it was far more elegant than that. Wide open.

Clouds were moving in from the west-southwest. It was nearly four in the afternoon. In that next half hour we passed over the very deepest part of the lake. In fact the depths of Christie Bay in Great Slave Lake are, at 2,014 feet, the deepest fresh water in the entire western hemisphere. Only the tiny water-filled volcano at Crater Lake in Oregon comes close at 1,946 feet. (Lake Superior's maximum depth is just over 1,300 feet.)

As we passed over what I reckoned to be the precise location of that deepest sounding, I stopped. This was something I had looked forward to—a chance to stand there on three or four feet of ice, 512 feet above sea level, and more than 2,000 feet above terra firma. The ice in that spot was free of snow, its top surface polished smooth by four months of wind. It was a window 40 inches thick, looking down on utter blackness. Like all the ice on the lake, the plate there was fractured with a spiderweb of cracks running at haphazard angles, reminiscent of a pickup-truck windshield in gravel-road country. Dividing sky above from depths below, that 40 inches was the merest of membranes. Yet there I stood solid and at ease, and upon that thin membrane the dogs and I would make virtually all of the 500-some miles of this western trip. I tried to be appropriately astounded at this, but I could only conclude that the mere act of standing on ice above incredibly deep water had long ago lost its ability to amaze me.

For just a moment I captured a feeling of peering downward into the vastness of inner space. I tried to imagine standing on the edge of a 2,000-foot precipice in the mountains, but that alpine image would not stick. It was more like peering into the mouth of a black cave than over the edge of a cliff. I wondered what was down there, so impossibly far below us in that liquid darkness. "Silt and rock, I suppose," I said aloud to the dogs. That broke the brief pause. At the sound of my voice somebody—almost certainly Eagle—gave a quick series of impatient yanks on the gangline. "Okay," I told him. "We'll go." I snapped a couple of photographs and we set off again.

By that evening, the close of day two, we had come about 30 miles from Shelter Bay. A layer of altostratus cloud had moved in, and the temperature was a pleasant minus 20 degrees. From our camp on the south coast of the Pethei Peninsula I could see the lights of Lutsel K'e, population about 320 souls, twinkling in the distance. There were not many lights, but there was movement among them as snow machines and the occasional pickup truck drove up and down the streets of the little town. On the high bluff just south of the airstrip a strobe beacon flashed a warning to incoming aircraft.

"Lutsel K'e on a Monday night...it can look quite cozy from the right distance. As Maupassant wrote, 'There's nothing prettier than the lights of a town seen from the sea.'"[5] I did not write much that evening, and what I did manage ended in a sleepy and illegible scrawl down the page.

Our camp was along a burned-over shoreline, reminiscent of my south trip with its long stretches of burned country. In 1994, all three of the tall escarpments that separate McLeod, Christie, and Wildbread Bays had been burned during an exceptionally hot dry summer. These subarctic forest fires are not very dramatic, because at this latitude even the mature timber is small and scattered by southern standards. But even though these taiga fires are usually not very hot, the regrowth following them takes a long time at latitudes so close to the northern limit of trees. I would hazard a guess that it will take sixty years for the swath of high ground which burned in 1994 to fully recover its sparse forest of spruce and pine.

The Kahochella Peninsula fire was nearly put out before it ever built up any size or momentum. On the evening of 21 June 1994, strikes of dry lightning (lightning not followed by heavy rain) had ignited many fires in a wide arc across the region. At first the small fire just east of Shelter Bay had been deemed worthy of some firefighting efforts, but the helicopter pilot who was sent from the nearest fire base to start bucketing water on it was soon called away by headquarters. There were more pressing concerns closer to the settlement at Lutsel K'e that afternoon. "Another forty-five minutes and that fire would never have gone anywhere," he told me later. "But they said to leave it, so I left it."

Through July and into August, fires on all three peninsulas flared and wandered with each shift of the winds, eventually burning most of the shoreline and higher terrain from Reliance to Taltheilei Narrows. The parting image of those fires is one I will always remember. By mid-August, as summer turns into autumn, our round-the-clock daylight gives way to a few hours of welcome darkness each night. On clear evenings when a north wind had cleared away the smoke, we could see across the bay. There the small spot fires and hot spots twinkled and flared on the crest of the cliffs, like streetlights along a 40-mile boulevard.

Low clouds moved in overnight with warmer weather. In the morning I woke to the gentle swishing sound of snow sliding off the tent fly every few minutes. I was headachy and groggy, still getting over our first late-night camp and shifting into the rhythm of trail life. I remarked to my journal that I wanted to *wander* west, and to avoid getting caught up in a mad dash for the lake's distant outflow, or any other faraway goal. Most of my winter trips on the lake have been made in "non-stop direct" mode, from Yellowknife to the Hoarfrost River or vice versa. I have made that 210-mile trek seventeen times over the years, once in just sixty hours with a ridiculously long string of twenty Iditarod dogs. Here was my chance to break that push-ahead habit, but the day before, out on Christie Bay, I had felt those urges creeping in.

While I had no intention of visiting Lutsel K'e or of stopping off in Yellowknife farther west, the twinkling town lights visible from my camp were thought-provoking. A sign of civilization so close at hand was certainly a far cry from my trips east, south, and north. I smiled very briefly when I realized I had not thought to bring any money along with me, for this led me to imagine hanging around the door of the local Co-op and post office, trying to panhandle enough change to buy a chocolate bar. Considering how many times I had been approached for "a couple dollars" by boozed-up friends on the streets of Yellowknife, I tried to find some wry humour in the scenario of turning the tables. But there was no humour there. When it comes to alcohol abuse and its reverberations through northern society, nothing is very funny to me anymore.

From the 15-mile remove of my camp north of Lutsel K'e I pondered my perplexity about the place. For over thirty years I have yearned to find some personal clarity of vision, some defining and inspiring empathy, when it comes to the indigenous cultures of the Far North. So far I have failed. Once the outer layers of upbeat pronouncements and politically correct turns of phrase have been stripped away, every settlement and hamlet from Labrador to Lac Brochet, from Attawapiskat to Anaktuvuk Pass, is a place of uncertainty and intermittent heartbreak. Rapid changes have been like a steady bombardment raining down on the Native people of Canada, and entire generations have been lost and damaged in the fallout. Beneath the confusion yawns a widening chasm between the much-talked-about "life on the land"—which in an honest view belongs these days to the realm of archetype and legend—and the daily realities of life in town: tedium and television; a suffocating dependence on corporate and government largesse; and family upheaval, much of it fuelled by alcohol and other drugs.

When it comes to my Native friends at Lutsel K'e, their past and present and future, I try to understand, and to arrive at some clear notion of a good way forward. It seems most vital to remain hopeful, and to try to be fair-minded in the face of cynicism. Vital also to remain skeptical enough to "penetrate the veils of bullshit," as one prominent northerner once categorized the palaver at a round of local meetings. As it is with the tumult in the far-off Middle East, covered day after day in the world "news," so it is with the close-up politics and polemics of the North: listening and watching, I am left utterly perplexed. As years go by I acquiesce to the realization that even in some local matters I may never have anything constructive to say. In the context of these pages and my journeys I will just acknowledge the ambivalence and perplexity that the twinkling lights of Lutsel K'e signified for me, and carry on past with my dogs, not stopping.

———

That morning, day three, I set off in search of one of the lake's more subtle and little-known passageways, this one new to me. For several winters I had noticed from the air a trail across a narrow cleft in Utsingi Point. It was being used as a shortcut by hunters heading west from Lutsel K'e to access some caribou wintering south of Taltheilei Narrows. I had visited the west end of this short portage briefly the year before while guiding some German tourists, but I had never looked for it from the east. In early afternoon we picked up an old track of several snow machines leading into the crossing. Once we were up off the ice and into the shelter of some thick spruce I stopped the dogs for a break. The wind was strengthening from the west and the low cloud was lifting a little. I sat on the sled, eating my lunch and thinking about that narrow trail and the old axe-cut blazes that marked it. These age-old connections are rarely noted on any official maps, and most of them are used only in winter, the main season for inland hunting and overland travel. Many of them are known to only a few hunters or to a family whose ancestors once trapped and hunted the area. Gradually the knowledge of all such passages is fading away.

I thought of the many trails we have cut and blazed around the Hoarfrost River and the north shore of McLeod Bay. Precise knowledge of most of those is recorded only in a few brains—between the ears of a few old lead dogs, and my own and Kristen's, and now our daughters'. It is the dogs who remember the details best, often with uncanny precision—but hey, they also live shorter lives and have less to remember! As Kristen and I get older, some of the trails we cut and blazed twenty years ago have fallen out of use. Old lead dogs die, and for years we do not need to use one route or another. Soon some of our trails that were in regular use many years ago will be extinct again. This is a loss, yes, but I resist the notion to portray it as cultural tragedy. It is just a simple fact of human life on a landscape: things change.

The trail I was parked on that day would probably stay in use for a long time, at least sporadically, depending upon the wanderings of the caribou herds. The crossing offers hunters a safe east–west passage and it avoids the thin ice and open water at the tip of Utsingi Point. Other such trails all across the north have constantly been created and forgotten over the span of one or two generations. Nowadays, though, trails being forgotten far outnumber trails being created.

Overhead, in the span of my half-hour lunch stop, two airliners and a smaller turboprop plane made their own shortcuts. The sound of their engines and the sight of those axe cuts on the trees made a striking contrast, but I was tired of trying to wring any profundity out of it all. "David, we're living in the future," my friend Ken liked to remind me. To which I often find myself replying, at least silently, "We are, and I sure as hell wish I found that future more enticing!"

We followed a good trail for most of the afternoon, passing through squalls of snow into a blustery west wind. It was a warm wind, though, about minus 12 degrees, with a feeling of spring in it. By nightfall we had come another 38 miles or so. Camp 3 was on the northeast tip of Narrow Island. The fast pace and longer miles were showing up as little aches and pains among the dogs. Steve had a sore shoulder, and by the end of the day Jasmine was favouring a tender wrist. I gave everyone a coated aspirin tablet and wrapped Jasmine's wrist with a wide neoprene band for the evening. Murphy had somehow cut his lower lip and he persistently reopened the wound by scooping bites of crusty snow as he ran. That night after feeding I knelt in front of him, drew his head up under my arm, and managed to slip in one quick suture across the laceration. Once Murph knew what I was up to, though, he would have no more of it—for which I could hardly blame him—and I had to give up with just the one stitch in place. I chuckled at his reaction, because he was an incessant barker when harnessed and I had often joked that I was going to sew his mouth shut. He probably thought I had finally decided to make good on my threats.

I was tired again that night. I suppose it is impossible to cover even 38 level miles on a dogsled without fatigue, when the chores involved are added in. It was a mild night, only in the mid-teens below zero, and a slender crescent moon was up. I did sit up long enough to make some notes in my journal, and was inspired to set off on a digression concerning the predominance of various forms of plastic and nylon in my gear:

When this era passes it will be known as The Petroleum Age, and we The Plastic Culture. Look at this "simple" romantic tableau—lone dog musher and team of faithful huskies—and imagine removing from it all things plastic and nylon and *directly* (never mind *indirectly*!) derived from petroleum...What remains is a comical sight: a heap of feathers instead of a sleeping bag, a camp stove with no fuel, a few slats of hardwood and bits of hardware instead of a sled, some pots and pans, myself—shivering in swatches of fur, wool, and leather—and the dogs with no harnesses, lines, or collars.

And if we take it a step further, none of those remaining things exist either, without petroleum-fuelled long-distance transportation, without petroleum-fuelled mining and harvesting and manufacturing. It all completely disappears. I disappear myself! We are indeed heading for some interesting times.

On that odd note I closed the journal for the night. I studied the map for a few minutes, then settled in for a deep sleep with the luxury of an open, frost-free sleeping-bag hood. Setting out later in the winter was certainly going to have some perks.

A noisy ruckus from the dogs woke me at dawn—one of the team was loose and scampering around the campsite. I could hear footfalls circling the tent. I spoke aloud, "Good morning, Eagle." The footsteps stopped, then moved away. I poked my head out of the tent door and saw that it was indeed Eagle. Of all the dogs I have ever owned, he has the most amazing knack for unsnapping himself from a picket line. I have no idea what his method is but he clearly has it mastered. Hidden thumbs? I went out to put him back on the line, which settled everyone down again. The morning was minus 24 degrees and the sun was not yet up. The view up and down the lake was stunning: The thin dark line of Utsingi Point, the black rounded brow of Sachowia Point, the cliffs of Et-then Island. The horizon beyond Utsingi was only ice and sky—there stretched the vast length and depth of Christie Bay, now behind us. I had been a little surprised the night before when Polaris and the dipper had shown me true north. On the big lake it is easy to fall into the assumption that the coast runs east–west, when in fact it is more northeast–southwest along many stretches, and very close to north–south up through Taltheilei Narrows. This explained the hardpacked snow of that campsite—the place received the full blast of every northeast gale. It had been a calm night, but the wind was already building strength that morning, and it was northeasterly.

Inspired by the sweep of the view and the alpenglow of dawn on the snow, I made an effort at photography. I put on my parka and got out the camera for a few shots of the camp. Back in the tent with my journal and coffee, I wondered again about perceptions, and whether trying to *share* a perception—in writing, speech, or image—in fact *deepens* that perception. I concluded, grudgingly, that it probably did, and wrote:

> So does this mean that, if this was an "online" expedition such as are now so popular, and were I composing my daily update on my trusty laptop, instead of with #2 pencil and dog-eared blue journal, I would actually push my thoughts into more coherency? Maybe, or maybe I would just skim along on the surface, playing to the crowd—trite, chipper, and banal: "beautiful sunrise this morning, pink and orange on the snow..." then log on, hit Send, and off to the satellite and on into cyberspace it would fly, and SO WHAT? But only in carefully recording my journeys do I seem compelled to probe whatever meaning and insight they have brought to my life. To write for others would force me to consider my thoughts from a more detached perspective, as I am in all honesty doing at this moment. Round and round we go. Still I am damned glad I am not out here sending daily updates to anyone!

From that camp it was 49 straight-line miles to the cache on Wilson Island—clearly more than I should ask of the dogs in a day, at least at this stage. I would have to camp short of the cache. This was day four. The Mackenzie River outlet was starting to look like an overly ambitious goal and I began trying to make my peace with setting it aside. "Do not hurry; do not tarry" seemed the best approach to such perfect sledding conditions. Once out of camp and free from journal notes and mundane chores, we swooped and skidded non-stop down the Hearne Channel for three glorious hours, chased by a steady northeast tailwind. Twice the sled tipped completely over as it bounced and slewed off the drift-tops, and when it did I simply hung on until my weight dragged the team to a stop. The dogs were clearly having a good time.

Eight miles west of McKinley Point a bulldozed access road heads inland to the Thor Lake mining camp. That camp, soon to be a mine, overlies a world-renowned deposit of rare-earth minerals valuable as ingredients for high-tech electronic equipment.[6] Beyond Thor Lake the road becomes a trail and continues north to a tourist lodge. I knew this area. Over the past five years I had driven teams of dogs to and from Blachford Lake Lodge, and some of our dogs had spent seasons giving sled rides to lodge guests there. I chose my lunch spot at the Blachford trailhead on the slim chance that someone would appear from up that trail and give me some midday company and conversation.

We were parked on the shoulder of the most prominent winter trail on the entire lake, a wide and hardpacked route that is established every year by snowmobile traffic between Lutsel K'e and Yellowknife. Since joining this wide main route at McKinley Point I had noticed some of the telltale spoor of modern winter travel: an empty vodka flask, a discarded red gas jug, and—vaguely disquieting—a lone running shoe. Signs of travel, but no travellers. In another ten miles, going west, I would turn off that main route into parts of the lake much less travelled. On my journey west—and in fact over all the miles of all four winter journeys, it was only on that tiny stretch of trail west of McKinley Point that I could realistically *expect* to meet up with anyone by chance. As I sat in the shelter of the cove, facing south in the warm sun, I truly yearned to hear the buzz of a snow machine approaching from some direction—east, west, or inland—but none came. (Of course the gentle *huff-huff* and jangle of bronze snaps that are the sounds of an approaching dogteam would have been even more interesting, but that was so far out of the realm of realistic possibility on that stretch of trail nowadays that I never gave it a thought.)

I knew that a detour of an hour's mushing up the inland trail and past the mothballed Thor Lake camp would have brought me to the lodge at Blachford Lake. For a few indulgent moments I let my daydreams wander up that way. I was no stranger to the lodge, having worked there from time to time, so I could fill in salient details as I snoozed in the sunshine: the smooth varnished tables of the main dining area; porcelain mugs of hot coffee in the morning and cool glasses of beer in the evening; smiling urbane guests padding softly through the main room, bound for the outdoor hot tub and a soak under the northern lights, swathed only in clean white terry cloth robes... *Geezus, Olesen, it must be time to get this dogteam moving again ...*

It was a glorious afternoon of sledding, running west-southwest with a ten-knot tailwind over all twelve of our shoulders. The team's pace was almost precisely matched to the wind's speed, so we moved in a perceived calm. I only noticed the following wind when we paused or when I happened to look down and see grains of snow skittering along beside us, like handfuls of sugar flung across the polished patches of bare ice.

Almost every winter a long pressure ridge forms along the north shore of the Hearne Channel. That day we paralleled it for several hours and the glimmering turquoise ice blocks were a magnificent sight in the sunshine. I watched the ridge, mesmerized for long minutes at a time while the dogs quickstepped down the wide trail with no need of my spoken guidance. One massive block of polished ice formed a perfect likeness of a wolverine's head—no sculptor could have bettered it. I considered stopping and trying to take a photograph, but even as I briefly pondered this we were rapidly leaving it behind. The dogs were gobbling up the trail, obviously enjoying themselves, and I was not inclined to break their rhythm. I noticed that Murphy's cut was open again and he was dipping bites of snow now and then as he ran. He clearly did not give a hoot, and he marked the trail with small smears of blood every 50 yards or so. That lip was not going to heal anytime soon.

Like most free and easy rides in life, our cruise down the Yellowknife–Lutsel K'e expressway ended abruptly and all too soon. Ten miles west of our lunch stop at the Thor Lake–Blachford trailhead, I called "Haw!" to the leaders. They took the command, but from the ranks of the team Steve and Murphy both looked pointedly back at me, as if to make sure I was serious. I suppose those older dogs had assumed we were on our way into Yellowknife, which from there was only 75 miles ahead.

Ernie and Kaltag were in lead though, and they had never been this far west, nor to Yellowknife, so at the sound of my command they veered south without hesitation. In an instant we left all traces of human passage and set off for a hundred miles or more of trackless mushing. I swallowed hard. *Here we go,* I thought. Maybe even *I* had subconsciously assumed we were headed for the lights of town!

The moment we left the trail the lake suddenly felt much bigger again. It was as if that narrow ribbon of hardpacked snow had compressed the experience of our journey into something akin to a drive along a country road, or a ride down a rural train track. Without that track I was busy steering again, with a steady string of spoken commands to Ernie and Kaltag. "Haw!" "Gee!" "Straight ahead!"—over and over, minute by minute. I was back at work after a brief respite. The effortless magic of the day's run had not ended for the dogs, though, and they drew me along southwest at a rollicking speed, the sled hammering and banging on hard drifts, fishtailing and skidding on patches of glare ice. The dark rises of the Westhead and Caribou Islands loomed up ahead and grew quickly larger as we sped along. The wind was still quartering behind us from the east, and we were making about ten miles an hour. With the ride so wild I had a death grip on the handlebar with both mittened hands. *Losing the sled was not going to be part of today's festivities*, I thought to myself.

Just before 5 p.m. I steered the dogs alongside the sloping shoreline of a small island north of Wilson. We had come 41 miles since morning. I was tempted to cross to the resupply cache that evening, but I knew what would come of that—a long night of setting up the more elaborate cache camp in the dark, finishing up weary and grumpy late at night. So we stopped and I made camp, without the need for snowshoes, and even before the daylight had faded I was into the tent for the night.

All day I had been sporadically belting out a raucous homegrown blues number that had its origins on the ice of Hudson Bay in 1979, on a trip I had guided with Will Steger. That night I wrote down the latest verse. A dear friend (the same one who had sent me the Mayan parable I had read on the trip south) had encouraged me to "listen for a song rising up from the land itself" as I made my winter journeys, but "Tundra Mama" was probably not what he had in mind:

(Chorus) Oh, won't you be my tundra mama,
My pack-ice piece of cake.
(Raucous blues riff, preferably on a cheap kazoo, then repeat first two lines)
I'll love ya clear from Churchill
All the way to Baker Lake.

Oh my lead dog's just tremendous
Don't get no ice balls on his feet.
(Repeat)
He pulls all day in a whiteout
On just about a pound of meat.

(Chorus)

Yeah we'll build ourselves an igloo
Just big enough for two
(Repeat)
Then we'll crawl inside and lay down
On the skins of the caribou

(Chorus)

[And the new verse...]

We're doin' the sastrugi boogie
We do it all day long
(Repeat)
We're just a-jumpin' and a-jivin' and
Singin' this stupid *song...*

(Chorus)

Yikes. At any rate, the dogs seemed to enjoy it.

That night I could clearly hear the arrivals and departures of jets at the Yellowknife airport, about 50 straight-line miles to the north. I convinced myself that I also heard a steady deep drone or hum, like that of a diesel power plant off in the distance. That proved impossible for me to pinpoint or even confirm. I mentioned it during my stopover at my friend Bill Carpenter's cabin several days later, and Bill immediately replied, "Oh, I know exactly what you hear—I hear it when I'm out there too. It's just inside your head, I think." I still wonder about it, and Bill may be right. There is this, too, from Elizabeth Hay's *Late Nights on Air,* a novel set in Yellowknife and out on the Thelon River: "Here on the Barrens there wasn't music, but a hum, a vibration, the sound of the earth, he thought, and she agreed. In moments of silence, she'd heard it too. It reminded her of Buddhist singing bowls vibrating at their lowest octave."[7]

It had been a smooth and easy day for me despite a few capsizes and our long mileage, and I was not worn out after dinner. I stayed up late in the tent writing and reading. One note I made to myself was that such "easy days for the musher are not always easy days for the dogs." We had camped early on a hardpacked shore where I could do my chores without snowshoes, and the day's miles had been covered in just two non-stop segments, three hours and then two hours, with a nice break in the middle. Still, the dogs had pulled a heavy load 41 miles in that time, and only 16 of those had been on flat smooth trail. The rest had been a choppy mix of snowdrifts, ice patches, and pockets of soft powder snow. Their speed, being a function of their innate eagerness, could easily have brought some sore shoulders and wrists. They would need an easier day soon, and some extra hours at rest in the sunshine, letting those minor aches and pains mend.

I remembered my friend Jerry Austin blazing into the checkpoint at Koyuk on the Iditarod one year, and someone remarking that his crossing from Shaktoolik had been remarkably fast. His reply was "Yeah, *too* fast,"

At the time it struck me as an odd comment from a competitor during a race, but over the years I realized what he meant. There is indeed such a thing as "too fast." We were on our own now, not running an organized race, so there would be no opportunity to leave a sore-shouldered dog behind at a checkpoint. I certainly was not interested in trying to carry a gimpy dog in the sled, though I have done that many times and will likely do it again. Sore dogs are not necessarily tired dogs, and keeping an energetic husky strapped atop a bulging sled load is not easy.

Little by little I came to terms with the realization that I should not try to reach the lake's outflow, despite the allure of such a tangible goal. "It looks pretty doubtful for making the Mackenzie. That would be about 420 miles from tonight's camp to our eventual arrival back at home, which averages to 35 miles a day with absolutely no allowance for weather delays or any layover." I needed to lower my sights a little, and I began thinking about a visit to Bill Carpenter's place on the west shore of the lake. Perhaps he could point me west onto one of his own broken trails for an overnight foray inland. "I have had a great trip so far," I wrote. "I don't want to throw away the notion of reaching the river, but neither do I want to push the dogs or become miserably tired and pressed for time...Miles, miles, and more miles—the lake is so huge."

A pair of ravens hung around that camp early the next morning, calling back and forth to each other as if waiting for something. They had appeared overhead within seconds of our arrival the night before. They were the first living things I had seen all day: 41 miles of lake and sky and ice, and two ravens. Their experience probably told them that at any moment I would start doing something appetizing, like pulling fish from a net or cutting up a moose or caribou.

I wrote about Ernie that morning. I was starting to realize that he probably was, for me, the once-in-a-lifetime sled dog that Lady Luck bequeaths on a lifelong musher. Born in June 1999, Ernie was sired by Riley, who came from the kennel of Iditarod legend Susan Butcher, and borne by my lead dog Jiminy, a great one herself and daughter of my Iditarod leader McDougal. Ernie was with me on all four solo trips, beginning as a two-year-old. On this trip west, at age five and a half, he was at or near the peak of his physical prowess. I do know this: I have never had a dog quite like Ernie. A young dog named Fletcher, who drowned in an accident on thin ice while leading a team in 1993, might, given time, have been that good, but I will never know.

From my journal: "I must savor every mile with Ernest Heming-dog, because I'm not sure I'll ever see the likes of him again. He has it all— speed, honesty, toughness, and a nearly insane *desire*. Often I think, as

I watch him run, 'Man, where were *you* those years when I was racing?' Maybe Kaltag, his protégé on this trip, will rise to 'the importance of being Ernest' but I doubt it. Ernie is simply a gift."[8]

———————

The day was not so completely simple after all. It should have been a leisurely couple of hours. I would probably have gone on lounging and writing in the sunlit tent that morning, but the subtle threat of a strengthening east wind got me up and moving. The dogs were spread out on a slope exposed to the east, and we would regret staying too long if the wind built up.[9] The crossing to Wilson Island was a pleasure and the dogs made short work of it. Remembering Alfred Lockhart's warning about thin ice, I swung wide of the island's tip and then turned east and north toward shore. The snow was sheltered on that south side of the island and the dogs were plowing slowly through deep drifts. But where precisely was the little cove where I had landed the plane and set out the cache supplies and the tent? A mile or so down the south coast of Wilson Island I decided I must have passed the cache cove. I called Ernie and Kaltag around and we doubled back. We swung in closer to the mouth of one inlet, but nothing there looked familiar. I had not thought to place a marker on the ice on the day I had landed to place the cache. As often happens, the cove had looked perfectly obvious from the air. From lake level though, peering intently at the steep rise of the island, I could not discern any obvious break in the shoreline.

Confused, I kept calling commands to the dogs. They marched back and forth in the deep snow. Nearly an hour went by. I grew concerned that I was wasting the dogs' strength and asking for a ridiculous amount of effort, all out of sheer stubbornness on my part. After all, I had in my sled bag the means to pinpoint that cache precisely. Finally, under the guise of stopping for lunch, I set the snow hook and unclipped the dogs' tuglines. "Time to check in with outer space," I muttered. I pulled the little GPS receiver out of its waterproof box in the sled and tucked it inside my innermost layer of sweater, right against my belly. It would warm up quickly there, and once it was warm it would only take a moment to show me the exact direction and distance to my cache.

My pride demanded that I at least pinpoint my own best guess before turning to "Command Central" for help. While I nibbled cheese and crackers I checked the time. I then drew a clock face in the snow beside the sled, with the hour hand pointed at the sun. Exactly halfway between the hour hand and the twelve on my snow-clock would be due south. I looked at my map (itself a tool from Command Central, lest I forget). The mouth of the cache cove had to be directly northeast of us, beyond that small peninsula that we had already passed twice. That was my theory.

The GPS receiver was warm. I pulled it out and turned it on and set it on the sled. I poured a cup of cocoa from the Thermos. Within ninety seconds the little screen showed a tiny map with a little black triangle— our position. I was where I thought I was. We were 0.4 statute miles from the cache, and it lay on a bearing of fifty-five degrees true. "Well," I told the dogs, "*that* was embarrassing!" Relaxed again, I sat and relished the beauty and simplicity of lunch time: nothing to cook, no stove or fire to tend. The sun shone. The dogs slept. I emptied, cup by cup, my one-litre Thermos of hot cocoa, and took long pulls from my plastic flask of warm Tang. I nibbled jerked bison meat, dried moose meat, crackers, and frozen pats of butter.

When a half-hour had passed I was glad that I had stopped to find my bearings, even if I had resorted to outside help. The break was perfect and I knew that once we did arrive at the cache I would slip immediately into work mode—putting up the big tent, cutting firewood, opening sup- ply barrels, and hanging gear out to dry in the sun. That year for my trip west I would stop at the cache twice—it was not the turnaround point. Instead of an old canvas wall tent, I had cached our big Arctic Oven tent, an Alaskan double-walled design, along with my resupply kegs. This effi- cient tent is one we use when guiding tourists and students. On past solos I had not wanted to risk setting it out at a cache, for fear of not retrieving it before it was needed for work at home. When I settled into it for the evening it felt downright hedonistic to have such warm spaciousness all to myself. I took sips from my flask of rum for the first time since night two.

A little humbled by it all tonight, especially by the difficulty I had locating the cache—I even overshot the place once *after* checking the GPS! The cove is much more narrow-throated than I perceived from the air. Then I lost my temper with Ernie and Kaltag as I tried to steer them in close to shore. Not fair to them—they had been slogging back and forth for well over an hour while I tried to figure out where the hell I was.

I am struck by how different this forest and shoreline is from McLeod Bay. I went out to gather firewood—normally a ten-minute process almost anywhere around home—and I literally *could not find* a dead spruce tree! Cut some sort of alder or willow, and some balsam poplar. Then when I tried to light the stove I realized the pipe was clogged with snow, and the tent filled up with thick smoke.[10]

Most humbling and thought-provoking, though, was my short walk along the shoreline on snowshoes. I had to round the little point and go into the smaller cove to retrieve the cache barrels and the big tent. Before bringing the dogs around I went to check the ice. I had seen a little slush in the narrows there in February when I had landed to place the cache. I had taxied the Husky right up through the inlet that day—a completely harmless-looking spot. Today the narrows were blanketed with a smooth layer of deep snow. I took a swipe at the snow with my axe to check the ice. And under that snow there was NO ice—nada, none! My axe-stroke swept through a foot of fluff right into liquid water. I broke off an alder branch and sounded the depth. It was about four feet deep there. Gulp. I guess Alfred knows whereof he speaks, with his warning about the ice around here.

I talked to Kristen on the radio that night, for the first time since leaving home. She reported that everything was fine there, Annika nearly finished with her third-grade home-school lessons, and a great grey owl seen nearby for the second time that winter. I told her where I was, and we signed off. I slept deeply but woke up chilled before dawn. Stoked the fire in the little stove and laid back in a half-awake daze watching the play of firelight on the tent walls. Sheer luxury. Once the day began to brighten I checked the weather: minus 30 degrees, calm, a few clouds. I made some calculations while taking a long look at the map. It was obvious that we should not lay over at that campsite for another night unless the weather forced us to. It was about 65 straight-line miles from the tip of Wilson Island across to the far west shore of the lake—more than a day's travel on a camping trip. I was still looking forward to making at least one overnight camp right on the open ice, out of sight of land. That was a vision I had long held for this trip west. As I could have foreseen, the lofty vision was one thing, the basic *doing* of it quite another. I hemmed and hawed. How was the weather? *Perfect.* How long would the open-ice crossing take? *About seven hours of travel time.* What other excuse might I dream up for not camping out there? *None.*

I left the big tent standing, tidied up the campsite, stowed the rest of the resupply back in the metal barrels, and we were under way before noon. An east wind continued to push us along as we crossed to the Outpost Islands. Just past them, on the very verge of the long open crossing, I stopped the dogs for our midday break. A deep fissure and a massive jumble of ice—blocks the size of cars and trucks—marked the north–south line of a pressure ridge. I walked ahead and found a spot

Jumbled ice of the big pressure ridge at Outpost Islands, just before heading west onto the open ice.

where we could cross it, then turned back toward the resting team. The dogs seemed suddenly humbled and mellow, as if to say, "We've talked it over and we're still with you, boss, but this looks like serious stuff." I felt the same way. That big ridge of ice was the boundary. We were leaving the East Arm. Ahead was the *sea* part of this inland sea.

I snacked and sipped, and the dogs rested. I was seized by a sudden inclination to touch up my knife blade with a pocket whetstone. As I did so I realized what was going on—I was postponing the inevitable. "What the hell are we waiting for?" I asked the dogs. No reply. "It's just ice, for cripes sake. Let's go."

The crossings of the open ice were the epitome of the trip west. Once we were under way my butterflies settled. Gradually the final glimpses of land all disappeared. The last to go was the bluff at Gros Cap, northeast of us, which seemed to be lifted up from the horizon by the refraction of warm air over the ice. This apparition becomes common in northern latitudes as spring progresses, because of cold surface air trapped under warmer air aloft, and at times very distant land is raised into sight from far beyond the usual limits of the horizon. Once we were west of the big pressure ridge and its freshly flooded ice we encountered only a few shards and blocks of upturned ice on the entire crossing. Wherever it was blown bare by the wind the ice appeared to be about three feet thick. It was a light tan colour and slightly opaque instead of clear and black. In the west end of the lake basin the water is tawny with sediment carried on the prodigious outflow of the Slave River.[11]

On the open ice, as on the open tundra, I navigated by dead reckoning. Using time and my best estimate of our speed, along with the sun's bearing, I kept a reasonably good estimate of our track and position. This lent an enjoyable layer of suspense to the evening ritual of flashing up the GPS, and letting it *inform* me of my precise location. That night as I began my journal entry, I recorded my estimate: "61° 40.5′ North by 114° 16′ West." Then the GPS computer chimed in: 61°40.547′ N X 114° 11.893′ W. As usual I had overestimated our speed slightly and had reckoned us about two miles farther west. But the simple clock-time estimate of the sun's bearing had again proven adequate—a good trick as long as the sun is visible. The GPS spit out other interesting details. We had come 35.4 statute miles from the cache on Wilson Island. It was 13.3 miles to Hardisty Island, which meant it should have been visible from that campsite. There was some haze off in that direction that evening, and I had not been able to discern any land on the horizon at dusk. I had not noted the precise time of sundown that evening, although the pure flat horizon would have given me a good chance to check the pronouncements of the GPS (sunrise 6:50 a.m., sunset 6:38 p.m.). Happy with that dose of trivia to mull over, I switched off the arrogant little black box. Back to pencil and journal and the candlelit world of the tent.

A breeze was still puffing out of the east, but with the temperature mild and the sky mostly clear, I was not worried about our wide-open camp. We were completely unsheltered on a vast plate of ice and snow, but I was enjoying our risqué devil-may-care exposure at that camp on such a night. Those stopovers on the open ice remain among my finest memories of the trip. It was a pleasure to simply stop, set the snow hook, pound in a couple of ice-climbing pitons to anchor the picket line, shift the dogs a mere three feet over from gangline to tie-out, put up the tent, melt snow and soak dog food, and watch the daylight fade from an entire hemisphere of sky. No staggering around on snowshoes, no chopping thin ice for a water hole, no cutting of boughs or sawing of firewood. "Here we are, staked down and not cowering in the bushes," we seemed to say. "Come what may." In those camps I could feel the allure of the High Arctic and Antarctic, which Will Steger had talked about in his visit to the Hoarfrost River the previous winter. On the ice the entire camp-and-travel routine was whittled down to its simplest elements: Stop, make camp, eat, sleep. Wake, eat, pack up, set out. Repeat ad infinitum. Will and his ice-cap rosaries again. I could understand.

The dogs and I were out of our element, though. I knew it and I suspect they did too. Staked out on a hundred-mile-wide pan of ice would have been a different story with a blast of the winds that had plagued the trip east two years earlier. The scant snow cover would have precluded the option of excavating a sheltering snow trench for the dogs, and life would have been a fiasco in the little red tent with eleven dogs and one musher all crowded in and around it for shelter.

In the twilight that evening I could see the sparkling lights of Yellowknife 55 miles to the north. The glow and twinkle of the entire city of eighteen thousand people was lifted by the inversion and refraction of warm air aloft. The sound of jets inbound and outbound from the airport was clear. Those sights and sounds, so clear on that first night out on the open ice, caused some worry and confusion for me later in the trip.

———————

Morning on the ice. Still mild, 15 below, with the wind still easterly at less than ten knots. As I moved around camp doing my chores, I noted something I had not spotted the previous day—within recent weeks all the snow there had been thawed to the melting point, and had refrozen with a thin crust. This underscored the fact that we were moving gradually into a warmer climate, for this thaw had never reached McLeod or Christie Bay, or even Wilson Island. We set off and the dogs broke from camp in a sprint. Clearly they had not enjoyed that feeling of absolute exposure quite as much as I had. The opaque haze still obscured the horizon to the west-northwest, and it underscored the sensation of being far from land. I was ticking off the miles and hours of the crossing, and at last the spruce-dark outline of Hardisty Island loomed into sight just north of our heading. It was a little anticlimactic. I had looked forward to crossing that stretch of open lake, and now we had done it. We had been lucky. "Well, guys, that was sort of a non-event, wasn't it?" I said to the team. A couple of heads turned briefly back toward me.

The crossing would have to be made again, eastbound, and the wind might yet play its hand. For the time being, though, it was sunshine and blue sky above, with the horizon milky and indistinct on all quadrants. The miles slid by. Low ground to our right, with low forest and a few gravelly spits jutting into our path. On one spit I pulled over for a break and the dogs sniffed curiously at a line of fresh fox tracks as we approached. They were the first tracks other than our own that I had seen for days. We had reached land—a clump of beach grass and some rounded stones blown clear of snow. The dogs settled in for their naps. I nibbled chocolate and jotted a few terse lines: "Islands along west shore reached 11:55. Shoreline brushy, nondescript."

We carried on west along the south shores of Hardisty Island and Long Island. As we coasted along hour after hour with the low shore-line to our right, I thought about many things. For a while I mulled over the different characters of the lake's various arms and reaches: the North Arm; the southwest outlet; the Slave Delta; Hornby Channel; Yellowknife Bay; the near East Arm; and the far East Arm—McLeod, Christie, and Wildbread Bays.

We were in a part of the lake where the commercial fishery is still under way, although sputtering for lack of interest. I mused about a fisherman's livelihood, one of the most alluring Walter Mitty-ish fantasies I hold. From what I hear, being a freshwater commercial fisherman in northern Canada is similar to being a bush pilot: a romantic way to work hard for modest pay, learning to live with uncertainty about weather and income, and all the while sweating equipment upkeep and clawing through a spider web of government regulations. Still, setting out nets, hauling in fish, and exchanging the catch for cash has always looked appealing when viewed from a soft-focus distance.

I mused about the book I was reading, *Infinite Life* by Robert Thurman, which may be characterized as a popularization of Tibetan Buddhism. Thurman made some thought-provoking points about the physical *inconsequence* of our "solid" physical world: the golf ball on home plate being the nucleus of an atom, tiny specks out in the bleachers its orbiting electrons. The vastness of the frozen lake seemed conducive to such an image. I tried to force that perception onto my reality of the moment, to see the dogs and the sled and the ice and sky as nothing but swirling, pulsating, essentially ephemeral fields of energy, but I could not hold the thread of that vision. The dogs seemed very real, huffing along ahead of me, and the ice beneath us was comfortingly solid. I wondered if I was destined to be forever a metaphysical flunky, out there "listening for a song from the land" and coming up instead with "Tundra Mama."

Mostly I did not think—I just watched the dogs run. I suppose only a true dog musher can watch a team of dogs run for three hours on per-fectly flat terrain without feeling bored, just as only a true pilot can make a five-hour flight alone in a small plane and be entirely content to do nothing but scan the instruments and daydream. Surely this talent for being so easily amused is an asset in some lines of work.

———————

Lonely Point was the name on the map for the low scrubby peninsula where we camped that night. "Lonely Point—no kidding," I wrote in my journal. The place had an eerie ambience that I could not seem to shake, and even now, years later, I recall the spot with a vague unease. Later I learned that for many years there had been a shack there, used by one of the local fishermen. Maybe some event there had tainted the place and its ambience.[12] Maybe I was just sensing that the dogs and I had arrived on an unfamiliar shore, a place different and very far from home.

After I finished the camp chores I took a walk on snowshoes back into the forest on the point. Spruce trees were interspersed with thick-trunked birches. Both were unusual. The spruce had been shaped by a pattern of seasonal gales sweeping in from the open lake. It looked as if all the big trees had at some time had their upper trunks lopped off in a windstorm, and had adapted to this by keeping all their growth low and protected. Some of them had trunks nearly 26 inches in diameter, with a bulbous growth of thick limbs and very little overall height, less than 20 feet. The birches were nearly black at the base and, like the spruce, their body shapes had been mutated low and round by the onshore winds.

As I snowshoed back into camp, I succumbed to the temptation for allegory, fittingly flavoured by Thurman and his Buddhism—something about striving rapidly upward, getting busted off by the wind, then turning toward a lower, fuller, more rounded version of fulfillment and survival. It was a notion that seemed to be trying to apply itself to my life. At first I resisted and tried to brush it off, but I recall standing outside the tent that night, looking at Lonely Point and the dogs, pondering for a long time in the dusk. Thwarted ambition could certainly make for new shapes, and could lead to a sturdy resilience. It was a reminder I needed in my middle years. I had tried for fifteen years to reach the upper echelons of the long-distance mushing world. I had poured myself into that effort, and had gleaned many gifts from the crusade—friends, moments, lessons. Now I was past that time, rounding out and widening my goals. Whenever I fly past Lonely Point these days I think of those trees and that night.

The next morning brought a blast of the wind that had convinced those trees on the point to revise their tall-spire aspirations. I woke to blizzard tent sounds: snow sliding off nylon at frequent intervals; fabric flapping in the gusty, eddying wind. At first it seemed as if travel would be out of the question. Once I clambered out of the Hillleberg for a brief assessment, though, I realized that the storm was not as bad as it sounded. The wind was not easterly off the wide-open ice, but out of the northwest. The temperature was a balmy minus 16 degrees. The overcast sky was surprisingly bright, and the clouds already seemed to be breaking apart. I retreated to the tent and went about my morning: coffee, journal, bacon, cereal. I was not enthused about the prospect of an entire day holed up at Lonely Point. I was keen to get out into the weather and make some progress. We were only about 17 miles from Moraine Point, where I knew there was a lodge and a family home—an establishment similar in many ways to our place at the Hoarfrost. I did not know whether Bill Carpenter or any of his family would be there that day, but I looked forward to finding out.

I went outside again for a look around. The sun was making brief appearances between low rows of scudding clouds. Beyond the shelter of the cove blowing snow was obscuring the lake's surface in a thick white blur. It was a strong wind, but it had no teeth. In such temperatures I was not worried about the dogs, their feet or flanks or undercarriages, no matter what the wind did. I decided to pack up.

The wind, which I had cursed so passionately on my southern and eastern trips, and the prospect of which had me trembling in anticipation on my trip north, became on that western trip mostly a welcome diversion to long miles of flat ice. Especially that day, it felt as though that gusty cross breeze from the northwest was helping to clear the cobwebs that had formed in my mood and thoughts as we made our way along the featureless west coast of the lake. It was the same for the dogs, I think, and when they pulled away from Lonely Point late that morning they seemed to be relishing the invigorating blast of moving air. Even while blowing up billows of snow that wind had a breath of spring in it. It was an utterly different creature from the murderous winds out on the Barrens at 30 and 40 below zero.

We crossed the ice toward Moraine Point in one long run and stopped for a break just offshore. A tall jutting headland—a leftover pile of glacial moraine—forms the prominent landmark there. Four tiny sparrow-sized birds tumbled in from the open lake, flapping valiantly head-on into that northwest gale. I marvelled at where they had come from and wondered how their little bodies could possibly store enough energy to move *against* that wall of wind, and to cross such an expanse of snow and ice. The sight of those tiny birds reminded me of a story a friend had told me about watching an exhausted raptor struggle to regain the northwest coast of Lake Superior. The hawk was flying right into the teeth of a strong west wind that must have blown it far off course, out over the open lake miles from land. It nearly made it back, but my friend watched as it ended the struggle by ditching into the waves—and hawks, I think it is safe to surmise, do not swim.

At least those little birds I saw had the choice of setting down on the ice for a rest, even if there was no food for them there. In May and June out in front of our home large flocks of migrating geese often land to rest on the ice of McLeod Bay. They sometimes sit on the white spring ice for many hours—sleeping with a sentry or two posted on the perimeter— before continuing their migration to the tundra.

A fox and two ravens came out from shore as we rested. Probably all three were "locals" at the Moraine Point homestead, and curious about our approach. After lunch we turned in toward land and rounded the point. The dogs seemed to sense that something unusual was ahead— their ears were up and there was a slight hesitation in their gaits. Clearly we had arrived at one of Great Slave Lake's few remaining winter outposts of civilization—buildings, trails, barking dogs, and the small moving figures of distant people up around the main house.[13] I tied the front of my gangline off to some small trees at the shoreline and walked up the path, feeling suddenly timid and uncertain about what sort of reception I would get. I was getting a taste of the same uncertainty that unan- nounced visitors to our place must feel when they first arrive. A generator was thumping away from somewhere nearby, and our arrival had not yet been noticed by anyone except one big dog. Suddenly Bill's wife Mary, who was up on the roof shovelling snow, saw me, waved, and disappeared into an upstairs door. Then Bill emerged from the doorway at ground level, a welcoming smile on his face. He shut off the generator, and my tension fell away.

"Hi, neighbour! Kristen sent me over for a cup of sugar."

He looked perplexed for a brief second and then laughed. Two hun- dred and fifty miles was a long haul between houses, and we were both aware that this arrival was a rare connection between two similar places, spread so far apart on the shores of the big lake.

I have known Bill for many years, and I have always liked him. His legacy in the Northwest Territories is long and varied. Beginning in the 1970s, he almost single-handedly set about to preserve the pure strains of Canadian Eskimo huskies from extinction. A biologist by train- ing, he for many years owned and operated a kennel and pet clinic in Yellowknife. His combined talents as a dog musher, conservation advo- cate, and businessman continued to focus his considerable energy. When I visited in 2005, he was sixty-three years old and had a paying gig as the northern representative for the World Wildlife Fund. Through the won- ders—and pitfalls—of a satellite-dish link to the Internet, he could work right from his desk at Moraine Point, many miles from the nearest road or post office.

I felt genuinely welcomed there that day. I was grateful for that because I know that any unexpected arrival to a remote household can bring a mixed bag of reactions. At times people must wonder, "What goes on out there, all day, each day, year in and year out?" They wonder because they cannot imagine what takes the place of meetings, phones, traffic, and commerce. Yet anyone who has lived full-time in the bush knows that, given a normal dose of zeal and interests, working days in the outback can easily become full almost to overflowing. Drop-in visits, especially in the middle of the day and particularly during seasons when they become daily events, can all too easily be viewed as a disruption and a distraction instead of as pleasures. Whenever I notice my curmudgeonly side coming through I try to take the warning—slow down and rethink the priorities of my life. There can be real joy in the arrival of passing strangers, especially when they pull in under their own steam by canoe or kayak, dog-team or ski. They always have a story to tell.

After chatting with Bill and Mary I picketed my dogs down along the shoreline. I took the added precaution of taping the bolts of the bronze snaps that connect the dogs' collar rings to the tie-out cable. With a few loose dogs around and Bill's own team of huskies staked out in the woods nearby, a loose stranger from my team had potential to cause chaos. Eskimo dogs like Bill and Mary's—and the breed is still officially called "Eskimo" huskies, not "Inuit" huskies—are hardy, loyal, and strong, but among mushers they are notorious for the ferocity of their pack instinct and their passion for fighting. In my team too were several ruffians who loved nothing better than a good brawl. With those scenarios in the back of my mind I kept my ears tuned for any alarmed barking throughout my visit to Moraine Point.

The afternoon and evening of my stopover were, in a word, busy. I offered to lend Bill a hand with his weekly chore of pumping water up to holding tanks high on the third floor of the main house. His method was an elaborate contrast to our bare-bones Hoarfrost system of wintertime water transport—the essential components of which are a hole in the ice, a lowly plastic pail, a handsled with a tow rope, an ice chisel, and muscle power. Bill's system involved many metres of thick flexible firehose, 300 feet of PVC pipe fastened in place up the hill, a big gas-powered water pump, a gas-powered ice auger, a snowmobile, a helper posted upstairs in the house to watch the water level at the tank, and steady back-and-forth communication on walkie-talkies. The end result of all this equipment and effort, though, was truly impressive: 350 gallons (2,800 pounds) of lake water ready to flow into the pipes of the house, and through on-demand propane heaters to faucets in an indoor bathroom, a kitchen, and a shower stall.

When we were done pumping water and draining hoses Bill gave me a tour of his home's systems, enthusiastically detailing everything right down to the bathroom's composting toilet. "Now the toilet, you see, has three separate fans but they're all very low amperage. This one here pulls air up and out of the holding tank, while this one on this big pipe draws warm air down from the upper floor of the house and warms the urine part of the system so that in winter the urine can still drain into the grey-water tank without freezing. And this one..." (My mind must have wandered because I cannot recall what the third fan did.) In my journal that night I remarked, "Our outhouse looks pretty simple and appealing in contrast. However, I have to admit that my hot shower felt wonderful."

Over dinner we talked about the area and about the country west of the lake. There are wood bison thriving on the west side of Great Slave Lake now, descendants of a small herd brought by barge from Wood Buffalo National Park in 1963. These are enormous creatures, some of the big bulls weighing nearly 3,000 pounds on the hoof—easily the largest land animals this side of Africa. The bison (usually called "buffalo"), along with woodland caribou, poplar trees, and shallow sulfur-smelling ponds, make the west and south shores of the lake distinct from the hardscrabble coastlines of the Canadian Shield to the north and east. Listening to the talk around the table I wished I could continue west for at least a day or two inland, but my supplies and the mileage back home dictated that Moraine Point would be our turnaround point.

Later that night, far too late for my own liking, Bill asked me to help dismantle the door of the kitchen's big Kenmore refrigerator. He wanted to change the direction of the door opening from right to left, or vice versa, I can't recall which. The next morning I wrote: "It was pretty funny. There I was, at the far end of Great Slave Lake at 10 o'clock on a winter night, sweating like a pig in ripe layers of trail clothes, two tool kits spread out on the floor and an instruction manual in my hand, extracting something like 54 little hex-head tapping screws from beneath the rubber door seal on a brand-new refrigerator. 'They've got all the modern inconveniences,' as my Dad would have said."

We never did get the door hinge reversed. Finally everyone crept off to sleep. I was shown to a palatial 24-by-40-foot log building, and I appreciated better than most what heating up such a big space for a guest represents to a homestead's wood supply. Thinking about Moraine Point and Hoarfrost River, and of what makes each place tick, I mulled over a theme that has been persistent during our years at the Hoarfrost River:

I often encounter a disparaging, "Well, it sure must be nice," attitude when people consider our lifestyle and situation. That wistful envy gets tiresome, and its follow-up line, "Oh and you have your own airplanes—wow!," only leads me to several unvarnished responses as the years go by. One is that I have honestly wondered at times whether we might be better off and happier *without* the planes.

Another response is a rhetorical question as to why more people in northern Canada *don't* own and fly their own small bush planes. The efficiency and freedom of a private plane and a pilot's licence for people like Bill and Mary at Moraine Point seems obvious. Their place is only about 50 air miles out from two major communities, Hay River and Yellowknife. With an older-model Cessna or Taylorcraft or Cub, many thousands of dollars in annual charter flying bills would disappear. (To be partly replaced, of course, by maintenance bills both expected and "surprise," insurance bills, fuel bills, and so on.)

There is that old phrase "choose your poison." I fly small bush planes and we manage to make a living at it; meanwhile we haul our water in pails and take our wintertime baths in the sauna. Bill calls up a flying service and charters planes when he needs them, and each plane can be chosen to suit the needs of that particular flight. He is thus free of the ongoing concerns of owning an airplane. He pumps his water and puts time and energy into maintaining his pumps, pipes, indoor toilet and on-demand water heaters—and of course that wide-door refrigerator! Once all the systems are up and running, his family and guests enjoy hot showers, and an opened can of milk can be set in the fridge until it is used up. Starting from a very similar "square one"—that is, transplanted white man with university education meets boreal-forest wilderness—our two lives and homes have naturally diverged according to the tastes, interests, and subconscious predilections of their inhabitants. It is cultural evolution in a nutshell. We make our choices, and like most people we sometimes question those choices and whine about them as we go along. The grass can look greener on the other side of the hill, because that is human nature. The various shades of green can be perplexing.

It was cold and clear the next morning. Time for the dogs and me to turn east. Before I packed my sled, Bill took me on a snowmobile tour up to the height of the Moraine Point bluff. We each drove a big wide-track machine selected from his fleet, and I was completely bamboozled by the gearshift on the one he lent to me, offering R, L, N, and H for Reverse, Low, Neutral, and High. This was a far cry from our little one-lung Tundra Skidoo at the Hoarfrost. Bill patiently got me under way; clearly he was eager for this chance to share his time and his place. We talked about the forest, the lake ice, summer windstorms, and his dwindling team of Eskimo dogs.

When I finally hooked up to leave, his family all gathered around. I gave a ride to several of the kids, Bill and Mary's grandchildren who were visiting on their spring break, for the first few hundred yards. When they jumped off I waved and rounded the point. The vista of the open lake spread out ahead of us. I was on our backtrail again, freed from calling commands to the lead dogs. As on every trip this was a profound pleasure. The silence and the space around me were a pleasure too, after hours of non-stop listening and talking.

Two and a half hours out from Bill and Mary's, I stopped at the campsite on Lonely Point. There I spent at least twenty minutes frantically churning up the snow in search of my two long aluminum pickets. I had missed them as I mentally accounted for my gear after leaving the hubbub of Moraine Point, looking down at the key items stowed at the back of the sled load: axe, rope, ice pitons, dog booties, spare necklines. Realizing that the aluminum stakes were not there, I figured I had left them at Moraine Point, or at the camp at Lonely.

I have never been very good at making departures—by dogteam, boat, or bush plane—while under the enthusiastic scrutiny of onlookers, however friendly or familiar. Something always seems to get lost or forgotten. My search at the campsite did not turn up the pickets, and I figured Bill would find them and put them to use. I decided to just sit and enjoy my lunch break.

That atmosphere of fanfare at departure is very distracting...just relax about 15 bucks worth of aluminum, Dave—you burned up at least that much in camp stove fuel over the past week...For Chrissakes just relax, period...Even 24 hours in the hustle and chatter of a household, and now I'm still mulling over snippets of conversation, remarks, underlying inferences...

One thing I was struck by is how relatively *simple* Kristen and I have kept things at home, and how we both seem generally happy with that approach. How rare that simplicity is in the mindset of these times, and this culture.

Now we are homeward bound. I can feel it. It's like hitting the coast on the Iditarod, except there's no race on.

I made camp right out on the sweep of the open ice again that night, far enough from land to impart the sense of vastness and exposure I was seeking. I could just make out the low eastern tip of Hardisty Island, about seven miles off. I had left Moraine Point thinking I might steer straight for Hardisty from there, a crossing of about 30 miles. But our back trail, just a wind-scoured pair of inch-and-a-half sled-runner tracks, had been too welcome to ignore and we had stuck to it. We had come 40 miles in five hours and forty minutes, for a speed of over seven miles an hour. The team was strong and happy, the day was sunny, the evening clear and calm. Over the afternoon I had relaxed back into the trip and the trail.

One odd facet of that second ice camp set me up for a few days of bizarre concern: I could not see the lights of Yellowknife from that camp. This struck me as strange, since they had been so plainly visible from the previous one. The two ice camps were in almost precisely the same place. The sight of them from the first camp must have been entirely a result of temperature inversion. I had thought that some of the city lights, or at least a glow, would be visible even without the lifting effect of warmer air aloft. More mysterious, though, and less easily explained, was the silence that night. On the evening of 16 March, and again the next morning, I had clearly heard the steady air traffic in and out of Yellowknife. "Like living alongside a railroad track," I had noted. But at that second ice camp on 19 March, there was nothing—not even the distant crackle of a jet far overhead, en route to anywhere—Frankfurt, Vancouver, Tokyo. Those two absences—no lights, no sound of air traffic—together led me into some speculations that I am a little shy about divulging. The first hint of them is in my notes from the morning of 20 March: "Still no airplanes. What, oh what, is going on 'out there?'"

That journal entry marks the start of a couple of days of low-grade absurdity, during which I became more and more thoroughly convinced that something very serious was going on—something along the lines of the immediate aftermath of the 9/11 attacks, when virtually all non-military air traffic in North America was suspended by official edict. Even the small floatplanes scheduled to fly north out of Yellowknife and retrieve trophy hunters from remote lodges were grounded for two days after that infamous 11 September. I suppose my ensuing agitation, out there on the ice of Great Slave Lake, is not something I should be embarrassed to admit, but it is. I simply could not explain why I had so plainly heard all those airliners bound in and out from Yellowknife on one night, and then, from virtually the same spot on the ice, in clear calm weather three nights later, I could hear absolutely nothing. It mystifies me to this day.

On down the tiresome menu of global disasters my imaginings went. There had been another attack, this one bigger, perhaps nuclear, perhaps widespread; clearly broad enough to affect the day-to-day life of Canada's most remote reaches. I remembered being at home in early November 2001 on a morning when I was to fly to Yellowknife in our little ski plane. I had the radio tuned to an AM station when suddenly the CBC's morning talk show cut to the crash of an airliner in New York City. It seemed all too familiar. My friend Ken sat in the house with me and we listened to the first few reports. "You better get on your way before they ground everybody again," he muttered. It seemed like good advice at the time, although that morning's New York crash turned out to be simply that—an airplane accident—with no jihadist lunatics on the flight deck.

This is an old theme with me. In fact, I have lived much of my life with the lingering subconscious expectation that our civilization was all going to come unravelled. In May 2005, a few months after the trip west and the mysterious missing lights and planes of Yellowknife, I wrote in my journal:

> I have spent my life thinking that someday soon this would all come tumbling down. I am not exaggerating and I do mean *all of this* in the largest sense. When I was in 7th grade, I had a social studies teacher who went out of his way to detail for us the effects of a nuclear attack on—for the purposes of his example—the city of Chicago, a mere 60 miles from our classroom. I seriously approached my father and made my case for a move to Michigan's remote Upper Peninsula. Gradually my expectations changed—environmental disaster would do us in: the air and water would be poisoned, a nuclear power plant would melt down, and so on down the list—the Cassandras are never short of dire predictions.
>
> Now, at 47, I realize that I still think this way, deep down, as if I had been brainwashed at the ripe old age of 12, not by some totalitarian or religious cult, but by that hip 1969 teacher's forecast of imminent doom. These years the mushroom-cloud threats have merged with others in a perfect storm: global warming, radical plots, economic collapse, and so on.
>
> At the same time I have finally grown weary—and wary—of this view, and of what it can breed: a festering, perverse *hope* that it will be vindicated by events. Especially now, with our children, I want to move past that doomsday view which has become such a habit. Actor and conservationist Peter Coyote, sharing a 1999 presentation with Gary Snyder, said: "Well, my sense of optimism has had the shit kicked out of it. But it's still kicking."[14] I should take courage from his words, and try to re-establish my own optimism.

From our home at the Hoarfrost River, arguably among the most remote family dwellings in North America, a person naturally begins to view world events as a spectator. That is wearisome. It is another version of my fellow pilot's remarks about the view out the Twin Otter window— there's no real connection to what's out there, it's more like watching a movie. That morning out on the ice, with no sound of jets moving in and out of the Yellowknife airport, the movie plot had made an odd digression.

Meanwhile, back in the little red tent:

Morning, Day 10, March 20th: the Spring Equinox. Ice camp off Hardisty Island. –20°, wind building from the east (oh boy!), sky clear, some cirrus on all horizons. A row of curled-up huskies. A sled, a tent, a shovel marking the spot where the dogs' cooler-full of breakfast is buried in the snow.

A phrase from folksinger Gordon Bok, I think: "you wait for the wind to tell you about your day…" Mushing or flying, hunting or sailing, it's right on the money. Story of my life.

This journey, and with it all four journeys together, now round the turn into the home stretch. This ice run back to Wilson Island, which might take us into tomorrow, feels like the final unknown of the entire endeavour. Beyond there the lake and route are all old-shoe familiar, and on the Hearne Channel we will be turning up the lane that leads to home.

The ice is making noise this morning—minor adjustments I suppose. Warming or cooling, shifting and settling. Last night I was about to drop the hook alongside a pressure ridge, with thoughts of having liquid water at hand for camp, or big blocks of ice for easy melting, but I changed my mind and went on. I did not want to lie awake in the tent at 2 a.m. with sounds of this massive plate of ice cracking and heaving beneath us.

"He crouched in the sleigh and raved all day / of his home in Tennessee," wrote Robert Service of the last day of sledding for stricken Sam McGee.[15] Day ten certainly saw me crouching, if not raving, as we forced our way east into a strong headwind. Compared to the deadly flash-freezer blasts of the trip east, though, the wind was little more than a steady presence, rising at times to the level of a minor annoyance. With that 2002 crossing from the Thelon back to Reliance as a benchmark (alongside a few memorable passages down the Bering Sea coast in my Iditarod years), I had a new standard. It seemed like it had become difficult to take any wind very seriously, as long as the temperature was above minus 25 degrees.

Still, it was a long crossing that day—seven hours of steady fast running for the dogs, seven hours of crouching low on the runners for me, broken only by three rest stops of about forty minutes apiece. I caught my first glimpse of the Outpost Islands about 2 p.m., and we passed abeam them at three twenty-five. The "big ice"—as I had come to think of it—was behind us. Home was less than 200 miles away, and on the calendar it was the final day of winter. At the second rest stop that day: "Far out on the big ice, miles from any land, I glanced to my right and spotted two birds the size of ravens or hawks, only a few feet above the ice, flapping hard into the wind and moving just barely faster than we were, perfectly parallel to our course." Astounding to me, these energy-extravagant journeys that creatures of all sizes undertake. Where were they going, those two, flying right into the teeth of that wind and making a groundspeed of barely nine knots? What was the big deadline for some destination upwind? I once thought that only we humans exhibited such stubborn wilfulness, but I have revised that notion. "Well hell, we talked about crossing the lake today, dear, so we may as well go..."

Benign though it was, the wind did eventually wear on my nerves, and the long hours of crouching took a predictable toll on my mood. By the time we reached the cache camp at Wilson Island, I was exhausted and shamefully short-tempered with my stalwart leaders Ernie and Kaltag. We had come 48 miles in straight-line distance for the day's run, and probably 50 on the ice, all of it straight into the teeth of the wind. Despite my pooh-poohing of the wind's ferocity early in the day, that night I had to revise my notions and admit this: a relentless wind, combined with almost any degree of cold, can sap a person's energy and resolve like nothing else in nature. The only thing that tops it, to my mind, is immersion in ice water. I suppose thin air would be on that miserable top-three list as well, but I have no experience with hypoxia except from the comfort of a cockpit.

The dogs were tired but they had handled the long crossing with perfect aplomb. Ernie was at the onset of his finest four years as a lead dog, and that day he stuck like a bloodhound to the tiny wind-scoured runner scrapes as they led east. In my thinking, that day the mantle of "main leader" was officially passed from Steve to Ernie, just as a few years earlier it had gone to Steve from Jiminy, who had received it from McDougal, who took it from Beaver, and on and on back through my decades of dog mushing. To witness this gradual and subtle passage of skill and knowledge from one generation of dogs to the next is one of the great joys of having a long connection to a kennel of sled dogs. With good bloodlines, a musher's task becomes more a matter of *discovering* that innate gift for leadership in certain dogs, instead of the step by step *training* of leaders. All we have to do is to give the veterans ample opportunities to mentor their proteges, and gradually the next generation is made ready to take over.

Thinking of those old lead dogs, most of them dead for many years, I realized with a jolt that on that precise date, 20 March 1981, I had first driven a dogteam onto the ice of Great Slave Lake, at Yellowknife Bay. It had been a low-key departure from a low-key part of Yellowknife's Old Town—a nondescript stand of alders and small shacks in the neighbourhood called The Woodyard. (In one of those odd circular coincidences of life's geography, nowadays I walk right through that piece of lakeshore on almost every trip to Yellowknife.) There were three of us in that group, woefully underpowered with only ten dogs altogether. We were eastbound for Reliance, the Thelon River, and—we hoped—the distant Inuit hamlet of Baker Lake, more than 600 trail miles from Yellowknife. Our two stout sleds, home-built monsters of oak and steel and polyethylene, were groaning with piles of heavy, ill-chosen, and downright superfluous gear. Mushing experience, dog-power, and high-quality rations for the dogs were among the main items in short supply. For example, our dog-feeding regimen on that trip still makes me shake my head in amazement. A scant pound of dry Purina kibble (and not the high-octane mix) tossed out on the snow for each dog, followed by a quarter-pound chunk of frozen lard, was each dog's daily fare. This we dutifully doled out once every twenty-four hours, without a drop of water.[16]

Six weeks later, after a journey of more than 600 miles, Kurt Mitchell and I arrived, not in Baker Lake, but back in Reliance. We had reached a bend in the Thelon River just upstream from Hornby Point before turning west in a humble, hungry retreat. Our third companion, John Mordhorst, had been flown out to civilization about two weeks earlier, when his mother down in Illinois had suffered a near-fatal stroke and word of this had reached us.[17] In retrospect that 1981 journey marked the start of a much longer journey for me—thirty-some years at this writing, and still counting. On our stopovers in Reliance I had a view north out onto the wide sweep of McLeod Bay—across to the rugged hills above the Hoarfrost River. That glimpse was, in the corny banter of greeting cards, the first day of the rest of my life.

Thinking back on that trip became a theme for the next several days as I travelled east up the lake toward home. The intervening years had certainly changed me, while the lake and landscape had changed only slightly—if at all. My memories of that trip and of what it began for me prompted some ruminations about fate, musings nudged forward by a line I read on my layover at Wilson Island. In Wendell Berry's novel *Jayber Crow* the title character, a small-town Kentucky barber, reflects, "But now it looks to me as though I was following a path that was laid out for me, unbroken, and maybe even as straight as possible from one end to the other, and I have this feeling, which never leaves me any more, that I have been *led*."[18]

After our windy ice crossing I decided we would rest for one full day at the cache camp on Wilson Island, no matter what the weather did. The next morning I slept until nearly eight thirty, completely dead to the world. The weather map for that date shows a low-pressure area centred on northern Alberta, surrounded by a tight ring of pressure isobars over Great Slave Lake. I woke to the steady roar of wind in the treetops. Outside, when I finally poked my nose through the tent flap, the sky was partly cloudy and the thermometer showed 16 below. I estimated the wind at 20 to 25 knots, although we were sheltered from it by the high ridge of Wilson Island rising up behind camp. I was delighted to have the crossing of the ice behind us. We had been very lucky.

Delightful too was the prospect of a complete day off from mushing—the first and only such day on that trip. I sat by the stove and wrote in my journal, a long and wandering entry with notes on dogs, the weather, and a long reminiscence about the big caribou skin that made one layer of the mattress beneath my sleeping bags.

I remember Liv and Annika scraping away on it with their little knives and scrapers, doing such a fine job that I have done nothing more to it. Annika and I waking in the little hut on Maufelly Bay early last September, looking out through a wet thick snowstorm and seeing two magnificent bulls standing on the flank of the esker just north of the hut. I downed one with an easy rifle shot from the porch. Annika burst into tears when the bull fell and lay kicking his last, his comrade standing motionless alongside. But her tears ended almost as quickly as they had started, and in five minutes she was out the door and at my side, chattering happily and helping me skin and butcher.[19] What a childhood our girls are living…How I miss them. How glad I am to be coming onto the home stretch of this *final* compass-point solo.

It had been months since I had taken a day completely off. That entire winter had been a steady procession of events and looming deadlines in our "simple" Hoarfrost life. My day of rest at Wilson Island posed the challenge of trying to shift a habit of mind that had become accustomed, perhaps even addicted, to the constant pressure of urgent priorities—what I think of as the "brush-fire" state of mind. Put out one fire and look around for the next. My stopover at Moraine Point had been a pleasant change of pace, but it had been filled with new faces and steady conversation, not solitude and rest. On Wilson Island I was alone. In late morning I took up with the predictable round of repacking, made some minor sled repairs, and took a careful look at the dogs' feet (all in good shape). After a pot of soup and a mug of real coffee I sat by the wood stove and read for a long time. The wind battered the tent with barrages of gusts, even there in the sheltered hollow of our camp.

In late afternoon I set off on a long snowshoe walk up over the crest of the island. My thoughts were all on home; I could tell that the pleasures of solitude were wearing thin. I reflected on the hustle and bustle of life.

We are all in a hurry, and at the same time all claiming we'd like to slow down. We are like Liv on her dogsled back at home, barrelling down the final hill onto the lake. As she comes flying into the steep turn I shout "Ride your brake, Liv!" and she dutifully stomps on the brake with one foot—and keeps on pedalling like mad with the other. That's all of us. If we could only devise and adopt ways of using our time *more efficiently*, we think, well then we could slow down and have *more* time—which we could then use *more* efficiently…Huh? We all seem to have forgotten the phrase that my 1981 mushing partner Kurt Mitchell used to attribute to old Gus D'aoust of Reliance: "When God made time, boys, he made plenty of it."

As sundown passed and evening twilight deepened I passed through the sombre narrows of nightfall. This was the first night of spring—who could possibly stay sombre? I felt my energy rebounding. Life was good. I had a warm tent and a good supper. My dogs were strong and happy. I was still nagged by that perceived hiatus in air traffic, although I had heard a turboprop plane somewhere in the distance in late afternoon. I chuckled at the realization that seventy-five or eighty years ago an airplane had likely never been seen from this spot on earth, so how could it now be that not seeing or hearing one for forty-eight hours made a person suspect the complete collapse of civilization?

I had asked Bill to pass a message to Kristen, changing our next radio check-in date to coincide with my night at the Wilson Island camp. At 8 p.m. I tuned in the transceiver but could hear only the lively chatter of

Inuit voices from up on the Arctic Coast—no Kristen at the Hoarfrost.
I read *Jayber Crow* and tried to write a few more lines in my journal.
"Drowsy now. A good day—I ... [illegible.]"

———————

Îles Basses, les Îles Terribles, Gros Cap ... the middle reaches of Great
Slave Lake are filled with landmarks named by the voyageurs of the
fur trade. The islands and channels where the wide western basin of
Great Slave narrows into the East Arm (the neck of the eastbound flying
goose that the lake's shape suggests) are a crossroad of navigation. The
points and channels there are imbued with the echoes of past travellers.
Akaitcho River, Matonabbee Point, Hornby Channel, Blanchet Island, all
named for people long gone. It is what I think of as the "old" part of the
lake. It is the oldest part of the lake in my own memory, too, because of
that first journey across the ice in 1981 and my first summer voyage out
to the Hoarfrost in July 1983.

The novelty of that stretch of lake has worn off. Over the years I have
mushed, boated, flown, and snowmobiled dozens of times past Blanchet
and Et-Then Islands, around McKinley Point and Narrow Island and up
through Taltheilei Narrows. And usually I have been intent on miles and
hours, on getting somewhere by some certain date or time: Yellowknife,
Blachford Lake, Lutsel K'e, or home. As I packed up to leave the layover
camp, I feared I would succumb to that "destination" mentality in the
final miles between Wilson Island and McLeod Bay. Once my cache barrels and the big yellow tent were all stowed in the shoreline alders for
retrieval by ski plane later that spring, I pulled the snubline loop. The dogs
surged out of the bay into the long reach lying south of the island. With a
couple of loud "Gee" commands I turned them west onto our tracks.

Instantly their momentum dwindled to nothing. The spark went out
of the entire team in the span of a hundred feet. I was mystified. Then I
realized—*they think we're going west again*—which of course we were.
They must have thought we were heading back out onto the big ice. I tried
to reassure them with some singsong chatter, but it was a lacklustre string
of huskies that plodded west out of that camp. Once we rounded the
tip of Wilson Island and turned north, then northeast, they grew more
energetic with every step. Clearly I was not the only one focused on home
sweet home by that point in the trip.

After that sputtering start, the day quickly evolved into one of those
purely magical days of dog mushing. The Hearne Channel had been
swept by those strong easterly winds for several days straight, and the farther northeast we went the harder and choppier the surface became. The

dogs ran faster and harder than they had for days, pounding me over the drifts and sastrugi at a breakneck pace. From the Caribou Islands to the spot where we joined the main Yellowknife-Lutsel K'e trail, the team was in high spirits. The dog-mushing slang for such moments is *rolling,* as in "they finally started rolling through that stretch," and the verb is perfect. There is a constant tip and lurch to the sled's motion over such uneven drifted snow, but at the right speed—fast, but not too fast—the team's momentum smoothes it all into a boisterous dance. It's the sastrugi boogie. You're *rolling.*

Almost as soon as we hit the main trail I saw a lone snowmobile and driver closing rapidly on us, westbound for Yellowknife. I stopped the team and anchored the snow hook in the firm trail. The driver stopped alongside my shying dogs and turned off his engine. This settled the dogs down, and we talked. He was Larry Nita, heading back to Yellowknife from Lutsel K'e. Liza Enzoe had died; she was his aunt and he had been to her funeral. He lit up a cigarette. He looked a little quizzical when I asked him if there was any big news in the world, gave it a few seconds of thought, and said no, not really. He told me there were two tourists on Tundras (the model name of a small Skidoo) a few miles to the east, near where the trail came down from Blachford Lake Lodge. He had left Lutsel K'e two and a half hours ago. He figured he would be about another hour and a half to Yellowknife. He flicked his smoke onto the snow and started his machine. We traded a version of the nonchalant forearm-and-mitten northern wave, which conveys something like, "Since we seem to be the only two human beings alive this afternoon in an area at least the size of Prince Edward Island or Massachusetts, I dutifully acknowledge your existence—but I'm sure as hell not going to get all warm and fuzzy about it..."

Lured ahead by the prospect of meeting the two tourists from Blachford Lodge, I carried on to the trailhead before taking our midday break. The dogs had made a three-and-a-half-hour run, full tilt and nonstop, since leaving camp, and they all sprawled for a rest in the sun. I ate my lunch. The tourists were nowhere to be seen, evidently already gone up the trail back to the lodge. I reviewed my conversation with Larry, as a person will do when it is the only such exchange in many days, but there wasn't much to rehash.

The light was coming back. At the winter solstice three months earlier we had turned the corner into the season of light, but now that we had passed the equinox we were rapidly and gleefully outstripping all points south in our daily measure of sunshine. We were plunging headlong toward the twenty-four-hour daylight of early summer. Sunglasses had suddenly become as vitally important as mittens. My eyes feasted on the vivid reds and blues of the dogs' harnesses, and my cheeks glowed in the warm touch of our wonderful star. A couple of ravens had been playing tag with us all the way across the Hearne Channel, and as we rested they landed on the ice and hopped around. I recalled a story I had heard about ravens leading wolf packs along for miles toward distant herds of caribou, in order to show the wolves the way to the caribou. Once the wolves and caribou met up, of course, the ravens could scavenge the wolf pack's kills.

Earlier in my life I had found that story hard to swallow, but the longer I live in raven country the more plausible such stories become. Watching the ravens, I wondered about this gradual softening or broadening of a person's acceptance of the unknown, especially as we glimpse facets of that deep mystery played out in the lives of our fellow creatures. Over time I have grown more, not less, open to such "soft" unscientific notions when it comes to dogs, moose, caribou, wolves, and ravens—not to mention women, men, and children. I have become more suspicious of the pat black-and-white pronouncements of our culture's new religion, Science with a capital S. I suppose this gradual opening to mystery could be the beginning of what is labelled "wisdom." Age and experience play into it—what seemed like clear straight lines become wobbly and indistinct. Even a hard-bitten dog musher becomes less *dogmatic.* The sum of my "wise" impressions that afternoon: "Ravens are awfully damned smart."

In an hour or less, at McKinley Point, I knew we would leave the smooth-packed Lutsel K'e highway and head northeast up the Hearne Channel. The whack and bounce of the sastrugi boogie would resume. I sat in the sun and made a few more notes: "What peace, 11 dogs sacked out...Moon must be nearing full by tonight—this full moon has something to do with the timing of the Easter holiday...Kaltag and Ernie are up and ready. It's time."

––––––––––

Camp that night, 22 March, was in a little cove named in my journal only as a set of latitude and longitude numbers "near Narrow Island." The deep fluffy snow near shore was a beautiful place to picket the dogs, with both ends of the tie-out cable secured to ice pitons. After hours punctuated by the banging of sled runners on wood-hard drifts, the billows of soft snow and the dim light of dusk were a sensuous salve for my muscles and nerves. It seemed as if the dogs felt the same way, as they burrowed and circled and fussed with their deep-powder beds along the line of the tie-out. As I set up camp I wondered why I was bothering with the tent at all, and not just sleeping out on such a night. I pondered this question further in my journal (from inside the tent!) and decided that I was getting soft and stodgy, suckered into all the accoutrements of life in the Hilleberg: candlelight, heat, eating my dinner without gloves or a hat, and writing at leisure with my legs wrapped up in the folds of my parka. The pleasures of life inside, the predictable routines and habits, easily offset the effort of putting up and taking down my tent, and outweighed the allure of a night sleeping out in the open beneath the stars. That could wait until spring truly arrived.

I was able to reach Kristen on the radio that night. She had not received my message from Bill about trying to change the radio schedule. As always it was a relief to learn that everything was fine at home and in the world at large. By the time we signed off I was assured that the Apocalypse was not upon us. She reported 25 below zero at the Hoarfrost, and overnight the temperature dropped at our camp. By morning it was minus 24 degrees, the coldest we had seen for eight days. The thick ice under the tent creaked and clicked all night as the cold deepened. We had made another 42 straight-line miles, with an additional three to five for wobbles and angles in the trail. The dogs were fit and strong, but they were all a little skinnier than I would have liked. Clearly the calorie count was not keeping up with our daily mileages, even in such mild weather. I felt fit and lean too, but not with the same intensity as on the previous trips. This trip west was turning out to be a fairly cushy ride for me, with the long days of lake running and the easy temperatures.

As we turned up the home stretch, I began to reflect on all of the four trips as a cohesive four-year endeavour. Was there to be a unifying thread or theme? With only two or three days to go I wondered whether I might be granted some sort of culmination. That brought to mind a notion that had come to me years earlier, a little phrase which seems to ring true in my life: "Culminations cannot be orchestrated." Culminations of journeys or experiences do not come on schedule. A journey, like a life or a career, culminates when and if it damned well pleases. It seems to me that the culminations of things—for there may be several—happen somewhere within or during a process, at those fleeting moments when everything is exquisite perfection. There, just then, and then gone. *That* was a culmination—did you catch it?

Perhaps we had caught one that day:

Ernie with his ears laid flat, like a running back threading a broken field of players, ducking and weaving, looking for the best line through, over, and around the steep hard drifts. A quietly spoken "gee" or "haw" from me every few seconds. The gait of every dog in the team right on that cusp between a trot and a lope, the miles just falling away behind us. Watching them run I thought, "They do not do this for me. They do it because, to them, running in harness in a team is the bedrock core of everything they love about life itself."

A quartering tailwind from the southwest pushed us along as we left camp next morning, and it backed into the south-southwest as we rounded Sachowia Point. There we left our outbound trail; we would not cross it again. I had decided early on that we would go home by my favourite route, through Taltheilei Narrows and northeast up the broad curve of McLeod Bay. In late morning a twin-engine Piper Navajo circled me overhead, then made a low pass with flaps down. I gave them a relaxed wave and imagined a young, slightly bored "sked" pilot (referring to a job flying only scheduled flights, although in Canada why are they not "shed" pilots?) making his daily run between Lutsel K'e and Yellowknife, probably snapping a photo to show the folks back home.

At Sachowia Point memories flooded back from a jumble of trips, including the voyage in the old wooden runabout in 1983, bound back to Yellowknife late in September. My friend Mitch and I had been windbound for several days just east of the point. The theme of those stormy days had been basic—we had ten hungry sled dogs on board and we were running low on food for them. A gale was blowing from the west and I was half-heartedly casting a big spoon out into the rollers. I hooked a big trout, and it made a slanting sideways run parallel to the big swells. I still remember the silvery flash of its trajectory as it sliced right through the crest of a breaking wave. It was an enormous, beautiful fish that we fed to the dogs as a thick soup with boiled corn meal, saving the trout cheeks as an hors d'oeuvre for our own supper of spruce grouse. At Sachowia Point I paused to give the dogs a break, although I noted happily that "these dogs are not the slightest bit tired." The point itself is a thickly wooded brow plunging steeply into the lake, but its beauty had been utterly marred within the past couple of days by a fresh claim post.

Right on the prow of the point, a few paces up from shore, the claim-staker had hacked down a spruce sapling and proceeded to festoon the squared-off stump with an entire roll of hot-pink flagging tape. This now-archaic method of claim-staking persists in the Northwest Territories. More enlightened jurisdictions have, in the age of GPS precision, switched over to "paper staking," whereby mineral claims can be registered simply by filing a list of exact coordinates. The time-honoured practice of blazing the claim boundaries with axe cuts and metal tags is a boon for stakers, pilots, and a few northern merchants, but it will surely fade away. I will miss it as a source of interesting flying jobs, but I will not miss those gaudy pink and orange ribbons.

The snow conditions deteriorated the moment we rounded Sachowia Point. The hard pack of the Hearne Channel was gone and our speed dropped off dramatically. The dogs put their heads down and churned forward. I had a pair of skis lashed atop my load, with which I might have helped ease the dogs' work, but one ski had been broken in half at Wilson Island when the sled had tipped completely over. Without my skis, the most helpful thing I could do for the dogs in that soft snow was to keep my weight centred on the sled runners. I pedalled and pushed whenever I could, and tried to just shut up and let them work. I could hear a small piston engine to the north of us, its sound coming in brief bursts between gusts of wind. I squinted and strained my eyes, first upward, then down along the shoreline alders, and there it was—a little Cub ski plane, not more than a hundred feet in the air. It landed, taxied, and soon took off again. We were barely creeping along in the deep soft snow, and it took us nearly an hour to come up to where I had seen it. The plane was long gone by then. I could see the flagging tape of claim lines marked along the shore, connected by deep furrows of snowshoe tracks. It looked as though the entire shoreline north from Sachowia Point was being staked, or re-staked.

At three forty-five I turned in to shore and unhitched the dogs' tug-lines. Half a mile ahead were the red-and-white buildings of the big fishing lodge at Taltheilei Narrows, and offshore from them a dark blue stripe of ice-free water. I have yet to see those narrows freeze completely, even at 50 degrees below zero. Evidently the flow of water through them is so strong, and the water wells up from such a depth, that it remains liquid. The customary route around the hazards of thin ice and open water is a treacherous skirting of the rocky shoreline right up to the lodge's dock, followed by a winding climb past buildings, beached boats, and parked trucks to join the narrow road out to the airstrip.[20]

For years I had followed this traditional nerve-wracking route past the narrows in winter, until in January 2002 bad weather forced me to take a low detour over the lodge on a flight home from Yellowknife. That day I noticed a narrow cutline through the spruce forest, a useful shortcut connecting the shoreline south of the lodge to the road which runs out to the airstrip. Later that winter a friend and I passed that way by dogteam and we took time to break open and blaze that cutline. I have used it ever since, and I have blithely assumed that other travellers would quickly catch on to the advantage of using it. To my surprise nobody has. Every winter the "locals" (i.e., the Lutsel K'e hunters) make their trail right down through the lodge, pick their way gingerly past the shoreline boulders on a scanty few inches of ice, and hug the shore south of the narrows. Old habits do die hard.

I left the team to rest in the sunshine and set off on snowshoes to break open "my" cutline. As expected, once I reached the airstrip road there were snow-machine tracks already on it, so I turned around and tramped back to the sled. The late afternoon had turned calm and mild. I paused as I came into sight of the shoreline: the sparkle of snow, the sleek fur of the curled-up dogs, the bright primary-colour spangle of my sled-cover and gear, all against the backdrop of the narrows and the sheer cliffs on the far shore...a culmination?

At that point in the day a sensible old woodsman, having broken out the trail on snowshoes, would have made camp and waited overnight for the snow to firm up, then crossed the portage next morning. Knowing this full well, I set about ignoring it. I wanted to camp beyond the narrows if we could. I hooked up the dogs and started over the soft trail, pushing and grunting, swearing and sweating. Dandy and Jasmine, churning along in wheel at the rear of the team, gave up on walking and resorted to dog-paddling through the powdery fluff. The sled moved forward at the pace of a very slow walk. Once we reached the airstrip road the old snowmobile tracks were firm enough for good sledding. We quickly rounded the little bay northwest of the lodge and pulled up alongside a big derelict wooden scow. It has been beached there since sometime in the 1960s. I had always wanted to examine it at leisure, and it was time to make camp. I could have a look at that scow in the light of morning.

Our camp faced across the small bay toward the main compound of the fishing lodge. I could see the three flagpoles that flank the picture windows of the dining room, where the Maple Leaf, the Stars and Stripes, and the flag of the Northwest Territories all flutter and freeze through the long off-season. An assortment of snow-covered vehicles—school buses, road graders, and pickup trucks—crowd around the buildings and along the apron of the long airstrip, like abandoned relics of a once-bustling colony. The lodge buildings and the tidy cabins for guest and staff are drifted in and boarded up. A frostbitten musher, driving a dogteam past the hibernating main dining hall, cannot help but muse upon the coterie of waitresses who smile there on warm July evenings. Ah, the plates of salad and steak, the heavy glass tumblers of bourbon, that jocular Rotarian sport-fishing camaraderie, all to the rustle of smooth blouses and skirts...In the icy twilight of a winter afternoon it is all melancholy and forlorn. I suppose this may be another reason why these days I prefer to bypass the main cluster of buildings and tramp through the woods on the cutline.

Just up the hill from my tent that night was one of the tall signposts popular in far-flung tourist destinations and military camps. Hand-lettered placards were nailed to the post, pointing off in various directions, indicating that the visitor to Plummer's Lodge is 93 miles from Yellowknife; 1,733 miles from Chicago; 1,902 miles from the North Pole; 2,000-something from Houston; 3,000-something from Hawaii. The weathered signs stacked on the white post assert the studied ambience of such lodges. Bastions of a distant civilization, quiet retreats for the world-weary movers and shakers, places defined mostly by their distance *away from* those other—and by tacit agreement more "real" and important—worlds.

Darkness came on and the dogs and I settled in for the night. A soothing peace seemed to drape itself over my shoulders that evening, tinged with a little sadness. The trip— and all the trips—now nearly done, and I was not overly eager to reach the end. Ahead was the length of McLeod Bay, a 75-mile arc of ice and snow as familiar to me as a winding country driveway, leading to home.

The morning of day fourteen, 24 March, was overcast and calm. An unremarkable morning, except for the mildness of the air: minus seven degrees. It would almost certainly be a warm journey up the western half of McLeod Bay that day. The prospect of such warmth and comfort was nearly intoxicating. My four most recent passages through that part of the lake had been savage struggles in headwinds and deep cold, and I had begun to consider the place jinxed. As I stood outside the tent with the slightest south breeze nuzzling my cheek, it was clear that the curse had lifted.

For some reason—maybe the caress of that breeze, maybe those boarded-up cabins—my notes and thoughts that morning as I sipped coffee were all about men and women, the fickleness and hazards of love and the human heart. "Odd thoughts for a wilderness journey winding down. Probably rooted in my musings yesterday about the 23-year-old Dave, out on the lake, heading for Snowdrift in 1981 . . . how life unfolds year by year, how young loves can so swiftly and haphazardly change the course of our early adult years, how chance meetings and journeys so dramatically shape the decades to follow." The clucking of a ptarmigan in the willows just outside the tent snapped me back to the here and now. It was downright warm inside the tent. Had I not become such a slave to my cozy tent-life routine I would have eaten my breakfast outside. Instead, I just threw open the door flaps.

I was acutely aware that morning of how much I had enjoyed the four solo journeys. It had been a real pleasure to travel alone with such good teams of dogs. With just one more person, with or without an additional dogteam, the ambience of the trips would have been utterly changed. Two people, and two teams of dogs, alone in the outback, are so intensely *aware* of each other. That awareness is first and foremost in all minds, canine and human. Huskies are intensely bonded to the team, which is their pack. Their intense focus on the other dogs, with humans a definite second in importance, is in striking contrast to, for example, the focus of a black Lab or a border collie. Among huskies only the truly exceptional lead dogs have a bond to their mushers that rivals the one-to-one bond of a trained bird dog to its human partner. I sometimes think that to a sled dog the human race is just a bothersome necessary component of a pretty good deal: "Will run and pull sleds (which I mostly enjoy anyway), in return for lifelong food and shelter."

Because the dogs are so attuned to each other, travelling alone with a single team is very different from travelling in a group of teams. When a group of teams do travel together it is much more pleasant when "together" means a loose confederation instead of a lockstepped march. The variables of team size, harnessing, sled-loading, and so on all make a simultaneous departure bothersome and difficult to plan. A more casual and anarchistic approach is preferable in many ways. Mushers and their teams pack up, depart, and travel essentially alone, only regrouping sporadically for rests and trail-breaking as the day goes on. I have noticed that this staggered start is the norm when groups of northern Natives set out by snowmobile, and perhaps it harks back to the era of winter travel by dogteam. To a non-Native, and certainly to a tourist adventurer, it seems more normal and comfortable to travel in a very close group— starting and stopping, moving as a pack. Of course, either approach works with machines, because they do not bark or harass each other at close quarters, or wear themselves out in an insatiable quest to close the gap on the front-runners (although there is plenty of that instinct in some snowmobile drivers.)

I took time that morning to make a thorough examination of the derelict scow that lay like a beached whale alongside the tent. In her day she (or perhaps he) was a stout wooden boat built hastily and heavily, about 40 feet long (eighteen axe handles, as measured that morning) and 12 feet across. Twin rudders, a wide blunt bow for pushing a barge, two big fuel tanks, bunks, and a simple head down below, wheelhouse high and forward, and a big gasoline engine sprouting no less than a dozen spark plugs. Using my repair-kit screwdriver, I pilfered a half-dozen antique porcelain light sockets, strung on copper wires running fore and aft the length of the boat. It would be good to give them a new life back at home, and their useful days aboard the old ship were clearly past. As I climbed into daylight from my tour of the scow, my eye caught the sparkle of sunlight on open water at the narrows. By late winter all eyes in the North are hungry for that glint of sun on waves. It sparks eagerness for the season of sails and paddles, of boats moving up and down the lake. It would still be another three months, but the sparkle enticed me.

I broke camp and started up the throat of the narrows, north from the fishing lodge and its huge runway. The day was so warm and altogether pleasant that I kept stopping to jot in my pocket journal. If every day of my solo trips had been so warm and pleasant, the sheer word count of those journals would have rivalled Proust or Dickens: "Now as I near home I am lost in thoughts of the *future* for minutes at a stretch; then I look around me and think, 'What a place!' Hard to take it all in, steadily and attentively, with home so close and this next traverse so familiar ... These journeys do have meaning, in and of themselves, without so much as a single line of journal notes or a haphazard photograph." I recalled Robert Service's poetic questions: "Have you suffered, starved, and triumphed, groveled down, yet grasped at glory, / Grown bigger in the bigness of the whole? / 'Done things' just for the doing, letting babblers tell the story, / Seeing through the nice veneer the naked soul?"[21]

"Babblers"? Ouch. Riding down the bay on that next-to-last day, I thought about that jab from Service (a babbler himself), fretted a little, then relaxed. These four journeys were worth preserving, if only as part of a record of this place in a specific context and time: here is how it was, for one man in this part of the North, in the winters 2002–2005.

The book will not be "it" anyway. "It" is the trips themselves, and my belief in the importance of them. "It" is Robert Lake, the Noman portage, 46 below at the Thelon cache, frozen dog dicks and frozen toes, the surprise of a mild February day way up on the Back River, our arrival at Moraine Point... "It" is the country deep down, felt and seen and slept with, mile by mile, by dogtrot and snowshoe step. The landscape is a part of me now in a way that it was not a part of me four years ago. "It" is that visceral connection, beyond the realm of language.

———————

Lines of caribou trails in snow dropped down from the steep prow of Gibraltar Point; "More a place for mountain goats than caribou," I remarked to the dogs. We had not crossed a caribou track since our passage down McLeod Bay on that first evening of the trip. By late afternoon we had picked up the traces of our outbound trail from that first night's run. The dogs clearly knew we were coming into the home stretch. A few hundred yards ahead of the lead dogs a wolverine loped across the ice, making as close to a flat-out sprint for safety as a wolverine can muster. We were no threat to it, but Spruce was eager to veer off and give chase. The long patch of glare ice abeam Shelter Point was still polished smooth. Ernie, the only dog in the team who was wearing booties that day, started to slip and skid wildly. I stopped and took his booties off, giving him back the use of his toenails for traction. "Feet heal faster than shoulders," as old Ray Gordon had once reminded me during a race.

That evening, rolling down the shore between Shelter Bay and Sentinel Point, the day's mild air gradually cooled as the shadow of the high cliffs fell over us. With the dogs still moving gracefully, almost effortlessly, a light north breeze puffing up, caribou and wolf tracks here and there...I wanted it never to end. A voice in my mind asked, *"Please can I just do this*—this right now—*forever? And never have to submit an amendment to an airplane maintenance schedule or pay my bills or buy groceries or consider what I am going to do when I am old and can't do this anymore? Can't we just run and run and then, in one perfect moment, like Mallory on the shoulder of Everest, just vanish forever into this cold clean air?"*

Long pause. *"Nope. You can't. You have to go in. Hell, let's face it Olesen, you* want *to go in."*

If no one had been waiting for us at home that night, I probably would have done just that—supper for the dogs and a two- or three-hour rest, then a final 25-mile run in the moonlight, angling northeast across the bay to Wolf Point...and home just before midnight. What convinced me to stop and pitch our final camp was just the imagined sight of a welcome from little Liv—for she had been sound asleep when I arrived from the North the previous winter. I wanted to see her and her sister Annika in broad daylight, tumbling and running down to the shore to greet us as we pulled in.

At that final campsite there was a small element of each trip. We were not very sheltered, just hugging the steep shore alongside a little patch of unburned spruce surrounded by fire-killed trees. A hundred yards out on the lake, parallel to the shore, ran a pressure ridge of shattered blue ice many miles long. Every year it forms along there, almost exactly the same distance out from shore; I do not claim to understand how or why. The beach just west of camp was blown clean, right down to fist-sized cobblestones, and even where the dogs were staked out the snow cover was scanty at best. Above us loomed the thousand-foot wall of the Kahochella. It was no place to weather a storm, and I chuckled as I imagined the consternation in the mind of my grumpy wheel dog Schooner: "What the hell? We're stopping *here*? Give yer head a shake, boss—what if the wind comes up?"

The wind stayed down. In fact the final night of that final trip was perfect in every way: minus 25 degrees, high broken cloud, a full moon, and dead calm. It was a pleasure to make and break camp without snow-shoes, and I admired the stark beauty of the fire-swept slopes above camp. Evening in the familiar small room of my tent, splurging with some lunch sausage cut up into the supper of rice and caribou meat. A few notes, some reading, and a warm sleep. Morning, 25 March came on pink and golden, the moon setting as the sun rose. SKC dominates the weather map for the entire Northwest Territories that day. The trip would end as it had started, with a broad area of calm high-pressure air centred on the Barrens just north of McLeod Bay. My final trail journal entry rambled from memories of my father to an attempt at humour with "ten lessons from the solo dogteam trips":

1. If you want to travel south of Great Slave Lake in winter, bring three Olympic athletes who enjoy snowshoeing.
2. Three sleeping bags are better than two.
3. Mr. Coleman Sr. of Wichita Kansas should have received a Nobel Prize for contributions to practical thermodynamics.
4. Likewise Mr. Bo Hilleberg the Tentmaker, from Sweden.
5. And let us not forget the unsung genius who invented Baby Wipes.
6. If you want to see northern and arctic wildlife up close in winter, take the kids to the Edmonton Zoo on Christmas vacation.
7. When setting out on a long solo dogteam trip in the subarctic, don't worry about your sled—any old wreck lying around the yard will do fine.
8. If it looks like a ridiculously huge portion of bacon, when you're packing out food in the warmth of your kitchen, it will be just right at 30 below and a little skimpy on all mornings colder than that.
9. If the Canadian military ever fights a winter war in the Arctic, with the infantry shod in their standard-issue boots with only standard-issue liners, the entire ground force will be useless within 48 hours.
10. Any item of clothing which, in the comfort of one's living room, does not look ludicrously wide, soft, and durable, should be left there prior to departure.

Finally, a paragraph on how we can never foresee what we will encounter on a trip in wild country, and how essential and wonderful that uncertainty is. This was prompted by the realization that one year earlier, on exactly the same calendar date, 25 March, in more or less precisely the same location, I had awakened at dawn to a brutal wind and a thermometer showing minus 44 degrees. Otto Bathurst, a London television director on holiday, was my client that morning. From the depths of his sleeping bags he called out, "What is the temperature?" I told him it was 44 degrees below zero, and he replied in his crisp British diction "Minus 44? Well now that is just fucking *stupid*!"

Stupid or not, there we were. A year later here we were again, minus Otto, and the same spot was like a slice of winter paradise. I lingered over more leftovers for breakfast, poured an extra cup of coffee, and finally closed the journal with "Four trips. Done. I've said it all now, at least once!"

The dogs knew where we were; there was no question of that. With the weather and snow conditions perfect, and with two weeks of steady running now behind them, they made short work of the final 25 miles. Ten miles out a snowmobile buzzed toward us from the east—Roger and his young son Gus, out to look for us and say hello on such a nice spring morning. I set the hook and we chatted for nearly an hour. Whenever a dog musher meets a snowmobile driver on the trail, there is a definite pattern: the Thermos bottles come out, the musher immediately sits down on his sled, and the snowmobiler takes the welcome opportunity to stand up. After I left Roger and Gus, a yellow ski plane droned eastbound above the cliffs of the south shore. It was caribou researcher Anne Gunn with pilot Perry Linton, busy carrying out the caribou-survey work I had opted out of in order to make this final solo trip. "Go ahead and rub a little salt in the wounds!" I shouted—but I was smiling. Work would always come and go; there is little certainty in the bush-flying business. *So be it*, I thought. I had done the trip and missed the work. As I watched the plane pass I was confident I had made the right decision.

Nine miles out from home we hit the north shore at Wolf Point. We have called it that since 1988, when Kristen had encountered a pack of wolves there. She had been running alone with a team of dogs at dusk, and for a few moments she had wondered what might transpire.[22] From there on, every little rock and island was familiar to me and to the dogs: Staircase Island, the mouth of Bag Bay, the shoals off the point at Early

Left to right: Annika, Kaltag, Ernie, Dave, and Liv. Final day, final trip, home sweet home.

Frost. Heavily rutted trails of caribou, tracks of hundreds of animals, criss-crossed the ice just three miles out from home.

In warm midday sunshine my sled snaked up the little hill behind the sauna, and we were into the dog yard. I pulled up in front of the barn and the girls and Ken and Kristen all gathered around. I kicked the hook into the packed snow. Hugs and kisses, handshakes and laughter. By mid-afternoon I was elbow deep in a sink full of plates and cups and warm dishwater, feeling cozy and sunburned and smug as outside a 20-knot wind blew from the northwest. Ken smiled when he saw me doing the dishes: "That warm soapy water feel pretty good today, Dave?" The ski plane landed and the pilot and biologist came up to the house for coffee. Home sweet home.

Two mornings later it was Easter Sunday, so there were chocolate eggs hidden around the room as I sat in our big chair of home-milled tama-rack boards. Everyone else was asleep upstairs. I listened to the cold wind outside. It was spring on the calendar, but winter had come around to give us another good kick. That seemed to be the pattern after every one of my returns, although the weather always looks and feels different from inside the walls and warmth of a house.

I had a new sense of the lake's enormous breadth and depth. It truly is The Big Lake, Tu Nede in the language of the Dene. For anyone living along its shores day to day and year to year, it would never need any other name. I had a surprising change of perspective, though, on that trip west: for all its miles of open water or open ice, the big lake was still just a lake. It was not an ocean, or even when you came right down to it, an "inland sea." Having crossed its wide basin all the way to that distant west shoreline, Great Slave had become tangible to me as a *lake*, once and for all. Hold any heading for more than five or six hours, even at just a few miles per hour, and soon enough land would rise up into sight.

And finally, from my chair by the window that Easter morning, journal and pencil in hand, there is this: "We live in a good place." Not very profound, that conclusion, but in the day-to-day realm of a person's life and times, what more comforting awareness can there be? "I can say I've had a good look around, and this place is by far the best I've seen. How fortunate we are to live here."

Afterword

On a warm summer morning I sit at my writing desk in the little log cabin by the workshop. I ponder the four journeys, now years into the past tense. Memories and my scrawled-pencil entries in journals, a few lacklustre photographs and a marked-up manuscript now transcribed to a screen. My life moves ahead season by season—Kristen and I have been here more than twenty-six years now, making a living, raising our children, travelling east and west along this rugged shoreline and inland up the home trails.

Sometimes it feels as if the land is under siege. Year after year, on every point of the compass, new schemes and changes loom and advance, subside and fall away. There is talk now of diamond and uranium mines to the north and east, of an enormous national park that could surround and change our home and thus our life, of hydroelectric projects on the Hoarfrost and high-voltage transmission lines marching north from other dams on the Taltson, squabbles over hunting rights and land claims. Worrisome, nagging, uncertain things—and enough of them to keep a man awake at night. Yet with these four long trips behind me, the country seems more spacious and resilient than ever. It is impossibly ancient, tough, and—above all—inscrutable. Every so often I think back to my walk on that rest day up at Maufelly Bay, and I see us all immersed in this brief interregnum. I relax. The ice king will return, or perhaps the throne will pass to a different dynasty for some time—warmth, drought, or another change beyond the ken of the mathematical models. Meanwhile, there is plenty to do, my brief life to live. I can relax in the face of all these uncertainties. I have changed.

Changed too, just as I had hoped, are all the horizons around this place. In every direction I know new routes, new secrets, and new passageways through the country. When I fly over the spots where the dogs and I struggled hard, and other stretches where we revelled in easy miles

and snug camps, those places are now distinct from the rest of the landscape. Our nights and days on the trail have made them precise and
unique to me; their lines and features have become as familiar as the vis-
ages of friends and family.

And there is this: those places are themselves somehow changed—in
some deep way which I am still trying to fathom—for my having been
there. It is a mysterious symbiosis: our lives on the land, lived well, enrich
not only us, but the land itself. We humans need not be doomed intrud-
ers here. We must be wary of the tiresome trap of forever demonizing and
alienating ourselves. If we try (and that is, I admit, a truly daunting "if"),
we may yet live in the North in some semblance of harmony, until the ice
returns and drives us away again. Sitting here, staring out as I have on
so many mornings, my tenuous new-found optimism is an unexpected
reward for the four journeys.

Out the south-facing window, white and brilliant, stretch the snow
and ice of McLeod Bay. The cliffs of the Kahochella Peninsula rise gun-
metal blue in the distance. Out the west-facing window are the dogs, dozens of them sprawled this morning on the roofs of their wooden houses.
Ernie, coming up on fifteen years old, deaf as a stone now and free to
roam the homestead at his leisure, still barks whenever the harnesses
come down off the rack. Eagle and his brother Kaltag are still out in the
main kennel, alive as ever, a little stiff but spry enough to run and pull.
Foxtail, Steve, Dandy, Riley, Flynn, B.J. and on down the list...all gone,
taking their long layovers up on the outcrop east of the river. Weathered
plywood name markers are nailed to a spruce tree there, like a totem pole
of the dog clan.

I wonder what the dogs thought of those trips we made together. As
near as I can discern, they simply enjoyed the going: the setting out, our
life on the trail, and the coming back home. In that imagined question to
the dogs, and in my version of their answer, lies a lesson for me. When all
is said and done the most enduring gift of such voyages may be just that
visceral *enjoyment*, uncluttered and unexamined. In my mind those two
beautiful poems of Snyder and Stafford are paraphrased and conjoined,
flavoured this morning by the sleeping dogs and their steady animal *presence*: Out there, over the boulders, eager, tasting the snow...those were
kinds of winter that we met.

Appreciations and Acknowledgements

Like the journeys it describes, this book has had its hard and easy days. It has been stuck in deep snow and delayed by weather and battered by headwinds. Sometimes the going has been easy, but for a few years the project seemed to be wandering on the tundra with a wind blowing, looking for a place to camp.

Many people have helped me along the way. With a note, a word of encouragement, or a good laugh at the right time, they have bolstered my confidence and helped me give my literary sled a heave and get it moving again. I appreciate them all. Whether your name is here or not, I thank you.

Especially I thank: Kathy Coskran, Lee Merrill, Lisa Quinn, Cynthia Brown, and Linnea Olesen—for careful reading, constructive criticism, and fact-checking; and John Parish, Ken Frew, Roger Catling, Miranda Casaway, Harry Turner, Duncan Storlie, Will Steger, James Olesen, and Bill and Mary at Moraine Point—for material support and doses of encouragement. Money toward a new tent from John; firewood and chores at home from Ken; caribou meat, hot tea, and more than one good trail from Roger and Miranda; a vintage down sleeping bag from Harry; books and thoughts and long-ago mushing lessons from Dunc and Willie; fatherly advice from Dad; Bill and Mary for a warm bunk and good meals; Dr. Mike English of Wilfrid Laurier University for helping connect me with WLU Press at just the right moment, and for his steady support of that connection along the way; Pam Schaus, cartographer at Wilfrid Laurier University, for her diligent work on the maps in this book; Graeme Shaw for a beautiful cover painting, and for his enthusiasm way back in 2001; Kristen Gilbertson Olesen for helping me select and fine-tune my trip photos; Gary Snyder for permission to quote his poem, and for the inspiration his life and writing continue to be for my own; Kit Stafford and the rest of the family of William Stafford, for permission to quote; Rob, Leslie, Clare, Lisa, and everyone else at WLU Press for professional bookmaking guidance and support; Carol Harrison for her brilliant editing.

My dogs, especially Ernie and Steve. None of them can read but, hey, they know.

And finally, my heartfelt thanks to Kristen, Annika, and Liv—for everything, every day, year after year. Onward.

Food, Gear, and Some Notes on Winter Camping

For those readers who might find it interesting, I will detail some key points of my food, equipment and clothing. Also I would like to toss out a few comments and nuances of my cold-weather camping techniques, developed and evolved over thirty-five years. Some specific details of dog feeding and care on the trail are covered separately in Appendix B.

FOOD

No one who has camped with me will ever accuse me of being a trail gourmet. I think my years of racing and training, along with a basic indifference to most things culinary (except eating) have led me to an extremely simple modus operandi when it comes to food on the trail. "Eat to live, don't live to eat," was a watchword around my house growing up, and I suppose that outlook has stuck with me. Also, a solo winter journey is more akin to a climbing trip than to a summertime canoe trip. Cold, darkness, fatigue, fuel rationing, and a small space with limited cookware (two billy pots and one small skillet, a fork, a spoon, and a cup) increase the appeal of keeping things simple in the kitchen department.

On the flip side, food is fuel and fuel is heat, so in winter the food had better go into the musher just as well as it does for the dogs (i.e., regularly and with gusto). Despite its apparent monotony, my trail menu on these solos remained appealing to me morning, noon, and night. Here is a checklist copied from my food pack-outs prior to the trips. The specific items changed slightly from year to year, but the key ingredients and methods remained the same.

Breakfast
- 2 tablespoons freeze-dried instant coffee
- $\frac{1}{4}$ pound bacon
- 1 ounce white sugar
- $1\frac{1}{4}$ cups basic granola (rolled oats baked with oil, margarine, honey, and brown sugar)
- $\frac{1}{4}$ cup raisins
- $\frac{1}{4}$ cup skim-milk powder (I prefer whole-milk powder, but it is difficult to find)

Totals approximately $12\frac{1}{2}$ ounces per day, about 1,700 calories.

Staples
Bannock mix:
- 1 cup flour
- $1/4$ cup canola oil
- 1 teaspoon baking powder
- $1/4$ cup cornmeal

Yields 8 ounces total for every four days. Average 2 ounces per day, or about 250 calories. (I did not make bannock very often.)

Ingredients for Daily Liquids:
- $3/4$ cup ($2^1/2$ ounces) cocoa powder (equal parts cocoa powder, milk powder, icing sugar, plus a dash of salt)
- instant soup powder for 2 cups (in bulk pack, about 3 ounces per day)
- 3 tablespoons Tang orange crystals with Vitamin C ($1^3/4$ ounces per day)

Totals $7^1/4$ ounces per day, about 560 calories.

Lunch and Trail Snacks
- 2 strips dry meat ($1^1/4$ ounces)
- 4 peanut butter balls (peanut butter, icing sugar, dry milk)
- $1^1/2$–2 ounces chocolate
- 2 ounces butter
- 8 wheat crackers (2 ounces)
- 4 ounces cheese
- $3/4$ cup peanuts ($3^1/2$ ounces)

Totals about $19^3/4$ ounces per day, about 1,850 calories.

Dinner
- 1 cup ($7^1/2$ ounces) broken jasmine rice (note: the broken rice makes a big difference for rapid cooking, which saves fuel and time—this is *not* "minute rice" but real rice, sold by rice wholesalers as "broken rice")
- 2 cups (8 ounces) pasta (I alternated rice and pasta each night)
- $3/4$ pound ground or finely diced caribou or moose meat, fully cooked before pack-out
- 2 ounces butter
- $1/2$ teaspoon each, salt and pepper

I mixed these ingredients together for each night's meal in one small plastic bag at pack-out. At camp, the entire bag's contents—rice or pasta, meat, butter, salt and pepper—were dumped into about four cups of water, heated to boiling, and simmered for five minutes until the rice or pasta was cooked. This was the complete main supper meal—total 22 ounces per day, about 1,800 calories. Usually there were additions to supper, gleaned from the lunch sack, like crackers, nuts, cheese, or chocolate. Also on some nights I had hot instant soup.

Miscellaneous
Special-occasion items for the entire 16- to 18-day trip
- $1/2$ pound real coffee
- 4 ounces whisky

Total weight personal rations as packed: about four pounds per day
Total calories packed: about 6,000 per 24-hour day

Not every morsel of food packed and carried was eaten. An estimate of my total daily caloric intake would be about 4,800–5,800. This proved adequate on most days and slightly low on others. I lost a little weight on all four trips, but only on the first two trips south and east did the ratio of input to output start to feel a little dicey at times. All in all, pretty normal for any long effort in deep cold. Interestingly this 5,000-calorie ballpark figure is almost exactly my estimate for the calorie ration for each dog per twenty-four hours, as detailed in Appendix B.

GEAR AND CLOTHING

Here is the master list that I used to pack gear and clothing for the 2003 trip east. Again, a few details changed from year to year but the main list was consistent and this one is typical.

Sled and Rigging
- sled
- snow hook
- snubline
- tie-out line for lead dogs
- two Snarg ice pitons
- 12-dog hollow-braid poly/cable gangline
- extra hollow-braid poly rope
- extra necklines and tuglines
- 11-dog cable picket line
- harnesses plus three spares
- caribou-hide muff on handle bar
- three two-foot angle-aluminum pickets
- dog "jingler" (beer bottle caps on a metal ring, used as a "giddyup" signal for the dogs)

Travel and Camp Gear
- Hilleberg Keron tent with vestibules
- blue poly tarp groundsheet
- axe
- saw
- extra saw blade
- shovel
- ice chisel (carried on first two trips only, jettisoned at my caches both times)
- snowshoes with bindings (see notes)
- skis (see notes)
- maps
- two compasses
- GPS
- eight pairs hand warmers (average one pair per two days)
- small plastic bottle of coloured beads and spare matches
- Remington 30-06 carbine with small cleaning kit and 18 rounds
- repair kit containing fids, screws and nails, spare bolts, nylon cord, brace and bit, screwdriver bits, small vise grip, small drill bits, galvanized wire, snare wire, tie wraps, hose clamps, and sewing kit

Cooking and Eating
- two-burner Coleman stove with a $^1/_2$-litre fuel bottle for pre-heating, metal funnel, and waterproof match container all nested inside
- second complete tank and generator unit for Coleman stove (one tank for evening, one tank for morning, both refilled each morning)
- collapsible aluminum windscreen, a cube about two feet on a side to cover the Coleman
- white-gas fuel in two five-litre jerry cans plus two one-litre aluminum gas bottles
- Sierra cup
- thermal mug
- one-quart Thermos
- two one-litre water bottles with insulated jackets
- one-quart and four-quart metal pots with carrying handles and lids
- small square skillet
- fork
- spoon

Light

- headlamp with belt pack (four D batteries)
- small LED Eternalight flashlight
- 18 candles and tin-can candle holder

(Halogen-bulb headlamps and big D-battery belt packs, like film cameras, have now gone the way of the dodo. LED technology has taken over completely in the realm of headlamps, digital in the realm of photography.)

Toiletries

- small signal mirror
- toilet paper
- toothbrush
- floss
- toothpaste
- small plastic bags with three to four baby wipes in each—one of these packets carried thawed in an inside pocket and replenished from the main frozen supply every couple of days.

Sleeping Gear

- down sleeping bag
- synthetic-fill overbag (two overbags plus main down bag on the final two trips)
- vapour-barrier inner bag
- Wiggy's Lamilite roll-up pad
- Crazy Creek chair (flattens at night for use as sleeping pad)
- one caribou hide

Pocket and Belt Gear

- sheath knife
- two match safes
- fire-lighting sticks in plastic bag
- handkerchief
- wool nose and cheek guard
- Channel Lock slip-joint pliers
- one pair hand-warmer packets
- roll of nylon cord
- carabiner
- dog snaps and necklines
- LED Eternalight flashlight (the same light already listed under Light)
- diamond whetstone

Dog Care and Feeding

- 7-x-16-x-10-inch 3¹/₂-gallon capacity, aluminum cooking pot with cover
- sturdy ladle
- big coffee-can scoop (that also served as my nighttime pee can for the tent)
- 12-quart insulated cooler with lid
- caribou-hide belly warmers
- fleece belly bands
- 20 dog jackets (for ten dogs)
- 150–300 dog booties (some at cache, some carried)
- dog-care kit:
    - two rolls Vet Wrap
    - Algavyl liniment
    - fifty 500-milligram Amoxicillin tabs
    - Imodium diarrhea medicine
    - coated aspirin
    - suture needle and thread (a veterinary stapler is preferable and I carry one now)

Writing, Reading, Photography

- two journals
- four pencils
- loose lined paper
- various books for reading (two per trip)
- camera and 3 x 36-exposure rolls of slide film

My post-trip notes state: "Always bring several good engrossing books, like novels with action and intrigue—don't skimp or be too 'lofty.' These are important to bolster patience when pinned down by bad weather."

First-Aid Kit

- first-aid manual
- Tylenol 3 with codeine
- gauze
- Band-Aids
- adhesive tape

When packing first-aid supplies I always remember a comment from a fellow Outward Bound instructor back in 1979. He had been a medic in Vietnam and his philosophy on first-aid kits was simple: "Really, all you need is a lot of tape."

Communication

- small VHF telemetry collar attached to sled stanchion
- HF radio with antenna
- one set of spare alkaline C batteries (11 in the radio for a total of 22—heavy!)
- personal locator beacon (406 mHz) on final two trips

Emergency Gear

(backup in case of tent loss—always stowed in sled)

- tarp
- down parka
- MSR stove
- spare fuel and matches
- beaver hat
- fleece mitts

CLOTHING

Clothing choices and specific items are personal and a detailed list of mine will not be that useful. A few essential items of clothing cannot be found in most modern high-tech outdoor shops. One is a set of supple, durable leather work mitts, simple and sturdy with no gauntlets, fitted with *removable* wool or wool-blend mitten liners. These "chopper mitts" are in nearly constant use. Leather is much more durable than any synthetic material when it comes to high temperatures (as in handling hot stoves and cook pots) and the wear and tear of dog handling and camp chores. Many spare socks and a complete spare set of inner layers (long johns top and bottom) are essential.

When it comes to clothing for travel in deep cold with constantly changing levels of exertion, the key points are *layering and bagginess*. Layering, especially on the upper body and the feet, allows for separating and drying the various parts and pieces of the clothing. It also allows for constant adjustment as intense effort is started and stopped through the course of the day's travel. Bagginess simply means room to wiggle, nothing tight or constricting or svelte!

If a winter boot or moccasin is roomy, at least somewhat breathable, with insulation made up of several independent layers that can be pulled apart in camp *each night*, the battle for warm feet in deep cold will be won. If the boots or moccasins are slim or form-fitting, and difficult or impossible to take apart into separate pieces, cold feet will be the result. I chuckle at the "warm to –100° F." claim on fancy boots that are rigid and slim, with heavy rubber over the sole and foot and a liner that is nearly impossible to remove. Yes, they might work down to minus 100 degrees for a day or so, but after that they will be lined with frost and steadily more miserable.

I will list in detail the clothing I had on during the coldest, windiest days of travel. The system was good, flawed only by the accumulation of ice and frost in the throat and chin area and along the sides of the parka ruff. This area of fabric should be removable for drying each night, and a spare should be carried.

Head and Neck
- trapper-style musher hat with beaver fur (chin strap is soft leather with soft fleece only)
- green army-surplus face-and-cheek protector
- simple fleece headband worn low over chin
- thin stretchy fleece neck gaiter (doubles as a hat)
- enormous insulated pullover parka (no front zip) with extra down-filled hood buttoned into the parka's hood. My parka is made by Apocalypse Designs in Fairbanks, Alaska. Both the inner and outer hoods have a ruff of wolverine fur.

Torso
- long-sleeve fleece top with zipper at throat
- lightweight fleece sweater with zipper only at neck
- light soft-wool sweater
- heavy hand-knit wool vest
- a second heavier fleece sweater with full front zip
- parka (see above)

Hands
- fingerless fleece wristlets
- two pairs wool mitts
- one pair hand-warmer packets opened in the morning on the very coldest days
- beaver and sheepskin mushing mitts, slung on a cord mitten harness

Lower Body and Legs
- medium-light polypro long johns
- Patagonia vapour-barrier long johns

- Alyeska down-filled pants
- medium-weight baggy military-surplus wool trousers
- breathable baggy wind pants with multiple pockets—*not* Gore-Tex! (cuffs down over moccasins)

Feet
- two pairs wool socks
- outer pair knee-high wool socks
- fleece or felt boot liners
- down booties with foam sole
- very large double-layer duffle liners
- *extremely* large and wide moose-hide and canvas knee-high moccasins

MISCELLANEOUS NOTES AND TIPS

Sleeping in Deep Cold

The main prerequisites for a good sleep in deeply cold weather are:

- a good multi-layered set of sleeping bags
- at least three layers of ground insulation (e.g., foam, caribou hide, and Wiggy's Lamilite sleeping pad)
- dry sleeping clothing, changed from the day's work clothes before bed if necessary
- a one-litre plastic hot-water bottle stuffed into the toe of the bag before bed
- some care given to making a hip and shoulder hollow in the snow pack as you set up the bed

If you follow these principles, a fancy thousand-dollar sleeping bag is unnecessary even at minus 45 degrees. In cold weather, I like to sleep with a light layer of long johns, bare feet (snuggling up to that hot-water bottle down in the far end of the inner sleeping bag), a down vest, and a thick fleece balaclava hood. In the pockets of the vest are light supple gloves. Come morning I am ready to sit up and partly extricate myself from the sleeping bags, don the gloves (for handling 40-below metal stove parts), light a candle, start up the heat source whether it is Coleman stove or wood stove, retrieve the water bottle from the warm depths of the sleeping bag, and sit there sipping from it as the coffee-water and the tent warm up. Bliss. Everything has to be immediately at hand for those cold morning start-ups, if that first half-hour is to be pleasant.

Snowshoes and Skis

I am amazed at the ludicrous little pads of lightweight metal and fabric that have started to appear in the outdoor shops as "snowshoes." Some of them are scarcely wider or longer than a size-14 boot. I gather that they must not be intended for deep unbroken snow, where the obvious purpose of snowshoes is to spread out the weight of the person wearing them. Snowshoes serve the same purpose as the enormous footpads of a lynx or a snowshoe hare, and they need to be sized for the weight of the animal atop them—the heavier the wearer, the greater the surface area of the shoe. The snowshoe's shape should be chosen with consideration of the work to be done. Long narrow snowshoes with tail "keels" are great for trail-breaking, but around camp a set of elongated oval bear paws with no tails are much handier. I like a compromise—a relatively wide shoe with a modest tail. For reference, see any of the guides from reputable makers of traditional ash and babiche (varnished raw leather) snowshoes. Faber and GV of Canada are two. The various traditional shoes I have from them are all excellent.

An aspect of snowshoes that deserves careful attention is the binding. Twenty-five years ago a friend showed me a homemade snowshoe binding that caught my eye, and since then it has been a pleasure to share it with other people and watch their eyes light up the way mine did. The elegantly simple binding is made from rubber bicycle-tire inner-tube material, cut to length and knotted. A toe loop is tied to the snowshoe, just behind the opening in the shoe (this opening lets the toe drop down through the plane of the shoe with each step) and a loose anklet of inner-tube rubber is slipped over the entire boot or moccasin *before* putting on the snowshoe. Once the toe is snug under the rubber toe loop, the front of the rubber ankle ring is pulled forward and down, locking beneath the front of the toe. This can all be easily done in seconds, and *without* taking off your mittens. The only slight drawback to this binding is that in deep cold the rubber gets very stiff, and a real effort is needed to stretch the ankle and toe loops. But the simplicity and durability of this binding still beats every other snowshoe binding I have seen.

Skis as accessories to a wilderness dogteam trip are mostly used as I used them on my trip south, as "Norwegian snowshoes." On skis a musher can glide along with one hand on a tow rope or on the handlebar of the sled, and this is a huge help to a dogteam pulling a loaded sled through deep snow. Used this way, to take the musher's weight off the sled runners, skis have the clear advantage over snowshoes of allowing a shuffling glide that is pleasant and efficient. For this purpose long wide wooden skis are best, and for shuffle-gliding beside the sled waxing is not necessary. A bare wooden ski with a pine-tar base will do fine in cold dry snow. A pocket-sized metal ski scraper is useful—overflow waits in ambush beneath some of that fluff.

I am still looking for a ski binding that accepts a bulky, truly warm moccasin or boot. The nearest I have found so far is the military-surplus cable binding made by Ramer, but it is good only with boots, not soft moccasins, because of the cable. Over the years I have had bad luck in deep cold with the toe-strap and heel-cup type of bindings (the flexible foot plate keeps snapping off in cold), but I am told that those are much improved recently. Berwyn is one brand.

The key point is that skis used on trips such as the ones I made cannot demand any special ski boots. To be useful to a musher, skis must be like snowshoes—ready to put on and take off at any point in the day's travel, easily and quickly, without any change in big warm footwear. One final note on skis is that they can be tricky to pack on a sled—they must be lashed down tightly or they will inevitably wriggle out to one side, catch on something, and break.

Caching Resupplies in Metal Barrels

A reliable cache-barrel system is easy and cheap to make with some old metal fuel drums, an electric jigsaw fitted with a metal-cutting blade, and some tapping screws. Cut a big round or square opening in the bottom of one drum. (I use the 11-gallon size most often, but also the full-size fuel drums for big caches. If the drums have been used recently for fuel, I rinse them out with soapy water before I start cutting and drilling.) Cut a bigger patch of metal from the bottom of another drum. Clean the inside of the drum and load with supplies. Place the lid piece over the opening, drill holes down through the lid and barrel, and screw the lid down tightly with tapping screws (woodscrews work almost as well). As the holes get worn with repeated uses, use the next larger size of screw.

Cache barrels made like this are simple to transport by plane or snow machine, and easy to reuse. Metal barrel caches have proven impervious to all the usual suspects except *Homo sapiens* armed with screwdrivers. I know that at least one grizzly bear has tried to get into one of my cache barrels (in springtime) and could not. Wolverines, martens, wolves, and foxes have all inspected my caches, but have never got into them. This is good peace of mind when caches are set out. A small keg holds about 40–50 pounds of supplies. A full-size fuel drum (called a 45 in Canada and a 55 in the United States, being 45 imperial gallons and 55 U.S.) holds up to about 200 pounds of supplies.

Water, Water Everywhere and Not a Drop to Drink

As I have written in the narrative, water is a theme of winter wilderness travel. Camping near open water or thin ice is a big advantage, especially if there are teams of dogs to keep well-hydrated. Often, though, thin ice or open water cannot be found at the night's camping spot, and with northern ice thicknesses sometimes well over four feet (I have seen seven feet), the easiest solution is to melt water. A few tricks can make the chore of melting water more efficient. One easy one is to dig down into the snowpack for the sugary "depth hoar" close to the ground, and use that for melting. Wind-packed snow is also preferably to light fluffy powder. Another dodge is to chop ice chips with the axe. Ice melts much more efficiently than snow, and should be used if fuel supplies are a concern. On big lakes a pressure ridge often has thin ice or open water on one side, and large upturned plates of ice can be knocked off with the axe and carried to camp for melting.

One trick that has helped me with the chore of water production is to bury a pot of water in the snow at bedtime, heap powdery snow over it and mark the spot with a stick or shovel. Amazingly, a four-quart metal pot of warm water buried like this will stay unfrozen overnight even at 40 below zero, because of the incredible insulating capacity of the snow mounded over it. This overnight storage of a kettle of water, along with a hot bottle or two in the toe of the sleeping bag, are a great help when travelling hard. The laborious water-melting process can be moved ahead during the evening, and this speeds up preparation for departure come morning.

The Dogs and Their Care

THE DOGS

The sled dogs of the Hoarfrost River are Alaskan huskies with a pinch of Canadian Inuit or Canadian Eskimo dog (both designations are used as the proper name for that arctic breed). That spice in the genetic mix has an interesting background.

Back in about 1979, Bill Carpenter had given or sold one of his Eskimo dogs to another musher in Yellowknife. That dog was Girlie. One March day in about 1982, my long-time friend and mushing mentor Arleigh Jorgenson was standing in the holding area of the Canadian Championship dog race, which he had just finished, and he noticed Girlie as she eagerly lapped up a bowl of cool, clear water—this at a temperature far below freezing. This was exciting to Arleigh, as it would have been to any long-distance musher, because water often has to be baited with food at those temperatures in order to entice a dog to drink. He struck a deal with the woman musher who owned Girlie—she happened to be another transplanted Minnesotan who had moved to the Territories—and he brought the dog south with him to Grand Marais, on the north shore of Lake Superior. There Girlie was bred to Otter, Arleigh's main leader and one of the foundations of his line of sled dogs. Otter harks back to many Iditarod dogs of the late 1970s and early 1980s, including a dog called Brownie from Rick Mackey of Nenana, Alaska. I was building up my own team at that time, and I was inspired by the prospect of this combination of Inuit and Alaskan husky breeds. Arleigh and I shared some litters of pups, and I ended up with some dogs descended from Otter and Girlie, which led to the foundations of our Hoarfrost bloodlines.

Steve, a gifted lead dog often mentioned in the narrative, was completely unrelated to those "Arleigh dogs." In 1996, Steve was a gift to me from mushing friends in Knik, Alaska—Dave and Donna Olson. Steve came from a small litter named for Dave and two of his good friends, Steve and Vern. Between 1991 and 1995 Kristen and I steadily bought and sold and traded dogs with other mushers, and ended up with several outstanding dogs harking back to the breeds of Iditarod champions Susan Butcher, Rick Swenson, and Martin Buser.

Which is all a long-winded, eyeball-glazing ramble leading to this: our dog yard, like the kennels of almost every long-distance musher in the circumpolar North, is an assortment of loosely related Alaskan huskies with nary a Kennel Club registration paper to be found. The guiding maxim is to breed good dogs to good dogs. The one unusual feature of our own teams is still that small dose of arctic husky genes, from Girlie and her long-ago litters with Otter.

For the record, my teams on each of the trips were:

- South 2002—Foxtail, Flynn, Ernie, Schooner (these four all litter-mates), Steve, Murphy, Tugboat, Dandy, and old reliable Riley;
- East 2003—Steve, Dandy, Foxtail, Gulo, Murphy, Jasmine, Schooner, Riley, Edelweiss, and Ernie;
- North 2004—B.J., Minnie, Fipke, Steve, Dandy, Foxtail, Flynn, Jasmine, Schooner, and Ernie;
- West 2005—Fipke, Steve, Dandy, Jasmine, Murphy, Spruce, Schooner, Ernie, Kaltag, Safire, and Eagle.

DOG FOOD AND FEEDING

On the trail the ongoing challenges of dog feeding are to keep up the caloric density and palatability of the feed, and to keep the dogs' water intake adequate. The dogs have to have plenty of fuel to stay warm on cold nights after working hard all day. Over a long trip they have to be able to build and replenish strength and body weight, and stay hydrated.

There are plenty of energy-dense dog foods and most of the foods on the high-price end of the "athletic" dog kibbles are going to work out. Dog-food brands rise and fall, and over my years as a musher many good mixes have come and gone. The main principles of working-dog nutrition are easy to research in other sources. Buy good dog food. The best you can afford. If the dogs eat it eagerly day after day on a long trip, with good digestion (i.e., solid poops, not splats), you are on the right track.

On a wilderness camping trip with a team of eight to twelve dogs, there are some challenges that make race-proven methods difficult to utilize. The weight of the dog food is a major consideration on expeditions, and that is the biggest difference from home-based runs and long-distance races. On races like the Iditarod the weight and bulk of a team's dog-food supply, prepacked weeks in advance and waiting for the team in big sacks at checkpoints, is not of any real consequence. On the trail, camping each night and with many days' travel between resupplies, weight and bulk become critical. Frozen raw meat and fish are the two

time-tested staples of a working dogteam's diet, but these are a problem
when weight becomes a factor. Most of the weight in a chunk of frozen
meat or fish, something like 80–90 per cent of the weight, is just water.
Great for hydration, but not workable for a nine-day sled load. When you
start packing water around in your sled you lose the weight battle pretty
quickly.

Given a choice, most sled dogs—in fact most dogs, period—would live
their entire life on almost nothing but fat and raw meat—muscle meat,
organ meat, fatty meat. Whole fish, like salmon or whitefish, would be a
second-choice daily diet for many northern dogs. Processed kibble from
a bag ranks a distant third. This preference may be changing, as kibble
becomes the mainstay in the diet of generation after generation of sled
dogs. Dog kibble is nothing more than a clever salvaging and repackag-
ing of by-products. It is made up of ingredients that cannot be easily sold
to finicky modern humans for their own dinners: cow blood, pig lips,
chicken parts, fish entrails, less-than perfect rice or wheat or corn...you
name it. All processed, baked and formed, and then supplemented by a
concoction of additives, minerals, vitamins, and preservatives. Kibble
quality varies immensely, from horrendous cheap blends ("chicken feathers, soybeans, and wood chips, and they're phasing out the chicken feathers," as one musher summed it up) to calorie-dense, nutritious mixtures
that working dogs find very adequate and palatable, on up to boutique
blends priced beyond the reach of mere mortals. Wal-Mart markets a dog
kibble called "Old Roy" that a musher from Alberta tried out for a while.
He laughed that it should be renamed "Old Splat" for its effect on the
chore of dog-yard cleanup.

In a nutshell, when it comes to kibble, get serious, shop around, and
open your pocketbook.

There are ways to use meat on the trail, and still keep the sled load
down. One is to use small amounts of frozen ground meat or ground
liver, as an added enticement melted into the main course of kibble, water,
and fat. This works well. Another is to use freeze-dried meat made for just
this purpose. Provit, made in Scandinavia, is one brand. It is very expensive, for obvious reasons. I did have some with me on my trips east and
north, and it worked out well. Raw dried meat, even if it is just partially
dried, is a help in reducing weight. Someday, maybe, I will be organized
enough to dry some meat for the dogs before a big trip.

Fat is the secret weapon on the trail, when it comes to keeping a dogteam's weight and energy levels up. Fat is the most calorie-dense of all
the food options. As a ballpark planning figure I use 4,000 kilocalories
per pound of fat. As mentioned in the book, another huge advantage of

fat is the metabolic water that it yields, at the rate of 110 grams of water produced for every 100 grams of fat digested. This is significant. (By comparison, the wizards of Wikipedia proclaim that the digestion of 100 grams of starch yields 55 grams of metabolic water. Protein does not yield any water for us mammals, because the metabolic water from protein digestion roughly equals the amount of water needed to excrete the urea that protein digestion produces.)

I use two kinds of fat: saturated-fat beef lard, sold wholesale in 20-kilogram (44-pound) boxes for use in restaurant deep fryers, and liquid (unsaturated-fat) canola oil which we buy in 16-litre pails. At home our routine is to cook fish, lard, and rice every morning in the barn, and mix this with kibble and canola oil before the evening feeding. For time on the trail, as on the journeys of this book, I prepare the fat component of the dog food by melting equal parts of the liquid canola oil and the solid beef lard together, then pouring it into wide flat blocks to cool and harden. In camp I melt snow or ice, or haul water if there is some nearby, and heat the water in a big rectangular aluminum cooker. Into the heating water goes the fat for the evening feeding, and the block of mixed canola oil and lard melts much more quickly than a block of straight lard. When the water-fat mix is hot and the fat is completely melted in it, I pour it into a plastic insulated cooler filled with kibble. The precise amounts of fat on a given night vary slightly, depending on the temperature and weather, the work the dogs have done, their condition, how well they are eating, and so on. I find that feeding the dogs lightly on the first night and morning of a trip, with little or no fat in the mix, helps ease them into trail life and trail eating, and they eat better for the rest of the trip.

Every experienced musher develops favourite methods and techniques for dog care. In a wilderness camp of unpacked snow the dogs are usually picketed overnight in a protected oasis of low bush and trees, on a cable tie-out with short individual chains. For a musher tending dogs while wearing snowshoes, it is difficult to ladle out bowls of soupy broth to the dogs, even though they might be accustomed to this at home. Yet they do need the water if they are to stay adequately hydrated. I get around this problem by mixing up a second batch of food every evening, immediately after I cook and serve the main feeding, and soaking that second batch of kibble with as much water and melted fat as it will absorb overnight—so much water that if it were any wetter, bowls would be needed. In the morning, after soaking all night in the cooler buried under the snow, I can dollop this breakfast out onto the cold packed snow along the picket line, where the dogs can gobble it up. On the trail I prefer this method to daily use of broth in bowls, although I still carry a few dog bowls if space and weight allow.

Dog Food 2004: Ten Dogs, Sixteen to Eighteen Nights

I will just wrap up with a list of my dog-food supplies, taken from my checklist before the trip north in 2004.

Per twenty-four hours:

- 17 pounds (11 large coffee-can scoops) high-performance kibble (I used Nutri-Source in those years, and as of this writing I use Distance Dog Food; see below)
- 3 small blocks Provit freeze-dried beef/fat
- 2½ pounds canola oil and beef lard mix (16 litres oil were melted with 20 kilograms lard, then refrozen into blocks)
- 3 blocks Science Diet Endurance (this was a custom-made mix packed in massive frozen blocks, developed for Will Steger's expeditions; he had left a supply of this with us when he passed through that winter)
- 1 pound Energy Pak powder (this is a concentrated high-energy supplement made and marketed by National Dog Food of Wisconsin)

Total weight dog food per 24 hours: about 26 pounds/ten dogs

My calorie estimates:

- 22,000 Nutri-Source kibble
- 1,500 Provit
- 9,000 oil-lard mix
- 15,000 Science Diet blocks
- 3,000 Energy Pak

Total 50,500 kilocalories/ten dogs = 5,050 per dog per day

As with my own food, not every speck of dog food packed out for each day was used. The temperatures on the trip north were extremely mild in comparison with the two preceding years. Because of that milder weather I left some dog food behind at both caches, and there was spare food in my sled as I pulled into home at the end of the trip. This list just gives an idea of what was packed and what my pre-trip calculations were. On the first two trips I used National's Competition Extra kibble, which is made in Wisconsin. I was generally pleased with that food and especially with its high density—less bulk in the sled. By 2004, supply lines to our homestead had dictated a change to Nutri-Source Super Performance, marketed through Manitoba and made in Minnesota. A few years later we switched to Inukshuk Pro, made in New Brunswick. Again a good product. As of this writing, we are feeding Inukshuk along with Distance

Dog Food, an excellent blend developed by Billy Snodgrass of Wyoming. On the trail Distance is perhaps the best kibble I have yet come across. Its only drawbacks are that it is not quite as energy dense or as physically dense as Inukshuk or National.

MISCELLANEOUS DOG-CARE NOTES

Jackets

A compression stuff sack crammed full of fleece-and-nylon dog jackets is useful on long trips with Alaskan huskies, especially in areas of tundra and open ice where cold winds can hammer a resting team. Here the Polar, Inuit, and Eskimo breeds come into their own, as discussed in the book. I have a wide assortment of dog jackets from my racing days, and they still see steady use in deep cold and wind. Some dogs are helped immensely by them, and others never need them. The "cold sleepers" in the team are easily spotted by looking at the circle of each dog's bed after a cold night. Some dogs have a hole melted deep into the snow, clear to the ground. Those hot-blooded dogs will benefit most from a jacket.

The problem with the fleece-and-nylon dog jackets used in racing is that after a night or two of use the moisture of melting snow renders them icy and almost useless. In a small tent with no wood stove they are impossible to dry. Twenty-five years ago Kristen sewed up some jackets from shiny silver-and-orange "space blanket" material. These jackets were windbreak shells with no fleece or cloth, and thus did not absorb any water. They were very compact and easy to use. We have lost them all over the years to wear and tear. They were a great idea for a long trip. One of these days, maybe when we are finished drying dog meat before a trip, we'll make some more.

Booties

The more years that go by from my retirement out of serious racing, the fewer dog booties I use. As of this writing, we are coming to the end of a very cold winter. Since January we have had up to thirty-eight dogs on the trail at a time with expeditions of students and tourists. The total number of dog booties we have used is something like ten. But the mileage on these large-group trips is not very high. Mushing three or four hours a day, with frequent stops when the dogs can clean ice and snow from their feet, is different from hard running. On a longer trip with longer mileage the dogs' feet must be watched closely. Booties remain a necessary evil of modern long-distance mushing with most breeds of husky. The best booties are now made from durable lightweight cloth, with Velcro tabs at the top. Kipmik in Anchorage is my favourite source. These booties are durable and easily dried for reuse.

Snow-Blindness in Dogs

I have not seen much reference to it, but every year in April and May, if we put in some long afternoons running teams directly into the glare of the sun and snow, southwest down the Hoarfrost River from the tundra, a few dogs will be afflicted with snow-blindness. We have tried smearing black grease or ash under their eyes, which makes them look like baseball players, but whether that has helped them or not is hard to say. I think it has helped a little. Doggie sunglasses are out on the market (of course), but we have yet to find a husky in our kennel who will put up with wearing them. Old arctic journals and books sometimes mention dark veils of cloth over the dogs' heads, and we have tried this too. The dogs have not enjoyed or tolerated wearing a cloth veil around their heads, especially in warm weather. The only answer is probably to be aware of this problem and to try to adjust the travel schedule or timing of certain passages. Having been afflicted with serious snow-blindness once, in 1980 after a very bright but overcast day on Hudson Bay, I know that it is extremely painful and debilitating. It must be the same for the dogs. On the trips described in the book, all made in February and March, the sun was not strong enough to cause a problem for any of us.

Some Tricks for Dead-Reckoning Navigation

As mentioned in the book, I used some simple techniques of dead reckoning to help with my navigation across featureless white expanses of tundra and ice, where map reading can be futile and frustrating. *Dead reckoning* is a term used in sailing and flying, for approximating one's position by keeping careful records of direction and speed. Beginning from some known or hypothetical location, and knowing how long you have been travelling, at what speed and in what direction, you can approximate your position.

For heading or direction, sometimes I use a magnetic compass, but more often I rely on a wristwatch and the position of the sun. Here are the important things to remember with this method:

- The sun passes through due south at "local noon" and this will be offset from real noon by a few minutes, depending on where you are in relation to the central meridian (of longitude) of the time zone. For instance, if you are west of the central meridian of your time zone, local noon will be later than twelve o'clock; and if you are east of it, local noon will come *before* twelve o'clock. At the east end of Great Slave Lake our local noon is about 13:15 (1:15 p.m.) Central Standard Time, because we are almost 20 degrees to the west of the central meridian of that time zone. The central meridians of the time zones from east to west across all of North America are:
  Newfoundland 52°30' W
  Atlantic 60° W
  Eastern 75° W
  Central 90° W
  Mountain 105° W
  Pacific 120° W
  Alaska 135° W

In order to use this method with any accuracy, you must understand local noon. You must also account for that bugaboo of modern timekeeping, daylight saving time (DT). The reason Daylight Time "saves" daylight is that it skews local noon by one hour, making the sunrise "later" and the afternoons and evenings last longer—at least on the clock. The Northwest Territories follows Mountain Time and its official time changes twice a year. Out at the Hoarfrost homestead we decided years ago that we prefer to remain on Central Standard Time (CST) all year long, following the lead of our wise neighbours directly south of us in Saskatchewan. This does away with the irksome "spring forward, fall back" clock changes. (Strictly speaking, Saskatchewan is far enough west that the entire province should be on Mountain Time, not Central. I suspect the province's timekeeping decision has to do with its rural populace and the same shift in perception I cite here.) We find that psychologically it is more pleasant during the darkest days of winter if the afternoons and evenings stay "longer." For example, on the shortest day of the year, the sun drops behind the south shore of McLeod Bay at about 2:25 p.m. MST. If we set the clocks to CST, which is the same as Mountain Daylight Time (MDT), the clock reads 3:25 p.m. when the sun goes down. Add the hour of usable twilight after sunset on to that, and even on those short December days it never gets truly dark until about four thirty in the afternoon. That is bearable. Of course there is no such thing as a free lunch, and the longer afternoons are offset by a protracted wait for daylight in the morning (sunrise at 11:05 on the winter solstice). This seems to be more suitable to our own daily routines, so we do it.

• The sun arcs above the horizon from east to west at a rate of 15 degrees per hour, making a full 360 degrees every twenty-four hours. So for instance at 9 a.m. *local standard time* it is halfway between east and south, or directly southeast, on a bearing of 135 degrees.

• This all boils down to the clockface trick—anytime between the hours of 6 a.m. and 6 p.m., with the clock set to standard time for your time zone, point the hour hand at the sun, and halfway between the hour hand and the twelve lies south. If your watch is set to Daylight Time, you will have to imagine bumping the hour hand back (standard time is one hour earlier) or you will be off by about 15 degrees.

• If you have a digital timepiece, draw a clock face on the snow or the ground, or keep a drawing of one on a little card for reference.

• Between 6 p.m. and 6 a.m. the method still works, but you have to reverse the outcome. Halfway between the hour hand and the twelve will be north, not south.

• On cloudy days with no glimpse of our dear star to guide you, the compass is the way to accomplish the same thing. However, you must account for magnetic declination, which is another can of worms and can be confusing. In this part of the world we have a declination of 20-some degrees east, which means that magnetic north (0 degrees) is actually 20-some degrees true, or north-northeast.

For speed estimates, a variation of the chip-log method used by sailors can be put to good use by dog mushers. A measured length of gangline takes the place of the boat's hull length, and a pocket watch (or even a careful mental "one-one thousand" verbal count) is used for the timing. My own method is this:

1. Measure out 39^1/$_2$ feet along the gangline, forward from its connection to the sled bridle (usually a carabiner or metal ring.) With the gangline dimensions we use, this 39^1/$_2$ feet just happens to be at the fifth pair of necklines, so in a ten-dog team it is right at the shoulders of the lead dogs.

2. Now dust off your math skills. This 39^1/$_2$-foot distance is 0.00748 of a mile (39.5 feet divided by 5,280 feet per mile). As you are moving, time the passage of that length of gangline with reference to a stationary point, using a stopwatch (preferably a watch with big buttons for use with mittens). For example, let's say that exactly three seconds pass from the time that fifth neckline passes goes by a chosen reference spot on the trail (a snow lump, a tree, a shadow, or a rock), and the time that the carabiner at the head of your sled passes the reference point. You have travelled 0.00748 miles in three seconds—three seconds being 3/3600ths of an hour, or 0.00083 hours, you are going 0.00748 / 0.00083—or almost nine miles an hour (a very good cruising speed for a dogteam). If it takes you five seconds for the team to cover those 39.5 feet between the lead dogs and that carabiner, the math will reveal that your speed is 5.4 miles an hour.

3. But you don't have to do all the figuring once you discover a pattern. In this example you simply need to time the team over that distance, and then divide that number of seconds into 27. Voila: 27 / 3 = 9 mph; 27 / 2 = 13^1/$_2$ mph (hang on to your sled!); 27 / 4 = 6^3/$_4$ mph, et cetera.

You can play with these numbers and with your own gangline (turn the numbers over to an eleventh-grade math student if you get confused), and come up with variations that suit you. In the years of my racing and my long trips I was almost always running at least a ten-dog gangline, so the magic formula of dividing into 27 to get my miles per hour was convenient. I made up a little laminated card with speeds corresponding to seconds, from about six seconds down to two seconds, by tenths. I still use it now and then and it is a good estimate of speed. Now that I am often without a stopwatch, I use a one-one-thousand count to get a rough estimate up or down from the magic three seconds, or nine miles per hour. Estimating speed is especially helpful at night or in poor visibility, because when your range of vision is limited it commonly feels as if you are moving much faster than you really are. An accurate speed check can be humbling.

Nowadays you can just say to heck with map reading and dead reckoning, pull out the little GPS computer, flash up the screen, fumble with freezing fingers to push the little buttons or move things around on the tiny screen, and join the burgeoning ranks of the "GPS junkies." I think dead reckoning and map reading are more fun and rewarding in the long run.

Notes

Compass Points, Over the Boulders, Eager...

1 After first attributing this quote to skier and climber Dick Dorworth, a patriarch of North American mountain culture, I discovered that the line is from the British icon of bare-bones climbing and sailing, H. W. "Bill" Tilman (1898–1977): "Any worthwhile expedition can be planned on the back of an envelope."

South

1. Henry David Thoreau, "A Winter Walk," in *The Portable Thoreau*, ed. Carl Bode (New York: Viking Press, 1975 [1947]).
2. My sombre musings that morning may have been a premonition. Lawrence was tragically asphyxiated by carbon monoxide, alone in his sweat lodge near his home in Lutsel K'e, in January 2009. We miss him.
3. John Haines, "With an Axe and an Auger," in *The Stars, the Snow, the Fire* (Minneapolis: Graywolf Press, 1989).
4. Henry David Thoreau, "A Week on the Concord and Merrimack Rivers, 1849," in *The Portable Thoreau*.
5. On July 4, 2014, during the final weeks of bringing this book through its editing and layout, a raging wildfire pushed by a 40-knot northeasterly wind swept into our home valley at the Hoarfrost River. That fire started about June 16th, with a brief and unremarkable lightning storm west of Pike's Portage and east of the Lockhart River. Ironically, in the two weeks before the fire reached our home, I had been working steadily with our planes, ferrying fire crews and equipment to protect the Fairchild Penninsula and the historic sites at the outlet of the Lockhart, about ten miles east of the Hoarfrost. No one, including Kristen or me, had any inkling of how quickly that fire would run toward us when the wind became a full gale on the fourth of July. As this book goes to press, the house and guest cabin I write of in these pages are nothing but piles of ash and rubble. The rest of our buildings and homestead remain. Two dogs perished in the smoke and mayhem of that summer night. The country is a charred moonscape for miles along the north shore of McLeod Bay, and far up into the hills toward treeline. In ten or twelve panicked hours our place and our lives here were utterly changed—but that is a story yet to be lived.
6. For astronomical reasons beyond my understanding, the full moons in winter trace the path of the sun in summer, or some approximation thereof. It is one of the perks of those moons that come during the shortest days of winter. The moon rises far north of due east, and then sails high above the horizon through the long night, setting in the northwest for a few hours before rising again.

7. As noted earlier, 40 below is the magic number where both the Celsius and Fahrenheit temperature scales almost precisely coincide. So 40 below is 40 below no matter what scale you are using. I wonder whether that is the reason it is such a common benchmark for the onset of capital-C Cold.

8. Thoreau, "A Winter Walk."

9. Years after that day I happened across a written account of another traveller who had cut across that divide between Noman Lake and the Snowdrift River. A British canoeist and adventurer named Steve Read passed that way in the summer of 1990. Later on that trip he camped overnight at the Hoarfrost—I was away at the time but Kristen met him. That next winter he sent us an account of his trip as printed in *Nastawgan*, an Ontario canoeing newsletter. Included was a sketch map of the "Route via Five Lakes from Noman Lake to the Snowdrift River," and this paragraph:

> Noman Lake is the last in this highway of lakes where little height is gained or lost. I now wanted to connect up five small lakes, a route of no little interest. The portages were fairly easy, and the last one rose through the trees and suddenly burst into the open on the edge of a scarp overlooking the Snowdrift valley. I could see the river meandering in the distance, with its sandy beaches glinting in the sunlight. Later from my camp on a bluff I watched a moose browse on the willows below.

His route-finding northbound was better than my own in the opposite direction. I strayed west of the easier lake-and-portage route, and only realized my mistake while returning to my camp late that day.

10. P.G. Downes, *Sleeping Island: The Story of One Man's Travels in the Great Barren Lands of the Canadian North* (New York: Coward-McCann, 1943; North Ferrisburg, VT: Heron Dance Press, 2004).

11. Peter Steele, *Backcountry Medical Guide*, 2nd edition (Seattle, WA: Mountaineers Books, 1999).

12. The antenna is two 80-foot strands of copper wire. Stretched end to end, they lead from a midpoint junction to a coaxial cable and from there to the radio itself. For the best reception, orient them at a right angle to the station you are trying to contact, and hang them at least six feet off the ground. Done right, and during periods with good solar electromagnetic "weather," the range of a small ten-watt radio is astounding. I once talked with Kristen over a distance of about 600 straight-line miles, from our homestead northeast to her campsite on the Arctic Ocean. On other days, with the same set-up, it is nearly impossible to transmit an audible message more than a few miles.

13. Henry David Thoreau, "A Winter Walk."

14. Sure enough, a week or so later, a television crew from the Discovery Channel came to film a Native caribou hunt, and—there being no caribou any closer to Lutsel K'e—they chose to follow my trail (although of course not

mine in any rational sense) up to Daisy Lake. Hearing this, I was surprised at how proprietary I suddenly felt about that little lane of packed snow. I don't think the Discovery Channel program made any mention of the fact that some far-flung native of Illinois had opened the trail that led to that herd.

East

1. William Stafford, "Old Dog," in *The Way It Is: New and Selected Poems* (Minneapolis: Graywolf Press, 1998).
2. Warburton Pike, *The Barren Ground of Northern Canada* (London: Macmillan, 1892).
3. Helge Ingstad, *The Land of Feast and Famine*, trans. Eugene Gay-Tifft (Montreal: McGill-Queen's University Press, 1992).
4. John Meade Haines, "On the Road," in *News from the Glacier: Selected Poems 1960–1980* (Middletown, CT: Wesleyan University Press, 1982).
5. John Meade Haines, "Foreboding," in *News from the Glacier.*
6. Joshua Slocum, *Sailing Alone Around the World* (New York: Blue Ribbon Books, 1900).
7. I have always been leery of the current fascination with "wind chill" elicited by TV and radio weather reports, since I think it is just another form of fear-mongering and sensationalism. We are, in my opinion, better off without it, so long as we simply know that cold and wind can work together to produce dangerously chilling effects. Nowadays far too many people seem far too inclined to stay indoors in winter, and shrill warnings like "wind chill of 45 below zero" at an ambient temperature of, say, 18 below, serve only to keep them inside.
8. Richard Nelson, *The Island Within* (San Francisco: North Point Press, 1989).
9. Thomas Hornbein, *Everest: The West Ridge* (Seattle, WA: The Mountaineers, 1998).
10. Joe Runyan, *Winning Strategies for Distance Mushers* (Anchorage, AK: Todd Communications, 2003).
11. Annie Dillard, *The Writing Life* (New York: Harper and Row, 1989).
12. William Stafford, "So Long," in *The Way It Is.*
13. The signal turned out to be a young female wolf that had been collared several years earlier, nearly a hundred miles to the northwest. She had evidently wandered south and east from her original range, and had not been located for several years. We tried again to locate her on a flight that September but could not pick up the signal.

North

1. Ken Frew, who is mentioned in passing many times in this narrative, was a dear friend of our family, and "Uncle Ken" to our girls although we were not related. He drowned in the Hoarfrost River at Lacy Falls in August 2010.

He was fifty-nine. We cherish the memory of this quiet, warm, capable man who for many years was such a powerful presence in our lives.

2. Kennady Lake, and the mine site there now renamed as Gahcho Kué, is as of this writing about to become the site of the Northwest Territories' fourth diamond mine. A property of the diamond-mining cartel De Beers, the mine is forecast to produce gem-quality diamonds for about twelve years.

3. Walmsley Lake, like Cook and Fletcher Lakes, Maufelly Bay, and dozens of other local landmarks, was named by Captain George Back of the Royal Navy, on his ascent of the Hoarfrost by canoe in the late summer of 1833. "The Reverend Doctor Walmsley of Hanwell" was evidently a supporter of Back's expedition, and Maufelly was one of his most reliable Native guides.

4. This nickname derives from the fact that such cheap and flimsy woodstoves can very quickly reach a cherry-red "meltdown" state, if the user does not pay close attention to the draft control after stoking—or toking.

5. John A. Shedd, in *Salt from My Attic* (1928), qtd. in *The Yale Book of Quotations*, ed. Fred R. Shapiro (New Haven, CT: Yale University Press, 2006).

6. One of the clues most commonly used to find kimberlites is an indicator mineral called pyrope garnet. These deep purple garnets are used in jewelry. The gem-quality versions from South Africa are called Cape Rubies.

7. According to the De Beers people, whom I have no reason to doubt (so far), the mine site will actually lie within the watershed of the Lockhart River. Kennady, the small lake at the Gahcho Kué mine site, sits on the divide between the Lockhart drainage and the watershed of the unnamed river, with the water draining north down a small creek to the Lockhart. I suspect there is a groundwater connection to both drainages.

8. Paul E. Lehr, R. Will Burnett, Herbert S. Zim, and Harry McKnaught, *Weather* (New York: St. Martin's Press, 2001).

9. Biologist Dean Cluff has for many years conducted an aerial survey of wolf-den sites in June, returning to occupied dens later each summer to count the puppies that each pack has raised. The big esker north of Aylmer is among the most remote of these den sites. I will never forget the sight of a pair of big white wolves we spotted there late on a June evening. They stood calmly, lit by the low-angled Arctic sun, watching our little plane overhead, their vast hunting grounds sprawled beyond them. The picture of them in my mind's eye has stayed clear for me over the many years since that evening. Calling it up never fails to give me a fleeting respite from the world's rampant varieties of craziness.

10. John Balzar, *Yukon Alone: The World's Toughest Adventure Race* (New York: Henry Holt and Company, 2001).

11. Colin Fletcher, *River: One Man's Journey Down the Colorado, Source to Sea* (New York: Knopf, 1997).

12. Colin Fletcher, *The Man Who Walked Through Time* (New York: Knopf, 1968).

West

1. Now as I write this from a still longer view, it is clear to me that my turning down of that contract work in March 2005 may have contributed to the fact that, by year's end, I had lost my position as a seasonal contract pilot with Air Tindi of Yellowknife. Twice more in the ensuing four months I had scheduling conflicts, and so three times in half a year I opted out of paid work—paid work not only for me but for the company. The handwriting on the wall is only plain to me now, after these years. Do I regret my decision? No. Having gone on to start our own small bush plane operation, Kristen and I only wonder why we did not do it sooner.

2. In north-central Alberta, north of Edmonton, lies Slave Lake, or Lesser Slave Lake—itself a sizable body of water but nowhere near the scale of its northern cousin.

3. This well-known stromatolite site is farther down the northwest shore of Christie Bay, on the Pethei Peninsula near Taltheilei Narrows. Broad bands of tightly swirled fossils in the sloping bedrock extend for about half a mile right along the water's edge. Geologists tell me that it was these blue-green algae, there fossilized, which over eons turned the earth's predominantly nitrogen atmosphere into a mixture with enough oxygen in it to support the next steps in the evolution of life.

4. James Galvin, *Fencing the Sky* (New York: Henry Holt and Co., 1999).

5. Guy de Maupassant, *Afloat*, trans. Douglas Parmée (New York: New York Review Books, 2008).

6. The mineral deposit referred to here as Thor Lake is now owned by Avalon Rare Metals, and the project now has been rechristened with the mandatory Dene-language moniker *Nechalacho* (I can only hope that this translates as "place where they dig up ingredients for cellphones"). The minerals in the deposit include cerium and terbium.

7. Elizabeth Hay, *Late Nights on Air* (Toronto: McClelland & Stewart, 2008).

8. Kaltag never did seriously threaten to surpass Ernie. He runs, works, and leads, but he doesn't have Ernie's spark. Over the years since 2005, as Ernie has aged, I have kept looking for his replacement. As of this writing Ernie is fully retired, but in February 2011 at age twelve, he led our daughter Annika to the finish line of her first Junior Iditarod race in Alaska. We had hardly thought it possible that he would even make that team, not to mention lead them in. His prowess is still unmatched in my experience, and if his successor is out there in our dog yard we have not spotted him or her yet. Deep down, I don't think we ever will.

9. I had again asked friends in town to save the daily weather maps for me, and on the map I can see the big *H* depicting a high-pressure centre, parked about a hundred miles north of Yellowknife beginning March 10th. On the maps it does not budge from that position until the 16th. The clockwise circulation of air around that centre explains the steady easterlies that pushed us along for those days of the trip.

10. This brings me to a story too good to pass up, from a night on the trail to Yellowknife in December 1990 with my friend Peter Arychuk. We had set the tent up but despite a good hot fire we could not get the wood stove to draw properly. Something seemed to be clogging the pipe. Suddenly it dawned on me: "Say, did you see that one-litre bottle of white gas that was nested inside the stovepipe?" Blank look; rapid action. Very warm and very full bottle of white gas plucked from stove pipe. Problem solved. Now *there* was a situation with potential for embarrassment—not to mention pyrotechnics.

11. The Slave, which is formed by the confluence of the Peace and Athabasca Rivers, carries an enormous amount of water into Great Slave Lake, in fact about 70 per cent of the lake's total inflow. The flow varies with season and weather, from 1,800 to about 10,000 cubic metres *per second*. Mike English, a professor at Wilfrid Laurier University in Ontario, told me that an average flow rate is close to 3,300 cubic metres per second. I tried to visualize this somehow, and came up with this: 3,300 cubic metres is a square box of water 15.5 metres (50 feet) on each edge, entering the lake *once per second*—and more than three of those every second at the highest flowage rates. All of this water remains only briefly in Great Slave Lake before starting down north for the Arctic Ocean, via the Mackenzie. If considered as one unified watershed, which it is despite its confusing series of name-changes, the Peace-Athabasca-Slave-Mackenzie is second in size only to the Missouri-Mississippi among North American rivers. It is the twelfth largest river system in the world.

12. In his memoir *Beyond the Great Slave Lake* (New York: E.P. Dutton, 1958), Tom Lodge describes Lonely Point from the perspective of his days as a hired hand to a commercial fisherman. His time there was marked by an unpleasant and gradually unravelling partnership. He eventually walked off the job, setting out alone over the autumn ice to join another crew of fishermen at Moraine Point.

13. Sadly the Moraine Point peninsula, including lodge and homestead, was destroyed by wildfire in August 2014, in the same fire season that claimed our own home. Bill and Mary had moved away a few years earlier. I flew past their old place on 29 August 2014, and there are no buildings standing, only rubble and char.

14. Peter Coyote, "Freewheeling the Details: A Conversation with Gary Snyder and Peter Coyote," *Poetry Flash*, 283 November/December 1999, http://www.english.illinois.edu/maps/poets/s_z/snyder/interviews.htm.

15. Robert Service, "Cremation of Sam Magee," in *Songs of a Sourdough* (Toronto: William Briggs, 1907).

16. It is true that the old-timers never bothered to water their dogs in winter, but it bears emphasizing that a frozen fish, for example, is about 90 per cent water by weight, and frozen meat of any kind has nearly that much water content. Fat is also a source of water, since metabolizing one gram of fat

yields an equal weight of water as a byproduct. This "metabolic water" is, for both dogs and people, a key to remaining adequately hydrated in deep cold.

17. The pilot who flew out to the Hanbury River on an April day to give John the message about his mother was Roger Catling, my neighbour now and often mentioned in this narrative. In that spring of 1981 Roger, along with his wife Theresa and their two young daughters, was living at a cabin on the upper Thelon River. That brief meeting was our first.

18. Wendell Berry, *Jayber Crow: The Life Story of Jayber Crow, Barber, of the Port William Membership, as Written by Himself* (Berkeley, CA: Counterpoint Press, 2001).

19. Such personal connections with pieces of gear make one of the differences between modern camping equipment and what I think of as *the real stuff*— hand-made and old, tried and true. A scraped caribou skin carries a story with it. I suppose the store-bought stuff can too, over time. The *old* aspect is more essential than the *hand-made*. (Or maybe "remember that day we drove to Mountain Equipment to buy that Ensolite pad? There was a six-car pile-up on the four-lane just before our exit—I thought we were gonna be there all week...")

20. In summer, chartered airplanes (for many years a Boeing 737 was the usual type) land at the 6,000-foot gravel runway once a week, picking up and dropping off a load of lodge guests and supplies for what is in essence a small town between mid-June and early September.

21. Robert Service, "Call of the Wild," in *Songs of a Sourdough*.

22. For decades the maxim among the wolf aficionados of North America was "there has never been an unprovoked attack on a human by a wild wolf in North America." This is, of course, an indefensibly sweeping statement. North America has been around for a very long time, and so have wolves and humans. In recent years there have been several such attacks, and there will be more. People who live cheek by jowl with wild animals soon realize the absurdity of such blanket pronouncements. The wolves that night veered off and stood at a distance while Kristen turned the team for home, and of course this is what she expected would happen. But it is scant comfort in such a situation to have read somewhere that an attack is utterly out of the question.

Glossary

Some informal definitions for a few mushing terms and local words that might not be familiar to readers.

Barrenlands or **Barrens**: The treeless tundra, especially common local parlance in the Northwest Territories.

booties: Cloth stockings for protection of dogs' footpads, secured with a Velcro strap around the dog's leg about three inches above the paw.

brake: Any style of braking device, usually with a metal edge, affixed to the back of a dogsled.

bridle: The loop of rope at the front of a dogsled, where a carabiner attaches the sled to the gangline, snow hook rope, and snubline.

broken, unbroken trail: "Breaking" a trail usually connotes making the first passage along a route through deep soft snow. The same trail can be "broken out" several times each winter, following periodic snowfalls and winds.

brushbow: A stout curved bumper bar of plastic or wood at the front of a dogsled. Helps to deflect the sled from a direct hit with a tree or rock.

esker: A long ridge of sand and gravel, deposited during the last glaciation by a stream flowing on or under the mass of glacial ice. Eskers are prominent features on the tundra and often have pockets of spruce timber growing along them, far beyond the local limit of continuous forest.

gangline: The main line connecting the dogteam's pulling power to the bridle and sled, with individual tuglines branching off from it to each dog's harness.

gee: The most common musher command to lead dogs, for a turn to the right.

haw: The opposite of "gee"; directs the lead dog(s) to go left.

krummholz: Short stunted spruce trees growing in clumps, surviving along or well beyond the treeline.

leader, lead dog: The dog or dogs running at the head of a dogteam, who respond to the musher's directional commands and set the pace for the team.

musher: The person driving a team of sled dogs. Derived from the French-Canadian start-up command to a dog team: *"Marche!"*

nautical mile: A unit of distance measurement most common in aviation and maritime navigation. It is a handy reference when using latitude and longitude, because it is almost exactly equal to one minute of latitude. Thus one degree of latitude is 60 nautical miles. Its precise measurement is 6,076 feet, or 1,852 metres. See statute mile, below.

neckline: A short supple line with a bronze snap that attaches a team dog's collar to the main gangline. Necklines are not stretched tight unless a dog is pulling hard to the side. They serve as tethers for resting dogs when the tuglines are detached from the dog's harness at a rest stop.

overflow: Water and slush lying in a layer on top of solid ice. The water has "overflowed" up through holes or cracks in the ice. Overflow is often insulated beneath snow cover and remains liquid at temperatures far below freezing.

pedalling: The rhythmic swinging and kicking of the musher's foot and leg, on either side of the sled, to help the dogs move the sled along (also helpful to warm up a cold foot).

picket line: Same as tie-out line. A lightweight cable with lengths of light chain attached at intervals. The chains end in a snap, which clips to a dog's collar. At each end of the cable is a length of rope for attachment of the picket line to trees, bushes, snow anchors or ice pitons. Used for overnight stops with a team.

pressure ridge: A long wall of broken ice where a fracture in the ice has led to the lifting of blocks with expansion of the ice sheet. Once frozen, ice is like any other solid; it expands with warming and contracts with cooling. A pressure ridge may start as a contraction crack in the ice after cooling. With the next warming trend, that crack becomes the relief area for the expansion pressures in the ice sheet.

sastrugi: Plural of *sastruga*, derived from the Russian word *zastrugi* for a long wavelike ridge of hard snow, sculpted by the wind in open terrain.

sled bag: A sled bag is the cloth container that contains and confines the load in a dogsled. Once loaded with gear its cloth covers are tightly lashed or buckled down.

snow hook: A two-pronged metal anchor hook for snow and ice, fitted with a long rope that is joined to the gangline by the carabiner at the sled bridle. Used by kicking it into the snow or pounding it into the ice to keep a team stopped.

snow machine: Common local parlance for snowmobile, as is "skidoo." Often "snow-go" in parts of Alaska.

snubline: A length of strong rope. Like the snow-hook line, the snubline attaches directly to the team and gangline at the bridle and carabiner. The snubline is used as a tow rope when the musher is running or skiing behind the sled, and is used to tie off the team to a tree or post at departure time.

spline: A thin strip of wood or metal used to reinforce a joint or to back up a damaged area. Damaged sled runners and stanchions can be splined or splinted with sticks of wood to make a quick repair.

stanchion: An upright support in the structure of a dogsled.

statute mile: The common "mile" which in Canada was supplanted by conversion to the metric system, but which is still in use in the stubbornly non-metric United States. Oddly enough, statute miles, not nautical miles, are used in aviation weather reporting and forecasting, and in some important details of the air traffic control system and air regulations. Its precise measurement is 5,280 feet, 1,609 metres, 1.609 kilometres.

straight-line miles: When I use the term *straight-line miles* I am contrasting that distance to actual trail miles, or miles travelled by the dogsled over the terrain. A straight-line mileage is mileage "as the crow flies" from point A to point B, not accounting for all the twists and turns of actual overland travel.

tie-out line: Same as picket line. A lightweight cable with lengths of light chain attached at intervals. The chains end in a snap that clips to a dog's collar. At each end of the cable is a length of rope for attachment of the tie-out to trees, bushes, snow anchors or ice screws. Used for overnight stops with a team.

toggle: A three-inch chunk of wood or plastic spliced to the back of a dog harness. The toggle slips through a loop in the tugline when a team is "hooked up" for departure. Bronze snaps can also make this connection. I prefer toggles since the sliding bolts in the metal snaps can freeze shut.

tugline or **tug**: The 40–60-inch length of rope that connects a dog's harness to the main gangline. The tension on the tugline tells the musher whether the dog is pulling, and how hard.

wheel position or **wheel dogs**: The wheel dogs are those closest to the sled, at the back of the team. They are often the bigger dogs, but it is sometimes better to have a nimble lighter dog in wheel, because the position can demand agility when the trail is narrow and flanked with obstacles. *Wheel* comes from the use of horses and mules in a team pulling a cart, with the "wheel horse" at the rear. It probably harks back to the Klondike era, when thousands of transplanted southerners, accustomed to driving teams of horses and mules, suddenly found themselves driving dogteams.

white gas: A generic term for naphtha, also commonly called Coleman fuel, because it is used for camp stoves and lanterns.

Books in the Life Writing Series
Published by Wilfrid Laurier University Press

Haven't Any News: Ruby's Letters from the Fifties edited by Edna Staebler with an Afterword by Marlene Kadar • 1995 / x + 165 pp. / ISBN 0-88920-248-6

"I Want to Join Your Club": Letters from Rural Children, 1900–1920 edited by Norah L. Lewis with a Preface by Neil Sutherland • 1996 / xii + 250 pp. (30 b&w photos) / ISBN 0-88920-260-5

And Peace Never Came by Elisabeth M. Raab with Historical Notes by Marlene Kadar • 1996 / x + 196 pp. (12 b&w photos, map) / ISBN 0-88920-281-8

Dear Editor and Friends: Letters from Rural Women of the North-West, 1900–1920 edited by Norah L. Lewis • 1998 / xvi + 166 pp. (20 b&w photos) / ISBN 0-88920-287-7

The Surprise of My Life: An Autobiography by Claire Drainie Taylor with a Foreword by Marlene Kadar • 1998 / xii + 268 pp. (8 colour photos and 92 b&w photos) / ISBN 0-88920-302-4

Memoirs from Away: A New Found Land Girlhood by Helen M. Buss / Margaret Clarke • 1998 / xvi + 153 pp. / ISBN 0-88920-350-4

The Life and Letters of Annie Leake Tuttle: Working for the Best by Marilyn Färdig Whiteley • 1999 / xviii + 150 pp. / ISBN 0-88920-330-x

Marian Engel's Notebooks: "Ah, mon cahier, écoute" edited by Christl Verduyn • 1999 / viii + 576 pp. / ISBN 0-88920-333-4 cloth / ISBN 0-88920-349-0 paper

Be Good Sweet Maid: The Trials of Dorothy Joudrie by Audrey Andrews • 1999 / vi + 276 pp. / ISBN 0-88920-334-2

Working in Women's Archives: Researching Women's Private Literature and Archival Documents edited by Helen M. Buss and Marlene Kadar • 2001 / vi + 120 pp. / ISBN 0-88920-341-5

Repossessing the World: Reading Memoirs by Contemporary Women by Helen M. Buss • 2002 / xxvi + 206 pp. / ISBN 0-88920-408-x cloth / ISBN 0-88920-410-1 paper

Chasing the Comet: A Scottish-Canadian Life by Patricia Koretchuk • 2002 / xx + 244 pp. / ISBN 0-88920-407-1

The Queen of Peace Room by Magie Dominic • 2002 / xii + 115 pp. / ISBN 0-88920-417-9

China Diary: The Life of Mary Austin Endicott by Shirley Jane Endicott • 2002 / xvi + 251 pp. / ISBN 0-88920-412-8

The Curtain: Witness and Memory in Wartime Holland by Henry G. Schogt • 2003 / xii + 132 pp. / ISBN 0-88920-396-2

Teaching Places by Audrey J. Whitson • 2003 / xiii + 178 pp. / ISBN 0-88920-425-x

Through the Hitler Line by Laurence F. Wilmot, M.C. • 2003 / xvi + 152 pp. / ISBN 0-88920-448-9

Where I Come From by Vijay Agnew • 2003 / xiv + 298 pp. / ISBN 0-88920-414-4

The Water Lily Pond by Han Z. Li • 2004 / x + 254 pp. / ISBN 0-88920-431-4

The Life Writings of Mary Baker McQuesten: Victorian Matriarch edited by Mary J. Anderson • 2004 / xxii + 338 pp. / ISBN 0-88920-437-3

Seven Eggs Today: The Diaries of Mary Armstrong, 1859 and 1869 edited by Jackson W. Armstrong • 2004 / xvi + 228 pp. / ISBN 0-88920-440-3

Love and War in London: A Woman's Diary 1939–1942 by Olivia Cockett; edited by Robert W. Malcolmson • 2005 / xvi + 208 pp. / ISBN 0-88920-458-6

Incorrigible by Velma Demerson • 2004 / vi + 178 pp. / ISBN 0-88920-444-6

Auto/biography in Canada: Critical Directions edited by Julie Rak • 2005 / viii + 264 pp. / ISBN 0-88920-478-0

Tracing the Autobiographical edited by Marlene Kadar, Linda Warley, Jeanne Perreault, and Susanna Egan • 2005 / viii + 280 pp. / ISBN 0-88920-476-4

Must Write: Edna Staebler's Diaries edited by Christl Verduyn • 2005 / viii + 304 pp. / ISBN 0-88920-481-0

Pursuing Giraffe: A 1950s Adventure by Anne Innis Dagg • 2006 / xvi + 284 pp. (photos, 2 maps) / 978-0-88920-463-8

Food That Really Schmecks by Edna Staebler • 2007 / xxiv + 334 pp. / ISBN 978-0-88920-521-5

163256: A Memoir of Resistance by Michael Englishman • 2007 / xvi + 112 pp. (14 b&w photos) / ISBN 978-1-55458-009-5

The Wartime Letters of Leslie and Cecil Frost, 1915–1919 edited by R.B. Fleming • 2007 / xxxvi + 384 pp. (49 b&w photos, 5 maps) / ISBN 978-1-55458-000-2

Johanna Krause Twice Persecuted: Surviving in Nazi Germany and Communist East Germany by Carolyn Gammon and Christiane Hemker • 2007 / x + 170 pp. (58 b&w photos, 2 maps) / ISBN 978-1-55458-006-4

Watermelon Syrup: A Novel by Annie Jacobsen with Jane Finlay-Young and Di Brandt • 2007 / x + 268 pp. / ISBN 978-1-55458-005-7

Broad Is the Way: Stories from Mayerthorpe by Margaret Norquay • 2008 / x + 106 pp. (6 b&w photos) / ISBN 978-1-55458-020-0

Becoming My Mother's Daughter: A Story of Survival and Renewal by Erika Gottlieb • 2008 / x + 178 pp. (36 b&w illus., 17 colour) / ISBN 978-1-55458-030-9

Leaving Fundamentalism: Personal Stories edited by G. Elijah Dann • 2008 / xii + 234 pp. / ISBN 978-1-55458-026-2

Bearing Witness: Living with Ovarian Cancer edited by Kathryn Carter and Lauri Elit • 2009 / viii + 94 pp. / ISBN 978-1-55458-055-2

Dead Woman Pickney: A Memoir of Childhood in Jamaica by Yvonne Shorter Brown • 2010 / viii + 202 pp. / ISBN 978-1-55458-189-4

I Have a Story to Tell You by Seemah C. Berson • 2010 / xx + 288 pp. (24 b&w photos) / ISBN 978-1-55458-219-8

We All Giggled: A Bourgeois Family Memoir by Thomas O. Hueglin • 2010 / xiv + 232 pp. (20 b&w photos) / ISBN 978-1-55458-262-4

Just a Larger Family: Letters of Marie Williamson from the Canadian Home Front, 1940–1944 edited by Mary F. Williamson and Tom Sharp • 2011 / xxiv + 378 pp. (16 b&w photos) / ISBN 978-1-55458-323-2

Burdens of Proof: Faith, Doubt, and Identity in Autobiography by Susanna Egan • 2011 / x + 200 pp. / ISBN 978-1-55458-333-1

Accident of Fate: A Personal Account 1938–1945 by Imre Rochlitz with Joseph Rochlitz • 2011 / xiv + 226 pp. (50 b&w photos, 5 maps) / ISBN 978-1-55458-267-9

The Green Sofa by Natascha Würzbach, translated by Raleigh Whitinger • 2012 / xiv + 240 pp. (5 b&w photos) / ISBN 978-1-55458-334-8

Unheard Of: Memoirs of a Canadian Composer by John Beckwith • 2012 / x + 393 pp. (74 illus., 8 musical examples) / ISBN 978-1-55458-358-4

Borrowed Tongues: Life Writing, Migration, and Translation by Eva C. Karpinski • 2012 / viii + 274 pp. / ISBN 978-1-55458-357-7

Basements and Attics, Closets and Cyberspace: Explorations in Canadian Women's Archives edited by Linda M. Morra and Jessica Schagerl • 2012 / x + 338 pp. / ISBN 978-1-55458-632-5

The Memory of Water by Allen Smutylo • 2013 / x + 262 pp. (65 colour illus.) / ISBN 978-1-55458-842-8

The Unwritten Diary of Israel Unger, Revised Edition by Carolyn Gammon and Israel Unger • 2013 / ix + 230 pp. (b&w illus.) / ISBN 978-1-77112-011-1

Boom! Manufacturing Memoir for the Popular Market by Julie Rak • 2013 / viii + 249 pp. (b&w illus.) / ISBN 978-1-55458-939-5

Motherlode: A Mosaic of Dutch Wartime Experience by Carolyne Van Der Meer • 2014 / xiv + 132 pp. (b&w illus.) / ISBN 978-1-77112-005-0

Not the Whole Story: Challenging the Single Mother Narrative edited by Lea Caragata and Judit Alcalde • 2014 / x + 222 pp. / ISBN 978-1-55458-624-0

Street Angel by Magie Dominc • 2014 / vii + 154 pp. / ISBN 978-1-77112-026-5

In the Unlikeliest of Places: How Nachman Libeskind Survived the Nazis, Gulags, and Soviet Communism by Annette Libeskind Berkovits • 2014 / xiv + 282 pp. (6 colour illus.) / ISBN 978-1-77112-066-1

Kinds of Winter: Four Solo Journeys by Dogteam in Canada's Northwest Territories by Dave Olesen • 2014 / xii + 256 pp. (illus.) / ISBN 978-1-77112-118-7